Adversary-Aware Learning Techniques and Trends in Cybersecurity

Prithviraj Dasgupta • Joseph B. Collins
Ranjeev Mittu

Editors

Adversary-Aware Learning Techniques and Trends in Cybersecurity

 Springer

Editors
Prithviraj Dasgupta
Information Management
and Decision Architectures Branch
Information Technology Division
U. S. Naval Research Laboratory
Washington, DC, USA

Joseph B. Collins
Information Management
and Decision Architectures Branch
Information Technology Division
U. S. Naval Research Laboratory
Washington, DC, USA

Ranjeev Mittu
Information Management
and Decision Architectures Branch
Information Technology Division
U. S. Naval Research Laboratory
Washington, DC, USA

ISBN 978-3-030-55694-5 ISBN 978-3-030-55692-1 (eBook)
https://doi.org/10.1007/978-3-030-55692-1

This Springer imprint is published by the registered company Springer Nature Switzerland AG
The registered company address is: Gewerbestrasse 11, 6330 Cham, Switzerland

Preface

Machine learning-based intelligent systems have experienced a massive growth over the past few years and are close to becoming ubiquitous in the technology surrounding our daily lives. Examples of such systems are abundant—intelligent consumer appliances such as automated home security systems, intelligent voice service-enabled software assistants such as Alexa, online recommender systems for social media feeds and e-mail spam filters, automated image and biometric data recognition software used for homeland security applications, and automated controllers on self-driving vehicles, all employ machine learning-based algorithms for making decisions and taking actions.

Machine learning-based systems have been shown to be vulnerable to security attacks from malicious adversaries. The vulnerability of these systems is further aggravated as it is non-trivial to establish the authenticity of data used to train the system, and even innocuous perturbations to the training data can be used to manipulate the system's behavior in unintended ways. As machine learning-based systems become pervasive in our society, it is essential to direct research towards issues related to security, trust, reliability, and robustness of such systems, so that humans can use them in a safe and sustained manner. The contents of this book address the overarching need towards making automated, machine learning-based systems more robust and resilient against adversarial attacks. The book comprises ten chapters around the theme of adversarial learning with a focus on cybersecurity. We have organized the book into the following parts focused on three complementary, yet closely related themes:

- **Part I:** Game-playing artificial intelligence (AI) and game theory-based techniques for cyberdefenses
- **Part II:** Data modalities and distributed architectures for countering adversarial cyberattacks
- **Part III:** Human–machine interactions and roles in automated cyberdefenses

In the rest of the preface, we summarize the salient aspects of the different chapters in this book under each theme.

Part I: Game-Playing AI and Game Theory-Based Techniques for Cyberdefenses

Games are essentially strategic interactions between two or more players, where the objective of each player is to overwhelm the remaining players and win the game. To establish superiority in the game, a player must be able to understand, anticipate, and predict its opponents' moves and respond appropriately to those moves towards winning the game quickly. A player that can perform these tasks adeptly is considered an intelligent player. In other words, *intelligence can be looked upon as a manifestation of sophisticated capabilities to dominate adversaries within game-like interactions*. This idea forms the premise of the three chapters in the first part of this book. In the chapter "Rethinking Intelligent Behavior as Competitive Games for Handling Adversarial Challenges to Machine Learning," the authors posit that modeling adversarial machine learning as games provides several desirable characteristics that can be leveraged to develop effective mechanisms to respond to and defeat adversaries. They also provide an overview of different AI game-based environments and techniques therein that are currently being used to develop human-level capabilities in machine intelligence and lay the foundation towards developing machine intelligence that can repudiate adversarial challenges.

The concept of game-playing intelligence to develop effective cyberdefenses for adversarial learning in attacker versus defender settings is highlighted in the following two chapters. A canonical problem in adversarial learning is to develop effective defenses against an attacker that modifies the data and its labels used to train a supervised machine learning-based AI model. In the chapter "Security of Distributed Machine Learning," Zhang and Zhu address this problem using game-theoretic formalisms and a distributed support vector machine (SVM)-based learning algorithm for attacks on machine learning algorithms, as well as for network-centric attacks such as denial-of-service type attacks. The subsequent chapter by Xu and Nguyen also considers an attacker–defender game setting. But here, the attacker employs deception to misguide the defender and prevents it from calculating an effective response strategy. This problem is analyzed within a game called Stackelberg Security Game (SSG) and the authors describe methods for the defender to respond adequately under constrained and unconstrained deception strategies by the attacker.

Part II: Data Modalities and Distributed Architectures for Countering Adversarial Cyberattacks

Supervised machine learning-based algorithms are "data hungry" and adversaries exploit the reliance of these algorithms on the data by modifying the data so that the predictions made by the supervised machine learning-based learner are erroneous and less reliable. Many machine learning-based systems that are currently deployed or being researched use data of predominantly two modalities: text and image. The first two chapters in this part of the book deal with adversarial machine learning techniques for these two data modalities.

Text data presents unique challenges in adversarial learning due to various reasons including multiple interpretations of the same word or phrase depending on its context, typographical errors introduced inadvertently by humans, and language-related constructs. In the chapter "Adversarial Machine Learning in Text: A Case Study of Phishing Email Detection with RCNN Model," Lee and Sharma address the problem of adversarial learning with text data by characterizing different types of attacks on text data during testing of a supervised machine learning classifier and evaluate the attack's effect on different performance measures for the classifier.

A recently popular technique that can be used by adversaries to generate synthetic data that mirrors real data with stark resemblance is generative adversarial network (GAN). GAN-generated synthetic data, especially fake images have recently been shown to successfully fool machine learning-based classifiers. In the chapter "Overview of GANs for Image Synthesis and Detection Methods," Tjon and co-authors survey different GAN-based techniques that have been proposed to generate fake images and video along with techniques to detect GAN-generated fake images and video. They conclude with open problems, benchmarks, and challenges in machine-enabled identification of GAN-generated fake images and video.

The final chapter under this part by Shukla and co-authors describes a concept called diversity as a solution for adversarial learning. Their proposed approach realizes different components of a machine learning-based system in a distributed manner across cloud servers while using blockchain technology to ensure the integrity of the distributed data and services, along with federated services and edge computing to enable accessibility to lightweight sensor nodes for Internet of Things networks.

Part III: Human–Machine Interactions and Roles in Automated Cyberdefenses

Effective detection of cyberattacks using AI and machine learning involves close interactions between human and machine in multiple roles: humans, on the one hand, can generate cyberattacks that can be thwarted by autonomous software agents. On the other hand, human and machine could act together as a team to improve defenses against novel cyber threats. Similarly, machines can be used by malicious human actors to automate attacks against humans and/or machines. The third part of this book consists of four chapters around this theme of human–machine interactions and human roles in AI and machine learning-based techniques for detecting cyberattacks.

In the chapter "Automating the Investigation of Sophisticated Cyber Threats with Cognitive Agents," Meckl et al. describe how logical inference techniques used by humans could inform automated software capable of detecting sophisticated cyberattacks called advanced persistent threats (APTs). The approach that they describe leverages a collection of several AI techniques to reliably detect cyberattacks by first generating hypotheses from suspicious activity data, and, then, using those hypotheses to collect additional evidence from the data and strengthen the detection of the attacks via more reliable inference from the hypotheses.

Zhao and Jones' contribution in the chapter "Integrating Human Reasoning and Machine Learning to Classify Cyberattacks" describes a technique where the role of humans in detecting cyber threats is more tightly coupled with machine intelligence—human input from the visualization of network activity between connected computers is integrated with an unsupervised machine learning technique called lexical link analysis to determine cyberattacks more effectively.

The chapter "Homology as an Adversarial Attack Indicator" by Moskowitz et al. describes a formalism from the field of algebraic topology called homology to detect adversarial data. Their technique's operation is illustrated on an automated classifier that is able to correctly identify adversarially modified handwritten digits.

Finally, in the chapter "Cyber-(In)security, Revisited: Proactive Cyber-Defenses, Interdependence and Autonomous Human–Machine Teams (A-HMTs)," Lawless and co-authors take an expository outlook towards the theories and fundamental principles that guide the detection of cyberattacks and cyber deception. They posit that these theories need to be revisited in a ground-up manner to be effective in AI-based systems involving autonomous human–machine teams (A-HMTs). As a case for their defense, they mention that established tenets of rational choice theory fail to adequately capture and explain interactions between A-HMTS and, then, prescribe several directions to address these shortcomings and develop more effective cyberdefenses for A-HMTs.

We envisage that the collection of chapters in this book will provide a solid foundation of the state-of-the-art techniques in different facets of adversarial machine learning. We hope that the material in this book will encourage readers to explore and develop novel approaches to solve open problems and challenges in this field towards building safer, more reliable, more robust machine learning-based systems that will enhance the quality and convenience of human life and society.

Washington, DC, USA   Prithviraj Dasgupta
                                                                                       Joseph B. Collins
May 14, 2020   Ranjeev Mittu

Contents

Part I
Game-Playing AI and Game Theory-Based Techniques for Cyber Defenses

Rethinking Intelligent Behavior as Competitive Games for Handling Adversarial Challenges to Machine Learning

Joseph B. Collins and Prithviraj Dasgupta

Abstract Adversarial machine learning necessitates revisiting conventional machine learning paradigms and how they embody intelligent behavior. Effective repudiation of adversarial challenges adds a new dimension to intelligent behavior above and beyond that exemplified by widely used machine learning techniques such as supervised learning. For a learner to be resistant to adversarial attack, it must have two capabilities: a primary capability that it performs normally; and a second capability of resistance to attacks from adversaries. A possible means to achieve the second capability is to develop an understanding of different attack related attributes such as who generates attacks and why, how and when attacks are generated, and, what previously unseen attacks might look like. We trace the idea that this involves an additional dimension of intelligent behavior to the basic structure by which the problem may be solved. We posit that modeling this scenario as competitive, multi-player games comprising strategic interactions between different players with contradictory and competing objectives provides a systematic and structured means towards understanding and analyzing the problem. Exploring further in this direction, we discuss relevant features of different multi-player gaming environments that are being investigated as research platforms for addressing open problems and challenges towards developing artificial intelligence algorithms that are capable of super human intelligence.

Keywords Game-playing AI · Adversarial learning · Human-level machine intelligence

J. B. Collins · P. Dasgupta (✉)
Information Management and Decision Architectures Branch, Information Technology Division, U. S. Naval Research Laboratory, Washington, DC, USA
e-mail: joseph.collins@nrl.navy.mil; raj.dasgupta@nrl.navy.mil

© This is a U.S. government work and not under copyright protection in the U.S.;
foreign copyright protection may apply 2021
P. Dasgupta et al. (eds.), *Adversary-Aware Learning Techniques and Trends in Cybersecurity*, https://doi.org/10.1007/978-3-030-55692-1_1

3

1   Introduction

What is intelligence? This is the fundamental underlying question that must ultimately guide research into artificial intelligence (AI). Even the proverbial man-on-the-street has an opinion here: we all think we know intelligence when we see it, and we each think we have intelligence to some degree. Similar to Clarke's Third Law [9], that a sufficiently advanced technology is indistinguishable from magic, our own conscious, intelligent behavior is sufficiently poorly understood so as to appear to many to have supernatural origins. Even though we each think we can recognize intelligence, do any of us really understand it? Intelligent behavior has no single definition but most examples of intelligent behavior are referenced to some human behavior and involve finding solutions to problems not previously encountered. The further removed an arbitrary, new problem is from prior experience, the more intelligent the agent seems that can solve it. Take, for example, machine learning classifiers based on supervised learning [3]. Their ability to correctly classify is called intelligent because their accuracy rivals human accuracy at the same task. Additionally, it appears to be based on the ability of the learning algorithm to generalize from the training data set to perform well on previously unseen cases [35, 36]. Many of the recent advances in machine learning have focused on supervised learning. The allure is that fairly abstract classification problems that have long resisted attempts at solution have given way to this approach. Supervised learning begins with a formally well-defined problem: *How well can a learning algorithm perform in classifying previously unseen data given a set of examples of human-classified data?* As surprisingly effective as deep machine learning algorithms have become at providing automated learners, it has become clear that this is not enough [1].

A large variety of machine learning solutions have been discovered and their remarkable performance in classification problems documented, rivaling and even exceeding human performance in classification accuracy on problems previously thought to be hard [14]. Almost as quickly, however, they have been criticized due to their poor performance under adversarial attack where they are frequently fooled into mis-classification by seemingly trivial perturbations to input data [22]. From a human perspective, the machine savants are quickly determined to be idiot savants when subjected to such attacks, their understanding appearing to be superficial. (Certainly our human bias tends to render dramatic each of these advances in understanding in this field.) These criticisms seem fair from a pragmatic perspective. Since the applications of artificially intelligent systems will inevitably involve interactions with humans, it is reasonably supposed that adversarial challenges will need to be dealt with. The question we raise is: are these criticisms fair from a theoretical perspective? The general approach to creating a supervised learning algorithm is to find a solution, approximate or exact, to an optimization function [3, 14]. Typically, the objective is to estimate a classification function by learning from a set of training data that are instances of input/output values of that function. The optimization problem is formulated to minimize the errors made by the estimated function on a set of test data which is different from the training data. To subsequently deal with the problem of adversarial attacks, one response has been to augment the training data with adversarially perturbed data and re-train [31]. While this may offer some improvement in performance, that improvement is not generally impressive.

By way of example, a classification problem of interest is email spam filtering [4, 23]. The volume of email is too great to use people to filter out email spam, so we want automated solutions. The performance of supervised learning solutions is typically quite high, say greater than 97% accuracy, although no reasonable researcher imagines these algorithms have great insight into the mind of the spammer. Adversarial examples are rather easy to generate, compromising the usefulness of spam detection algorithms, and re-training using adversarially perturbed data has only modest usefulness in addressing the problem. The problem with the supervised learning approach to dealing with spam filtering is that while it begins by solving a well-defined optimization function, the problem of dealing with adversarial challenges is a kind of bolt-on afterthought. It is unfair from a theoretical perspective to criticize the supervised learning methodology since the supervised training is structurally incapable of providing solutions to dealing with adversarial challenges. Supervised learning only utilizes a single objective function.

Introducing the idea of an adversarial challenger is reasonable from a pragmatic perspective. In the case of the spam detection problem, the whole purpose of the spammer is to insert unwanted email into our inboxes, i.e., the spammer is an adversary. The true nature of the interaction between spammer and email recipient is actually that of a game, where there are two players with competing objectives. The problem with the standard supervised learning framework is that it does not take account for two competing objectives in the solution it provides. While supervised learning is a great illustration of intelligent behavior, as currently used, it does not provide a good solution to game-like problems such as spam filtering. Indeed, it may well be that most useful applications of artificial intelligence will require resistance to adversarial attack, and that the useful examples of artificial intelligence must incorporate game-playing intelligence. If this is indeed true, we would essentially be redefining intelligence by necessitating resistance to adversarial attack as part of the definition.

2 Limitations of Supervised Learning in Handling Adversarial Instances

The recent advances in deep learning have definitely achieved several milestone events: much improved performance at classification problems that were long considered difficult, exceeding the performance of alternative models and even exceeding human performance. The lack of formality of the neural network modeling approach causes some frustration because there is no well-defined, specific set of parameters for building one. On the other hand, their effectiveness over large ranges of meta-parameters is suggestive as to how evolution has stumbled onto the biological neural networks that the machine learning algorithms are modeled after.

There have been many attempts at modeling intelligence to create artificial intelligence, but, to be tractable, many modeling approaches tend to have fairly simple, uniform structures. At an abstract level, supervised learning models are thought of as universal function learners. In practice, there is a rather *ad-hoc*, empirical engineering recipe to follow for building and training them. One consequence of this lack of formality is that we are left being unable to prove that their remarkable performance should have been expected, and so they appear somewhat magical. Another consequence is that applying the underlying principles to solving more complex problems is not necessarily straightforward. Reflecting back on the structure of the brain, the relatively simple and uniform structure of deep learning models was in part inspired from focusing on the neural tissue structure at a relatively fine scale [16, 17]. Looking at the brain on a larger scale, we find many distinct larger structures with specialized functions, suggesting a significant complexity, despite the fact that these structures are generally made of neural tissue. In order to determine what would be required of a more complex structure for a learner, we must look more carefully at what we are trying to achieve, i.e., what kind of intelligent behavior we seek.

Upon reflection, the real problem of susceptibility to adversarial challenge is that the original training process in supervised learning presumes a benign setting, and, consequently, does not account for solving the adversarial attack problem. So, one should not be surprised that the algorithm would be susceptible to adversarial challenge. Nevertheless, since the applications of artificially intelligent systems will inevitably involve interactions with humans, it is reasonably supposed that adversarial challenges will need to be dealt with. The introduction of a requirement to be resistant to adversarial challenges dramatically changes the nature of the problem to be solved and, we argue, the underlying definition of intelligence. In adversarial learning, the product of supervised learning, the learner, is being called upon to withstand adversarial challenges. Originally, deep learning models were not really designed or trained to be resistant to adversarial perturbations. They were developed for taking a finite empirical sampling of input data and output labels and producing a learner that performs accurately on both its training inputs and some test inputs. While one can automate the generation of adversarial examples from a given set of input data, one cannot reliably automate the generation of correct classification labels for those adversarial examples. The process using existing training data to generate adversarially perturbed data for the purpose of additional training of the original algorithm is more of a bolt-on afterthought rather than a process for arriving at a solution. As such, in order to deal effectively with this inherent limitation, we posit that to move beyond the limitations of the supervised learning, the learner must be a game-playing intelligence.

What are other essential characteristics of intelligent behavior? Intelligent behavior is generally that which advances towards a goal, where the more expeditious the progress, the more intelligent the behavior seems. In other words, learning can be interpreted as supplanting less efficient goal-seeking behavior with more efficient behavior. In a classification task using supervised learning, the replacement of less efficient behavior is part of the training algorithm that has been designed by humans. For example, the structure of a decision tree, or, the margins of a support vector machine, or, the weights in a neural network, are refined in a predetermined manner to minimize the error in classifying recent data instances under the guidance of the training algorithm. While the learner does learn, it is itself not in control of its learning. A more intelligent learner would be one that itself decides and acts to replace less efficient goal-seeking behavior with more efficient behavior.

Another feature of supervised learning is that the learner's future behavior is strictly a result determined by past instances. The consequence of this is that the future behavior of the learner is unlikely to stray very far, if at all, from the domain of past instances. If the learner is challenged in novel ways by the adversary, the learner will be unable to respond in novel ways. To remedy this, the learner cannot be purely limited by its past experience; it must also have some understanding of its possible actions, and be able to introduce experimental variations into its future actions that are not entirely dependent on its past experience.

Supervised learning also separates the intelligent behavior into two phases: a learning phase and a deployed, performing phase. One weakness of this approach is that the intelligent learner does not continue to learn during its interactions after deployment. While an adversary may have benefit of prior knowledge of how a given learner will perform based on known data, the adversary's knowledge may be incomplete or nonexistent. In such cases, the adversary can also probe the learner to learn more about how it will perform. In such a case there is an ongoing interaction where the adversary is learning more and more about the learner. If during this interaction the learner does not take the opportunity to learn more about the adversary, then it will be at a disadvantage. To gain this capability we believe that, ultimately, intelligent behavior requires a mechanism that allows a learning algorithm to learn in the absence of human-in-the-loop training mechanisms.

3 A Game Playing Intelligence

From the discussion in Sect. 2, the principal conclusion that must be drawn is competition is one of the principal enablers of human intelligence and to achieve machine intelligence get at par with human intelligence, we should focus on developing intelligent learners that learn via competitive game-playing. In other words, the AI should be able to strategically handle situations where there are multiple competing objectives present. Clearly, the problem posed by a requirement to learn resistance to adversarial challenges is significantly more complex and challenging than a straightforward application of existing machine learning techniques including supervised and unsupervised learning. A game-playing, intelligent learner needs to have an in-built mechanisms that can effectively engage in game-playing behavior to understand and intelligently respond to an adversary with an unpredictable nature, and, simultaneously incorporate the learning process into its game- playing behavior. Below, we identify a set of fundamental requirements towards creating a game-playing, intelligent learner:

- **Bi-level Optimization.** In supervised learning, the machine learning model is constructed by optimizing a single objective function with a precisely defined objective, e.g., to minimize the learning agent's classification error function over a finite empirical sampling of previously evaluated input data. The introduction of an adversarial challenger creates a second, competing objective: to make the learner commit classification errors. This second objective is held by a different intelligent agent. This transforms the adversarial machine learning problem from optimizing a single objective function by one learning agent to a pair of objective functions, that are conflict with each other, being solved in an interdependent manner by the learning agent and the adversary agent respectively. While the general problem of adversarial learning may be considered to be a multi-player game with different adversaries trying to subvert a machine learning model, we restrict our discussions to two player games, while assuming that different adversarial players could be virtually combined into a single adversarial agent that possesses different adversarial behaviors.
- **Game Moves and Game Duration.** With the introduction of two intelligent agents with competing objectives, the next step is to define what a game consists of, say in terms of moves, A very simple game such as matching pennies consists of one move for each player. More complex games may be either games with many, but finite number of moves called rounds, or, repeated games where multiple rounds of the game are played successively, resulting possibly in an unending sequence of moves.
- **Intelligent Play.** When does the game-play become intelligent? We may, for example, consider the process to be open-ended where there is repeated game play and learning continues over an indefinite number of games. One widely-used marker for defining intelligence in game playing is by comparison to humans: when a game-playing intelligent agent can competitively play against humans they are usually deemed intelligent. Since the process may be considered to be open-ended, where there is a second intelligent agent inventing new challenges, in principle the learning can continue as long as there is capacity in the learning data structures to acquire additional knowledge. In such a situation, measuring intelligence in competitive game-play is generally based on statistical, relational methods, with the Elo rating system the most widespread methodology. The Elo system [13], commonly used for zero sum games including Chess, Go, and several online video games, assumes an underlying distribution, typically a normal distribution for a human population, and provides a scoring mechanism that, when updated using the results of pairwise game-playing matches, eventually converges to a rating for each player. As players learn to play better,

their rating improves. However, Elo ratings are defined only for zero-sum games. Commensurate measures for intelligent play needs to be investigated for non zero-sum games in the context of adversarial learning.

- **Incremental Learning.** In a turn taking game, each move by a player that is observed by its adversary can serve to incrementally reveal the player's objective and strategy. Each move may also be considered as a probe, where the player wants to learn how the adversary's subsequent moves might be modified as a response. The desired effect, i.e., an intelligent learner that will be able to take advantage of these effects, can only be achieved if the learner is able to learn on a move-by-move basis, i.e., the learning process must be interactive, where the state of knowledge within the learner is always being updated.

- **Combining Past Experiences with Foresight.** Another distinct requirement is that the learner cannot be purely limited by its past experience, but must also have some understanding of its possible actions, and be able to introduce experimental variations into its future actions that are not purely dependent on its past experience. What this means for a game-playing learner is that incorporated into its design is an understanding of the rules of the game and some capacity to explore any move allowed by the rules.

To summarize, we posit that to properly address the problem of dealing intelligently with adversarial interactions, a learner must: (a) learn from past examples of behavior by a combination of memory and generalization (as in supervised learning); (b) incorporate learning as part of its regular behavior, i.e., learn interactively; and, (c) learn within the context of a game, i.e., to play a game with an objective of winning against another, potentially adversarial player. As a consequence, for a two-player game, the learning process will be a two-sided optimization problem for finding a pair of strategies where each player's strategy corresponds to its best response strategy given the strategy being played by its opponent player. In general, each player has an objective, and each player chooses its moves so as to advance towards its own objective, attempting to estimate the effects of the other player on its progress. If there were no contention, then both players would attempt to independently maximize their own utility. There generally is some contention, and so strategies for dealing with that become important. We discuss more about what type of game to learn to play in the next section.

4 What Game to Play?

There are a variety of complex games that have been played by humans such as chess, Go, or Shogi. These games have long challenged both humans and computers. Nevertheless, the competitive activities we engage in every day have characteristics that go beyond these games [20, 24, 28, 29]. A key difference is that many board games have *perfect information*, where each player is assumed to have complete knowledge of the state of the game including the moves made by the opponent. In real life competitive activities we seldom have perfect information about the opponent's past move(s) and the state of the game. It is more the opposite, where the only information we have is obtained by sensing and storing that information and with limited resources, both in time and storage, for doing so. A consequence of this limitation is that the competing player may change the state of the game in ways that, cumulatively over time, will degrade a player's understanding of the state of the game unless they continue to spend resources to maintain an accurate understanding of the game's state. Another key difference is the range of actions we have in real competitive activity. In simple board games there is a very limited range of actions available to players, while in real games we have a very large number of options available. Is there such a thing as a game that is general enough so as to represent any game?

4.1 Core War: A Programming Game

We believe that a more general form of game may defined by what we will call the Turing Game. First, the Turing game is defined by a Turing machine, with the addition of a second Finite State Automaton (FSA). Each of the two FSAs on the Tape define the position of one or the other of the two players. Each FSA may make moves about its environment (Move-Left or Move-Right on the Tape) and may sense its immediate environment (Read-Value), and modify its immediate environment (Write-Value). It is intended that the only interference each FSA may have on the other is via one player executing a Read-Value on a particular location that was previously left as a Write-Value action by the other player. In a general version of this game, each player has the objective to survive, i.e., continue operating, even if at the expense of the other. It is possible that a value written by one player may, when read by the other player, cause that other player to halt, which introduces contention into the game. This idea of the Turing Game is not novel: one instantiation of this idea is called Core War, a programming game created by Jones and Dewdney [10–12]. In Core War, two programs, or *warriors*, compete for control of a memory space, called Core. The programs are written in an simple assembly-like language, named Redcode. Core War was inspired by an earlier game called Darwin by Vyssotsky, Morris and McIlroy [21]. These games are essentially Von Neumann architecture renditions of this type of idea.

   The intent here is to create a game that has similarities with normal games, e.g., with two players (for simplicity), each making moves on a game-board (here one-dimensional), and each player being completely ignorant of the state of the game-board at the beginning, and only imperfect knowledge after visiting any position. The similarity to a Turing machine is intended to suggest, admittedly without proof, that any computable game may be so represented.

4.2 StarCraft-II

StarCraft-II (SC2) is a two-sided, real time strategy game developed by Blizzard Entertainment, and played between two opposing, even-sized teams. Each team can comprise between 1 and 4 players. The objective of each player is to capture and overpower the units and resources of its opponents by strategically deploying its own units and resources. The game has been studied as an attractive platform for AI-enabled game play because of several features that represent many aspects of real-life interactions between two adversaries:

- **Limited visibility of opponent moves and game state.** Each player can perceive its opponents activities and resources only within a finite range of its units. This provides partial visibility of the opponents moves, and, consequently, of the game state.
- **Large state and action spaces and complex actions.** The state space for a SC2 game corresponds to a map within which the game is played; the map size varies from 120×120 to 190×190 cells depending on the size of each team. A player in SC2 can belong to one of three races: Zerg, Terran and Protoss, which are roughly commensurate with the player's capabilities. Each race is characterized by different mobile and stationary units, each with specific capabilities. Every unit has a set of actions that it can perform. Examples of actions include harnessing energy from energy sources, selecting locations to construct buildings utilizing collected energy, moving constructed buildings inside the environment, training and deploying assets to reconnoitre or attack opponent resources, etc. Every action must satisfy certain pre- and post-conditions before it can be executed. For example, a possible strategy for attacking the enemy in a Terran race consists of the following steps that have to be executed in order: first, select space construction vehicles (SCVs) to collect resources like minerals from the environment. Then use the SCVs to construct a building called supply depot followed by another building called a barrack. A barrack can host basic attack units called marines. Thereafter, marines have to be organized or rallied to get them ready for training, followed by the training itself. Upon completion of training the marines can be directed to attack the enemy. The pre-requisites between different steps of the attack strategy require careful coordination between them. Moreover, actions can be coordinated between teammates in multi-player games. Each player in SC2 has an action set of about 10^{26} actions [34]. The combination of action pre-conditions, coordination of actions between teammates and strategically responding to actions of the opponent team makes the set of joint actions extremely complex.
- **Synchronous and asynchronous actions.** Actions can be both synchronous and asynchronous in SC2. For example, actions such as building barracks followed training marine units that have to be performed in sequence are executed synchronously, while actions such as collecting energy and constructing buildings by multiple units of the same or opposing teams could be done in parallel, and executed asynchronously.

- **Large number of rounds.** An SC2 game continues until one team defeats its opponent by destroying all its units. In other words, a game could continue for a very large number of rounds. Average times for games last between 15 and 20 min, with expert players playing upwards of 300 actions per minute.
- **Interface support.** SC2 has an open-source client interface for programming software bots that can interact with the SC2 gaming software via a client protocol called protobuf and play the game as surrogate humans. Researchers and developers have developed a wide variety of interfaces that enable programming of automated AI-based agent to play SC2 against the game or against each other. Notable among these are SC2 learning environment (SC2LE) and its Python component, PySC2 [33], Python-based sharpy-SC2, and interfaces in commonly used high level programming languages including C++, C#, Java and JavaScript.

Evidently, with the enormous size and complexity of the action space, brute-force and enumerative approaches are infeasible to solve an SC2 game. Researchers have recently proposed AI and machine learning-based techniques to develop automatic game playing AI. In [33], authors described a reinforcement learning based agent that automatically improves its playing strategies by learning from its past moves along with sequences of game plays between humans or human-machine teams playing SC2. Subsequently, the same researchers proposed a technique using multi-agent reinforcement learning with self-play [34] to further improve the performance of the AI agent to achieve grandmaster level while playing against human players and placing among the top 99.8% of human SC2 champions. Pang et al. have utilized hierarchical reinforcement learning architecture using macro-actions and transfer learning to achieve 93% success against the most difficult level of SC2. In [25], authors have proposed a multi-agent StarCraft-II challenge as a benchmark problem for developing new multi-agent reinforcement learning algorithms and testing their performance. While the complexity of the SC2 game poses a steep learning curve for AI developers not familiar with the game, the similarity of SC2 to many real-life competitive settings including battlefield scenarios makes it an attractive game-based environment for investigating adversarial AI techniques.

4.3   Reconnaissance Chess

Reconnaissance chess (RC) [19] is a two-player game where the game play rules follow chess but the information availability rules are motivated by a century old war game called *Kriegspiel*. The information availability rules introduce the following constraints on the chess game rules:

- **Large Action Space.** RC is played on a standard 8×8 chess board with regular chess pieces. In a seminal paper on computer chess [27], Shannon estimated a lower bound on the number of possible actions or game plays in chess as 10^{120}. Removing suicidal or deliberately game-losing moves, 10^{40} actions are possible in chess.

- **No information about opponent.** Each player cannot see its opponent's pieces or their locations and has no information about its opponent's moves.
- **Limited information about game state.** Each player only has partial information about the current game state or game board. This partial information corresponds to a 3 × 3 subset of cells that a player could reveal via making a probe at any location on the board, before taking its turn. No other cell on the game board is visible to a player. When a player's piece is captured by its opponent, the player cannot see the opponent's piece that made the capture. Similarly, when a player captures one of its opponent's pieces, the player is only revealed the location where the capture occurred, but not the opponent piece that was captured.
- **Time-limited.** The game continues for a finite time of 15 min. A player wins if it is able to capture its opponent king within this time, otherwise, the game ends in a draw. Repeated plays of the game does not retain or transfer information between successive games plays.

RC has gained popularity recently as an AI-based gaming platform for adversarial machine learning as it supports development and evaluation of automated game playing strategies in an incomplete information, competitive gaming environment, with an annual competition where RC-playing bots programmed by different human teams compete against each other.

4.4 Poker and Hanabi

Over the past two decades, AI and game theory-based game-playing strategies have been successfully developed for playing multi-player card games like computer poker and its variants such has Texas Hold ém Poker [30]. Here we give a brief overview of Texas Hold ém Poker to illustrate its complexity. The game is played between two (called heads up), and, usually, up to seven players. At the start of the game, each player is dealt two cards that the player can see. The information availability rules specify that a player cannot see its opponents' set of dealt cards nor the un-dealt cards. Consequently, a player has no information about opponents' cards or about the state of the game. The game continues for three rounds. At its turn during a round, a player can select an action such as call, raise, bet, check or fold, depending on the round and actions taken by other players before it in that round. Between rounds four cards from the un-dealt deck of cards are revealed as community cards. The winning player is the player than can combine the community cards with its two cards to form winning combinations that are given by a set of showdown rules. The possible set of states in heads up Texas Hold ém Poker is of the order of 10^{13}. Several automated game theory-based techniques that represent Texas Hold ém Poker as an extensive form game with imperfect information and solve it using techniques including linear programming, excessive gap technique and counter factual regret (CFR) minimization [26] have shown promising results in calculating game-winning strategies. Recently, Bowling et al. reported of solving heads up Texas Hold ém Poker: the first extensive form game with imperfect information to be solved, using an AI-based algorithm called CFR$^+$ minimization [5, 32]. Using CFR$^+$ and related game theoretic and optimization techniques such as self play, regret-based pruning and safe subgame solving, Brown and Sandholm developed AI-based software Liberatus [6] and Pluribus [7] that are capable of defeating human players at Texas Hold ém Poker with up to six players.

Recently, researchers have also proposed a multi-player card game called Hanabi [2] as a challenge problem for AI cooperative game playing. Hanabi, which means fireworks in Japanese, was introduced in 2010. The game contains five suits colored red, blue, green, yellow and white. Each suit has ten cards: three 1-s, two each of 2-s, 3-s and 4-s and one 5, along with eight information tokens and three fuse tokens. As in Poker, the information availability rules of Hanabi only allow limited information about player's cards and the game state. But unlike Poker, in Hanabi, a player can see its opponents' cards, but cannot see its own cards or the un-dealt cards. Also, unlike poker, Hanabi allows players to reveal information at each turn by viewing opponent cards and verbally revealing information such as number of cards of a certain color or number. At their turn, each player discards a card and plays one of their cards by revealing it to all other players, while accruing information and fuse tokens according to the game rules. Exhausting all fuse tokens ends the game with a loss for all players, while all players win if the 5-s of all suits have been played. Hanabi requires cooperation among players. The game state is incrementally revealed making it a sequential game with partial information. Currently, an open source Python-based programming interface called Hanabi Learning Environment [15] is available for research on this game. Researchers have proposed techniques using self-play and reinforcement learning using deep Q-networks [8] and enhancing self-play using symmetries in the mathematical formulation of the game [18] as techniques for Hanabi-playing AI. However, the AI is still far from human level capability and challenging issues in cooperation, reasoning and strategic action selection are open research problems towards developing skillful, Hanabi-playing AI.

5   Conclusions

In this paper, we have posited that conventional supervised learning techniques appear to be inadequate for addressing adversarial learning. The fundamental issue being that the main optimization problem in machine learning needs to be transitioned from a single optimization problem to a bi-level optimization problem with competing objectives between two players, to make it amenable for an adversarial setting. Our discussion on different competitive games along with characteristics that make them amenable for modeling real-life interaction scenarios representing competitive play between humans enunciates the fact that developing automated AI and machine learning techniques that can play and win these games could serve as a suitable means for building AI that is capable of matching or even exceeding human level intelligence. We envisage that with the directions set forth in this chapter, researchers will be able to investigate novel techniques at the intersection of machine learning and competitive game-playing as an enabler for human-level machine intelligence that is resilient to adversarial challenges.

References

1. Abbe, E., Sandon, C.: Provable limitations of deep learning. CoRR abs/1812.06369 (2018). http://arxiv.org/abs/1812.06369
2. Bard, N., Foerster, J.N., Chandar, S., Burch, N., Lanctot, M., Song, H.F., Parisotto, E., Dumoulin, V., Moitra, S., Hughes, E., et al.: The Hanabi challenge: a new frontier for AI research. Artif. Intell. **280**, 103216 (2020)
3. Bishop, C.M.: Pattern Recognition and Machine Learning. Springer, Berlin (2006)
4. Blanzieri, E., Bryl, A.: A survey of learning-based techniques of email spam filtering. Artif. Intell. Rev. **29**(1), 63–92 (2008)
5. Bowling, M., Burch, N., Johanson, M., Tammelin, O.: Heads-up limit hold'em poker is solved. Science **347**(6218), 145–149 (2015)
6. Brown, N., Sandholm, T.: Libratus: the superhuman AI for no-limit poker. In: Sierra, C. (ed.) Proceedings of the Twenty-Sixth International Joint Conference on Artificial Intelligence, IJCAI 2017, Melbourne, August 19–25, 2017, pp. 5226–5228. ijcai.org (2017). https://doi.org/10.24963/ijcai.2017/772
7. Brown, N., Sandholm, T.: Superhuman AI for multiplayer poker. Science **365**(6456), 885–890 (2019)
8. Canaan, R., Gao, X., Chung, Y., Togelius, J., Nealen, A., Menzel, S.: Evaluating the rainbow DQN agent in Hanabi with unseen partners (2020). Preprint arXiv:2004.13291
9. Clarke, A.C.: Hazards of Prophecy: The Failure of Imagination (in the Collection Profiles of the Future: An Inquiry into the Limits of the Possible), 1st edn. Harper & Row, New York (1962)
10. Core war: The ultimate programming game. https://corewar.co.uk/index.htm. Accessed 30 April 2020
11. Corewars - king of the hill. http://www.koth.org/index.html. Accessed 30 April 2020
12. Corno, F., Sánchez, E., Squillero, G.: Evolving assembly programs: how games help microprocessor validation. IEEE Trans. Evol. Comput. **9**(6), 695–706 (2005)
13. Coulom, R.: Computing "elo ratings" of move patterns in the game of go. ICGA J. **30**(4), 198–208 (2007)
14. Goodfellow, I., Bengio, Y., Courville, A.: Deep Learning. MIT Press, Cambridge (2016)
15. Hanabi learning environment. https://github.com/deepmind/hanabi-learning-environment. Accessed 4 May 2020
16. Hecht-Nielsen, R.: Neurocomputing: picking the human brain. IEEE Spectr. **25**(3), 36–41 (1988)
17. Hinton, G.E.: How neural networks learn from experience. Sci. Am. **267**(3), 144–151 (1992)
18. Hu, H., Lerer, A., Peysakhovich, A., Foerster, J.: Other-play for zero-shot coordination (2020). Preprint arXiv:2003.02979
19. Markowitz, J., Gardner, R.W., Llorens, A.J.: On the complexity of reconnaissance blind chess (2018). Preprint arXiv:1811.03119
20. Newborn, M.: Kasparov Versus Deep Blue: Computer Chess Comes of Age. Springer Science & Business Media, Berlin (2012)
21. Null, A.: Computer recreations: Darwin. Softw.: Pract. Exp. **2**(1), 93–96 (1971)

22. Papernot, N., McDaniel, P., Jha, S., Fredrikson, M., Celik, Z.B., Swami, A.: The limitations of deep learning in adversarial settings. In: 2016 IEEE European Symposium on Security and Privacy (EuroS P), pp. 372–387 (2016)
23. Paudice, A., Muñoz-González, L., Gyorgy, A., Lupu, E.C.: Detection of adversarial training examples in poisoning attacks through anomaly detection (2018). arXiv:1802.03041
24. Rubin, J., Watson, I.: Computer poker: a review. Artif. Intell. **175**(5–6), 958–987 (2011)
25. Samvelyan, M., Rashid, T., Schroeder de Witt, C., Farquhar, G., Nardelli, N., Rudner, T.G., Hung, C.M., Torr, P.H., Foerster, J., Whiteson, S.: The starcraft multi-agent challenge. In: Proceedings of the 18th International Conference on Autonomous Agents and MultiAgent Systems, pp. 2186–2188. International Foundation for Autonomous Agents and Multiagent Systems (2019)
26. Sandholm, T.: The state of solving large incomplete-information games, and application to poker. AI Mag. **31**(4), 13–32 (2010). http://www.aaai.org/ojs/index.php/aimagazine/article/view/2311
27. Shannon, C.E.: Xxii. programming a computer for playing chess. Lond. Edinb. Dublin Philos. Mag. J. Sci. **41**(314), 256–275 (1950)
28. Silver, D., Schrittwieser, J., Simonyan, K., Antonoglou, I., Huang, A., Guez, A., Hubert, T., Baker, L., Lai, M., Bolton, A., et al.: Mastering the game of go without human knowledge. Nature **550**(7676), 354–359 (2017)
29. Silver, D., Hubert, T., Schrittwieser, J., Antonoglou, I., Lai, M., Guez, A., Lanctot, M., Sifre, L., Kumaran, D., Graepel, T., et al.: A general reinforcement learning algorithm that masters chess, shogi, and go through self-play. Science **362**(6419), 1140–1144 (2018)
30. Sklansky, D.: The Theory of Poker. Two Plus Two Publishing LLC, Las Vegas (1999)
31. Szegedy, C., Zaremba, W., Sutskever, I., Bruna, J., Erhan, D., Goodfellow, I., Fergus, R.: Intriguing properties of neural networks (2013). Preprint arXiv:1312.6199
32. Tammelin, O., Burch, N., Johanson, M., Bowling, M.: Solving heads-up limit Texas hold'em. In: Yang, Q., Wooldridge, M.J. (eds.) Proceedings of the Twenty-Fourth International Joint Conference on Artificial Intelligence, IJCAI 2015, Buenos Aires, July 25–31, 2015, pp. 645–652. AAAI Press (2015). http://ijcai.org/Abstract/15/097
33. Vinyals, O., Ewalds, T., Bartunov, S., Georgiev, P., Vezhnevets, A.S., Yeo, M., Makhzani, A., Küttler, H., Agapiou, J., Schrittwieser, J., et al.: Starcraft ii: a new challenge for reinforcement learning (2017). Preprint arXiv:1708.04782
34. Vinyals, O., Babuschkin, I., Czarnecki, W.M., Mathieu, M., Dudzik, A., Chung, J., Choi, D.H., Powell, R., Ewalds, T., Georgiev, P., et al.: Grandmaster level in starcraft ii using multi-agent reinforcement learning. Nature **575**(7782), 350–354 (2019)
35. Wang, Y., Yao, Q.: Few-shot learning: a survey. CoRR abs/1904.05046 (2019). http://arxiv.org/abs/1904.05046
36. Wang, W., Zheng, V.W., Yu, H., Miao, C.: A survey of zero-shot learning: settings, methods, and applications. ACM Trans. Intell. Syst. Technol. **10**(2) (2019). https://doi.org/10.1145/3293318

Security of Distributed Machine Learning

A Game-Theoretic Approach to Design Secure DSVM

Rui Zhang and Quanyan Zhu

Abstract Distributed machine learning algorithms play a significant role in processing massive data sets over large networks. However, the increasing reliance on machine learning on information and communication technologies (ICTs) makes it inherently vulnerable to cyber threats. This work aims to develop secure distributed algorithms to protect the learning from data poisoning and network attacks. We establish a game-theoretic framework to capture the conflicting goals of a learner who uses distributed support vector machines (SVMs) and an attacker who is capable of modifying training data and labels. We develop a fully distributed and iterative algorithm to capture real-time reactions of the learner at each node to adversarial behaviors. The numerical results show that distributed SVM is prone to fail in different types of attacks, and their impact has a strong dependence on the network structure and attack capabilities.

Keywords Adversarial distributed machine learning · Game theory · Distributed support vector machines · Label-flipping attack · Data-poisoning attack · Network-type attacks

1 Introduction

Recently, parallel and distributed machine learning (ML) algorithms have been developed to scale up computations in large datasets and networked systems [2], such as distributed spam filtering [30] and distributed traffic control [8]. However,

Taken partially from the dissertation submitted to the Faculty of the New York University Tandon School of Engineering in partial fulfillment of the requirements for the degree Doctor of Philosophy, January 2020 [40].

R. Zhang (✉) · Q. Zhu
New York University, Brooklyn, NY, USA
e-mail: rz885@nyu.edu; qz494@nyu.edu

they are inherently vulnerable to adversaries who can exploit them. For instance, nodes of distributed spam filter system can fail to detect spam email messages after an attacker modifies the training data [33], or disrupts the network services using denial-of-service attacks [38].

ML algorithms are often open-source tools and security is usually not the primary concerns of their designers. It is undemanding for an adversary to acquire the complete information of the algorithm, and exploits its vulnerabilities. Also, the growing reliance of ML algorithms on off-the-shelf information and communication technologies (ICTs) such as cloud computing and the wireless networks [17] has made it even easier for adversaries to exploit the existing known vulnerabilities of ICTs to achieve their goals. Security becomes a more critical issue in the paradigm of distributed ML, since the learning consists of a large number of nodes that communicate using ICTs, and its attack surface grows tremendously compared to its centralized counterpart.

Hence, it is imperative to design secure distributed ML algorithms against cyber threats. Current research endeavors have focused on two distinct directions. One is to develop robust algorithms despite uncertainties in the dataset [15, 20, 28]. The second one is to improve detection and prevention techniques to defend against cyber threats, e.g., [23, 24, 36]. These approaches have mainly focused on centralized ML and computer networks, separately. The investigation of security issues in the distributed ML over networks is lacking.

The challenges of developing secure distributed machine learning arise from the complexity of the adversarial behaviors and the network effects of the distributed system. The attacker's strategies can be multi-stage. For instance, he can reach his target to modify training data by launching multiple successful network attacks. Furthermore, the impact of an attack can propagate over the network. Uncompromised nodes can be affected by the misinformation from compromised nodes, leading to a cascading effect.

Traditional detection and defense strategies for centralized ML and networked systems are not sufficient to protect the distributed ML systems from attacks. To bridge this gap, this work aims to develop a game-theoretic framework to model the interactions of an attacker and a defender to assess and design security strategies in distributed systems. Game theory has been used to address the security issues in centralized ML, e.g., [22, 25], and those in computer networks [21, 27, 31] and cyber-physical networks [9, 11, 12, 35]. The proposed game-theoretic model captures the network structures of the distributed system and leads to fully distributed and iterative algorithms that can be implemented at each node as defense strategies.

In particular, we use game models to study the impact on consensus-based distributed support vector machines (DSVMs) of an attacker who is capable of modifying training data and labels. In [41, 42, 45], we have built a game-theoretic framework to investigate the impacts of data poisoning attacks to DSVMs, we have further proposed four defense methods and verified their effectiveness with numerical experiments in [48]. In [43], we have proposed a game-theoretic framework to model the interactions between a DSVM learner and an attacker who can modify the training labels.

In this paper, we extend our previous works by studying a broad range of attack models and classify them into two types. One is ML attacks, which exploit the vulnerabilities of ML algorithm, and the other one is Net-attacks, which arise from the vulnerabilities of the communication network. We then build the game-theoretic minimax problem to capture the competition between a DSVM learner and an attacker who can modify training data and labels. With alternating direction method of multipliers (ADMM) [7, 44, 46], we develop a fully distributed iterative algorithms where each compromised node operates its own sub-max-problem for the attacker and sub-min-problem for the learner. The game between a DSVM learner and an attacker can be viewed as a collection of small sub-games associated with compromised nodes. This unique structure enables the analysis of per-node-behaviors and the transmission of misleading information under the game framework.

Numerical results on Spambase data set [19] are provided to illustrate the impact of different attack models by the attacker. We find that network plays a significant role in the security of DSVM, a balanced network with fewer nodes and higher degrees are less prone to attackers who can control the whole system. We also find that nodes with higher degrees are more vulnerable. The distributed ML systems are found to be prone to network attacks even though the attacker only adds small noise to information transmitted between neighboring nodes. A summary of notations in this paper is provided in the following table.

Summary of notations	
$\mathcal{V}$, v, $\mathcal{B}_v$	Set of nodes, node v, set of neighboring nodes of node v
$\mathbf{w}_v, b_v, \mathbf{r}_v$	Decision variables at node v
$\mathbf{x}_{vn}, y_{vn}$	n-th data and label at node v
$\mathbf{X}_v, \mathbf{Y}_v$	Data matrix and label matrix at node v
ω_{vu}	Consensus variable between node v and node u
θ_v	Indicator vector of flipped labels at node v
δ_{vn}	Vector of data poisoning on the n-th data at node v

2 Preliminary

Consider a distributed linear support vector machines learner in the network with $\mathcal{V} = \{1, .., V\}$ representing the set of nodes. Node $v \in \mathcal{V}$ only communicates with his neighboring nodes $\mathcal{B}_v \subseteq \mathcal{V}$. Note that without loss of generality, any two nodes in this network are connected by a path, i.e., there is no isolated node in this network. At every node v, a labelled training set $\mathcal{D}_v = \{(\mathbf{x}_{vn}, y_{vn})\}_{n=1}^{N_v}$ of size N_v is available. The goal of the learner is to find a maximum-margin linear discriminant function $g_v(\mathbf{x}) = \mathbf{x}^T \mathbf{w}_v^* + b_v*$ at every node $v \in \mathcal{V}$ based on its local training set

$\mathcal{D}_v$. Consensus constraints $\mathbf{w}_1^* = \mathbf{w}_2^* = \ldots = \mathbf{w}_V^*, b_1^* = b_2^* = \ldots = b_V^*$ are used to force all local decision variables $\{\mathbf{w}_v^*, b_v^*\}$ to agree across neighboring nodes. This approach enables each node to classify any new input $\mathbf{x}$ to one of the two classes $\{+1, -1\}$ without communicating $\mathcal{D}_v$ to other nodes $v' \neq v$. The discriminant function $g_v(\mathbf{x})$ can be obtained by solving the following optimization problem:

$$\min_{\{\mathbf{w}_v, b_v\}} \frac{1}{2} \sum_{v \in \mathcal{V}} \| \mathbf{w}_v \|^2 + VC_l \sum_{v \in \mathcal{V}} \sum_{n=1}^{N_v} \left[1 - y_{vn}(\mathbf{w}_v^T \mathbf{x}_{vn} + b_v) \right]_+ \tag{1}$$
$$\text{s.t. } \mathbf{w}_v = \mathbf{w}_u, b_v = b_u, \forall v \in \mathcal{V}, u \in \mathcal{B}_v.$$

In the above problem, the term $\left[1 - y_{vn}(\mathbf{w}_v^T \mathbf{x}_{vn} + b_v) \right]_+ := \max[0, 1 - y_{vn}(\mathbf{w}_v^T \mathbf{x}_{vn} + b_v)]$ is the hinge loss function, C_l is a tunable positive scalar for the learner. To solve Problem (1), we first define $\mathbf{r}_v := [\mathbf{w}_v^T, b_v]^T$, the augmented matrix $\mathbf{X}_v := [(\mathbf{x}_{v1}, \ldots, \mathbf{x}_{vN_v})^T, \mathbf{1}_v]$, and the diagonal label matrix $\mathbf{Y}_v := diag([y_{v1}, \ldots, y_{vN_v}])$. With these definitions, it follows readily that $\mathbf{w}_v = \widehat{\mathbf{I}}_{p \times (p+1)} \mathbf{r}_v, \widehat{\mathbf{I}}_{p \times (p+1)} = [\mathbf{I}_{p \times p}, \mathbf{0}_{p \times 1}]$ is a $p \times (p+1)$ matrix with its first p columns being an identity matrix, and its $(p + 1)$ column being a zero vector. Thus, Problem (1) can be rewritten as

$$\min_{\{\mathbf{r}_v, \omega_{vu}\}} \frac{1}{2} \sum_{v \in \mathcal{V}} \mathbf{r}_v^T \Pi_{p+1} \mathbf{r}_v + VC_l \sum_{v \in \mathcal{V}} \mathbf{1}_v^T \{\mathbf{1}_v - \mathbf{Y}_v \mathbf{X}_v \mathbf{r}_v\}_+ \tag{2}$$
$$\text{s.t. } \mathbf{r}_v = \omega_{vu}, \omega_{vn} = \mathbf{r}_u, \quad v \in \mathcal{V}, u \in \mathcal{B}_v,$$

where the consensus variable ω_{vu} is used to decompose the decision variable $\mathbf{r}_v$ to its neighbors $\mathbf{r}_u$. Note that $\Pi_{p+1} = \widehat{\mathbf{I}}_{p \times (p+1)}^T \widehat{\mathbf{I}}_{p \times (p+1)}$ is a $(p + 1) \times (p + 1)$ identity matrix with its $(p+1, p+1)$-st entry being 0. The term $\{\mathbf{1}_v - \mathbf{Y}_v \mathbf{X}_v \mathbf{r}_v\}_+ := \max[\mathbf{0}_v, \mathbf{1}_v - \mathbf{Y}_v \mathbf{X}_v \mathbf{r}_v]$, which returns a vector of size N_v. The algorithm of solving Problem (1) can be shown as the following lemma from Proposition 1 in [18].

Lemma 1 *With arbitrary initialization* $\mathbf{r}_v^{(0)}, \lambda_v^{(0)}$ *and* $\alpha_v^{(0)} = \mathbf{0}_{(p+1) \times 1}$, *the iterations per node are:*

$$\lambda_v^{(t+1)} \in \arg \max_{\mathbf{0} \leq \lambda_v \leq VC_l \mathbf{1}_v} -\frac{1}{2} \lambda_v^T \mathbf{Y}_v \mathbf{X}_v \mathbf{U}_v^{-1} \mathbf{X}_v^T \mathbf{Y}_v \lambda_v + (\mathbf{1}_v + \mathbf{Y}_v \mathbf{X}_v \mathbf{U}_v^{-1} \mathbf{f}_v^{(t)})^T \lambda_v, \tag{3}$$

$$\mathbf{r}_v^{(t+1)} = \mathbf{U}_v^{-1} \left(\mathbf{X}_v^T \mathbf{Y}_v \lambda_v^{(t+1)} - \mathbf{f}_v^{(t)} \right), \tag{4}$$

$$\alpha_v^{(t+1)} = \alpha_v^{(t)} + \frac{\eta}{2} \sum_{u \in \mathcal{B}_v} \left[\mathbf{r}_v^{(t+1)} - \mathbf{r}_u^{(t+1)} \right], \tag{5}$$

where $\mathbf{U}_v = \Pi_{p+1} + 2\eta |\mathcal{B}_v| \mathbf{I}_{p+1}, \mathbf{f}_v^{(t)} = 2\alpha_v^{(t)} - \eta \sum_{u \in \mathcal{B}_v} (\mathbf{r}_v^{(t)} + \mathbf{r}_u^{(t)})$.

Note that ω_{vu} has been solved directly and plugged into each equations. λ_v and α_v are Lagrange multipliers. The ADMM-DSVM algorithm is illustrated in Fig. 1.

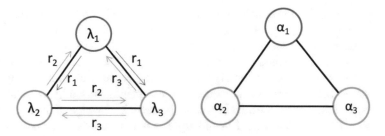

Fig. 1 DSVM example [43]. At every iteration, each node v first computes λ_v and $\mathbf{r}_v$ by (3) and (4). Then, each node sends its $\mathbf{r}_v$ to its neighboring nodes. After that, each node computes α_v using (5). Iterations continue until convergence

Note that at any given iteration t of the algorithm, each node $v \in \mathcal{V}$ computes its own local discriminant function $g_v^{(t)}(\mathbf{x})$ for any vector $\mathbf{x}$ as $g_v^{(t)}(\mathbf{x}) = [\mathbf{x}^T, 1]\mathbf{r}_v^{(t)}$. Since we only need the decision variables $\mathbf{r}_v$ for the discriminant function, we use the **DSVM**$_v$ as a short-hand notation to represent iterations (3)–(5) at node v:

$$\mathbf{r}_v^{(t+1)} \in \mathbf{DSVM}_v\left(\mathbf{X}_v, \mathbf{Y}_v, \mathbf{r}_v^{(t)}, \{\mathbf{r}_u^{(t)}\}_{u \in \mathcal{B}_v}\right). \tag{6}$$

The iterations stated in Lemma 1 are referred to as ADMM-DSVM. It is a fully decentralized network operation. Each node v only shares decision variables $\mathbf{r}_v$ to his neighboring nodes $u \in \mathcal{B}_v$. Other DSVM approaches include distributed chunking SVMs [32] and distributed parallel SVMs [26], where support vectors (SVs) are exchanged between each nodes, and distributed semiparametric SVMs, where the centroids of local SVMs are exchanged among neighboring nodes [32]. In comparison, ADMM-DSVM has no restrictions on the network topology or the type of data, and thus, we use it as an example to illustrate the impact of the attacker on distributed learning algorithms.

3   Attack Models and Related Works

In this section, we summarize and analyze possible attack models from the attacker. We start by identifying the attacker's goal and his knowledge. Based on the three critical characteristics of information, the attacker's goal can be captured as damaging the confidentiality, integrity and availability of the systems [29]. Damaging confidentiality indicates that the attacker intends to acquire private information. Damaging integrity means that the data or the models used by the learner are modified or replaced by the attacker, which can not represent real information anymore. Damaging availability indicates that the attacker, which is an unauthorized user, uses the information or services provided by the learner. In this paper, we assume that the attacker intends to damage the integrity of the distributed ML systems by modifying either the data or the models of the learner.

The impacts of the attacker are affected by the attacker's knowledge of the learner's systems. For example, an attacker may only know the data used by the learner, but he does not know the algorithm the learner use; or he may only know some nodes of the network. To fully capture the damages caused by the attacker, in this paper, we assume that the attacker has a complete knowledge of the learner, i.e., the attacker knows the learner's data and algorithm and the network topology.

The attack models on distributed ML learner can be summarized into two main categories. One is the machine learning type attacks (ML-attacks) [1], the other one is the network type attacks (Net-attacks) [13]. In the ML-attacks, the attacker can exploit machine learning systems which produces classification or prediction errors. In the Net-attacks, an adversary attacks a networked system to compromise the security of this system by actions, which leads to the leak of private information or the failure of operations in this network. In this paper, we further divide ML-attacks into two sub-categories, training attacks and testing attacks. Note that the attack models described here are generally applicable to different machine learning algorithms. The focus of this work is to investigate the impact of these attack models on DSVM, which provides fundamental insights on the inherent vulnerability of distributed machine learning.

3.1 Training Attacks

In the training attacks, an adversary attacks the learner at the time when the learner solves Problem (1). In these attacks, communications in the network may lead to unanticipated results as misleading information from compromised nodes can be spread to and then used by uncompromised nodes. One challenge of analyzing training attacks is that the consequences of attacker's actions may not be directly visible. For example, assuming that the attacker modifies some training data $\mathbf{x}_{vn}$ in node v, the learner may not be able to find out which data has been modified, and furthermore, in distributed settings, the learner may not even be able to detect which nodes are under attack. We further divide training attacks into three categories based on the scope of modifications made by the attacker.

3.1.1 Training Labels Attacks

In this category, the attacker can modify the training labels $\{y_{vn}\}_{n=1,...,N_v}$, where $v \in \mathcal{V}_a$. After training data with flipped labels, the discriminant functions will be prone to give wrong labels to the testing data. In early works [4, 39], centralized SVMs under training label attacks have been studied, and robust SVMs have been brought up to reduce the effects of such attacks. In this work, we further extend such attack models to distributed SVM algorithms, and we use game theory to model the interactions between the DSVM learner and the attacker. We verify the effects of the attacker with numerical experiments.

3.1.2 Training Data Attacks

In this category, the attacker modifies the training data $\{\mathbf{x}_{vn}\}_{n=1,\ldots,N_v}$ on compromised nodes $v \in \mathcal{V}_a$. Since the training and testing data are assumed to be generated from the same distribution, the discriminant function found with training data on distribution $\mathscr{X}$ can be used to classify testing data from the same distribution $\mathscr{X}$. However, after modifying training data $\mathbf{x}_{vn}$ into $\widehat{\mathbf{x}}_{vn}$, which belongs to a different distribution $\widehat{\mathscr{X}}$, the discriminant function with training such crafted data is suitable to classify data of distribution $\widehat{\mathscr{X}}$. Thus, the testing data $\mathbf{x} \in \mathscr{X}$ are prone to be misclassified with this discriminant function.

The attacker can delete or craft several features [15, 28], change the training data of one class [14], add noise to training data [3], change the distributions of training data [25], inject crafted data [5], and so on. However, these works aim at centralized machine learning algorithms. In distributed algorithms, the information transmissions between neighboring nodes can make uncompromised nodes to misclassify testing data after training with information from compromised nodes. In [41], an attacker aims at reducing a DSVM learner's classification accuracy by changing training data $\mathbf{x}_{vn}$ in node $v \in \mathcal{V}_a$ into $\widehat{\mathbf{x}}_{vn} := \mathbf{x}_{vn} - \delta_{vn}$. This work shows that the performances of DSVM under adversarial environments are highly dependent on network topologies.

3.1.3 Training Models Attacks

The DSVM learner aims to find the discriminant function with the lowest risks by solving Problem (1) with local training sets $\mathscr{D}_v$. However, the attacker may change Problem (1) into a different problem or he can modify parameters in Problem (1). For example, when the attacker changes C_l in Problem (1) into 0, the learner can only find $\mathbf{w}_v = \mathbf{0}$, which does not depend on the distribution of training data, and thus, the learner will misclassify input testing data in the same distribution.

With training attacks, the DSVM leaner will find wrong decision variables $\widehat{\mathbf{w}}_v^*$ and $\widehat{b}_v^*$ in compromised node $v \in \mathcal{V}_a$. However, the consensus constraints $\mathbf{w}_1^* = \mathbf{w}_2^* = \ldots = \mathbf{w}_V^*, b_1^* = b_2^* = \ldots = b_V^*$ force all the decision variables to agree on each other. Hence uncompromised nodes with correct decision variables will be affected by misleading decision variables from compromised nodes. As a result, the training process in the network can be damaged even the attacker only attacks a small number of nodes.

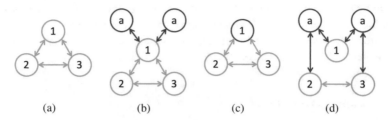

Fig. 2 Network attacks examples. (**a**) No attack. The learner uses a fully connected network with 3 nodes. (**b**) Node capture attacks. The attacker controls Node 1 and make modifications on it. (**c**) Sybil attacks. Two red malicious nodes are generated by the attacker and pretend that they are in the training network. (**d**) MITM attacks. The attacker creates adversarial nodes (depicted in red) and pretend to be the other nodes on the connections

3.2 Testing Attacks

In testing attacks, the attacker attacks at the time when the DSVM learner labels new input $\mathbf{x}$ into $+1$ or -1 with $\mathbf{w}_v^*$ and b_v^* from the solved Problem (1). The attacker can conduct three different operations in testing attacks.

Firstly, the attacker can directly change the given label y of the testing data $\mathbf{x}$ into $-y$, and thus a wrong label is generated with this operation. Secondly, the attacker can replace the testing data $\mathbf{x}$ with crafted $\widehat{\mathbf{x}}$, or he can modify that into $\widehat{\mathbf{x}} = \mathbf{x} - \delta$ [6]. In such cases, the learner gives the label of $\widehat{\mathbf{x}}$ rather than the label of $\mathbf{x}$, which leads to misclassification. Thirdly, the attacker can modify or replace $\mathbf{w}_v^*$ and b_v^* into $\widehat{\mathbf{w}}_v^*$ and $\widehat{b}_v^*$, and thus the compromised discriminant function $\widehat{g}_v(\mathbf{x}) = \mathbf{x}^T \widehat{\mathbf{w}}_v^* + \widehat{b}_v^*$ will yield wrong results. A simple example is that the attacker can set $\widehat{\mathbf{w}}_v^* = -\mathbf{w}_v^*$ and $\widehat{b}_v^* = -b_v^*$, thus $\widehat{g}_v(\mathbf{x}) = -g_v(\mathbf{x})$, which leads to contrary predictions.

Testing attacks can cause disastrous consequences in centralized machine learning algorithms as there is only one discriminant function. However, Testing attacks are weak in distributed machine learning algorithms as uncompromised nodes can still give correct predictions, and compromised nodes can be easily detected as they have higher classification risks.

3.3 Network Attacks

Network attacks can pose a significant threat with potentially severe consequences on networked systems [13]. Since distributed machine learning algorithms have been developed to solve large-scale problems using networked systems [18], network attacks can also cause damages on distributed learning systems. Network attacks include node capture attacks, Sybil attacks, and Man-In-The-Middle attacks, which are illustrated in Fig. 2.

In node capture attacks (Fig. 2b), an attacker gains access into the network, and controls a set of nodes, then he can alter both software programming and hardware configuration, and influence the outcome of network protocols [37]. When the attacker conducts node capture attacks on a DSVM learner, he can modify either the data in the compromised nodes, or the algorithms of the learner. Both of the modifications can lead to misclassifications in compromised nodes. Moreover, the attacker can also send misleading information through network connections between neighboring nodes, thus even uncompromised nodes can be affected by the attacker.

In Sybil attacks (Fig. 2c), the attacker can create an adversarial node in the middle of a connection, and talk to both nodes and pretends to be the other node [34]. If such attacks happen on the network of a DSVM learner, nodes in compromised connections will receive misleading information, and thus, the classifications in these nodes will be damaged.

In Man-in-the-Middle (MITM) attacks (Fig. 2d), the attacker can create an adversarial node in the middle of a connection, talk to both nodes and pretend to be the other node [16]. If such attacks happen on the network of a DSVM learner, nodes in compromised connections will receive misleading information, and thus classifications in these nodes will be damaged.

There are many other network attack models, such as botnet attacks [49] and denial of service [38], which makes it challenging to analyze and defend attacker's behaviors. Though distributed systems improve the efficiency of the learning algorithms, however, the systems becomes more vulnerable to network attacks. Thus, it is important to design secure distributed ML algorithms against potential adversaries.

With various types of attack models, a distributed machine learning learner can be vulnerable in a networked system. Thus, it is important to design secure distributed algorithms against potential adversaries. Since the learner aims to increase the classification accuracy, while the attacker seeks to reduce that accuracy, game theory becomes a useful tool to capture the conflicting interests between the learner and the attacker. The equilibrium of this game allows us to predict the outcomes of a learner under adversary environments. In the next section, we build a game-theoretic framework to capture the conflicts between a DSVM learner and an attacker who can modify training labels and data.

4   A Game-Theoretic Modeling of Attacks

In this section, we use training attacks as an example to illustrate the game-theoretic modeling of the interactions between a DSVM learner and an attacker. We mainly focus on modelling training labels attacks, and the training data attacks.

4.1 Training Labels Attacks

In training labels attacks, the attacker controls a set of nodes $\mathcal{V}_a$, and aims at breaking the training process by flipping training labels y_{vn} to $\widehat{y}_{vn} =: -y_{vn}$. To model the flipped labels at each node, we first define the matrix of expanded training data $\widehat{\mathbf{X}}_v := [[\mathbf{x}_{v1}, \ldots, \mathbf{x}_{vN_v}, \mathbf{x}_{v1}, \ldots, \mathbf{x}_{vN_v}]^T, \widehat{\mathbf{1}}_v]$ and the diagonal matrix of expanded labels $\widehat{\mathbf{Y}}_v := diag([y_{v1}, \ldots, y_{vN_v}, -y_{v1}, \ldots, -y_{vN_v}])$. Note that the first N_v data and the second N_v data are the same in the matrix of expanded training data. We further introduce corresponding indicator vector $\theta_v := [\theta_{v1}, \ldots, \theta_{v(2N_v)}]^T$, where $\theta_{vn} \in \{0, 1\}$, and $\theta_{vn} + \theta_{v(n+N_v)} = 1$, for $n = 1, \ldots, N_v$ [39]. θ_v indicates whether the label has been flipped, for example, if $\theta_{vn} = 0$ for $n = 1, \ldots, N_v$, i.e., $\theta_{v(n+N_v)} = 1$, then the label of data $\mathbf{x}_{vn}$ has been flipped. Note that $\theta_v = [\mathbf{1}_v^T, \mathbf{0}_v^T]^T$ indicates that there is no flipped label.

Since the learner aims to minimize the classification errors by minimizing the objective function in Problem (2), the attacker's intention to maximize classification errors can be captured as maximizing that objective function. As a result, the interactions of the DSVM learner and the attacker can be captured as a nonzero-sum game. Furthermore, since they have same objective functions with opposite intentions, the nonzero-sum game can be reformulated into a zero-sum game, which takes the minimax or max-min form [43]:

$$
\begin{aligned}
\min_{\{\mathbf{r}_v, \omega_{vu}\}} \max_{\{\theta_v\}_{v \in \mathcal{V}_a}} \ & K(\{\mathbf{r}_v, \omega_{vu}\}, \{\theta_v\}) := \frac{1}{2} \sum_{v \in \mathcal{V}} \mathbf{r}_v^T \Pi_{p+1} \mathbf{r}_v \\
& + V C_l \sum_{v \in \mathcal{V}} \theta_v^T \{\widehat{\mathbf{1}}_v - \widehat{\mathbf{Y}}_v \widehat{\mathbf{X}}_v \mathbf{r}_v\}_+ - V_a C_a \sum_{v \in \mathcal{V}_a} \theta_v^T [\mathbf{0}_v^T, \mathbf{1}_v^T]^T
\end{aligned}
$$

$$
\begin{aligned}
\text{s.t.} \quad & \mathbf{r}_v = \omega_{vu}, \omega_{vn} = \mathbf{r}_u, && v \in \mathcal{V}, u \in \mathcal{B}_v; && \text{(7a)} \\
& \theta_v = [\mathbf{1}_v^T, \mathbf{0}_v^T]^T; && v \in \mathcal{V}_l; && \text{(7b)} \\
& \mathbf{q}_v^T \theta_v \leq Q_v, && v \in \mathcal{V}_a; && \text{(7c)} \\
& [\mathbf{I}_{N_v}, \mathbf{I}_{N_v}] \theta_v = \mathbf{1}_v, && v \in \mathcal{V}_a; && \text{(7d)} \\
& \theta_v \subseteq \{0, 1\}_{2N_v} && v \in \mathcal{V}_a. && \text{(7e)}
\end{aligned}
$$

(7)

In (7), $\widehat{\mathbf{1}}_v = [1, 1, \ldots, 1]_{2N_v}^T$ denotes a vector of size $2N_v$, $\mathcal{V}_l$ denotes the set of uncompromised nodes. Note that the first two terms in the objective function and Constraints (7a) are related to the min-problem for the learner. When $\theta_v = [\mathbf{1}_v^T, \mathbf{0}_v^T]^T$, i.e., there are no flipped labels, the min-problem is equivalent to Problem (2). The last two terms in the objective function and Constraints (7c)–(7e) are related to the max-problem for the attacker. Note that the last term of the objection function represents the number of flipped labels in compromised nodes. By minimizing this term, the attacker aims to create the largest impact by flipping the fewest labels. In Constraints (7c), $\mathbf{q}_v := [0, .., 0, q_{v(N_v+1)}, \ldots, q_{v(2N_v)}]^T$, where $q_{v(N_v+n)}$ indicates the cost for flipping the labels of $\mathbf{x}_{vn}$ in node v. This constraint indicates that the capability of the attacker is limited to flip labels with a boundary Q_v at a compromised node v. Constraints (7d) show that the labels in compromised nodes are either flipped or not flipped.

The Minimax-Problem (7) captures the learner's intention to minimize the classification errors with attacker's intention of maximizing that errors by flipping labels. Problem (7) can be also written into a max-min form, which captures the attacker's intention to maximize the classification errors while the learner tries to minimize it. By minimax theorem, the minimax form in (7) is equivalent to its max-min form. Thus, solving Problem (7) can be interpreted as finding the saddle-point equilibrium of the zero-sum game between the learner and the attacker.

Definition 1 Let $\mathscr{S}_L$ and $\mathscr{S}_A$ be the action sets for the DSVM learner and the attacker respectively. Then, the strategy pair $\left(\{\mathbf{r}_v^*, \omega_{vu}^*\}, \{\theta_v^*\}\right)$ is a saddle-point equilibrium solution of the zero-sum game defined by the triple $G_z := \langle\{L, A\}, \{\mathscr{S}_L, \mathscr{S}_A\}, K\rangle$, if $K\left(\{\mathbf{r}_v^*, \omega_{vu}^*\}, \{\theta_v\}\right) \leq K\left(\{\mathbf{r}_v^*, \omega_{vu}^*\}, \{\theta_v^*\}\right) \leq K\left(\{\mathbf{r}_v, \omega_{vu}\}, \{\theta_v^*\}\right), \forall v \in \mathscr{V}_a$, where K is the objective function in Problem (7).

To solve Problem (7), we construct the best response dynamics for the max-problem and min-problem separately. The max-problem and the min-problem can be achieved by fixing $\{\mathbf{r}_v^*, \omega_{vu}^*\}$ and $\{\theta_v^*\}$, respectively. With solving both problems in a distributed way, we achieve the fully distributed iterations of solving Problem (7) as

$$
\theta_v^{(t+1)} \in \arg\max_{\theta_v} VC_l\theta_v^T\{\widehat{\mathbf{1}}_v - \widehat{\mathbf{Y}}_v\widehat{\mathbf{X}}_v\mathbf{r}_v^{(t)}\}_+ - V_aC_a\theta_v^T[\mathbf{0}_v^T, \mathbf{1}_v^T]^T
$$

$$
\text{s.t.} \begin{array}{ll} \mathbf{q}_v^T\theta_v \leq Q_v, & \text{(8a)} \\ \left[\mathbf{I}_{N_v}, \mathbf{I}_{N_v}\right]\theta_v = \mathbf{1}_v, & \text{(8b)} \\ \widehat{\mathbf{0}}_v \leq \theta_v \leq \widehat{\mathbf{1}}_v. & \text{(8c)} \end{array} \tag{8}
$$

$$
\mathbf{r}_v^{(t+1)} \in \mathbf{DSVM}_{v,L}\left(\widehat{\mathbf{X}}_v, \widehat{\mathbf{Y}}_v, \mathbf{r}_v^{(t)}, \{\mathbf{r}_u^{(t)}\}_{u\in\mathscr{B}_v} | \theta_v^{(t+1)}\right) \tag{9}
$$

Problem (8) is a linear programming problem. Note that integer constraint (7e) has been further relaxed into (8c). It captures the attacker's actions in compromised nodes $v \in \mathscr{V}_a$. Note that each node can achieve their own θ_v without transmitting information to other nodes. Problem (9) comes from the min-part of Problem (7), which can be solved using similar method in [18] with ADMM [7]. Note that $\mathbf{DSVM}_{v,L}$ differs from $\mathbf{DSVM}_v$ only in the feasible set of the Lagrange multipliers λ_v, In $\mathbf{DSVM}_{v,L}, \mathbf{0} \leq \lambda_v \leq VC_l\theta_v^{(t+1)}$, where $\theta_v^{(t+1)}$ indicates whether the label has been flipped, and it comes from the attacker's Problem (8).

With (8) and (9), the algorithm of solving Problem (7) can be summarized: Each compromised node computes θ_v via (8), then compromised and uncompromised nodes compute $\mathbf{r}_v$ via (6) and (9), respectively. The iterations will go until convergence.

4.2   Training Data Attacks

In training data attacks, the attacker has the ability to modify the training data $\mathbf{x}_{vn}$ into $\widehat{\mathbf{x}}_{vn} := \mathbf{x}_{vn} - \delta_{vn}$ in compromised node $v \in \mathcal{V}_a$. Following a similar method in training label attacks, we can capture the interactions of the DSVM learner and the attacker as a zero-sum game which is shown as follows:

$$
\min_{\{\mathbf{w}_v, b_v\}} \max_{\{\delta_{vn}\}} K \left(\{\mathbf{w}_v, b_v\}, \{\delta_{vn}\} \right) := \tfrac{1}{2} \sum_{v \in \mathcal{V}} \|\mathbf{w}_v\|^2
$$
$$
+ V_l C_l \sum_{v \in \mathcal{V}_l} \sum_{n=1}^{N_v} \left[1 - y_{vn} (\mathbf{w}_v^T \mathbf{x}_{vn} + b_v) \right]_+
$$
$$
+ V_a C_l \sum_{v \in \mathcal{V}_a} \sum_{n=1}^{N_v} \left[1 - y_{vn} (\mathbf{w}_v^T (\mathbf{x}_{vn} - \delta_{vn}) + b_v) \right]_+ \tag{10}
$$
$$
- V_a C_a \sum_{v \in \mathcal{V}_a} \sum_{n=1}^{N_v} \|\delta_{vn}\|_0
$$
$$
\text{s.t.} \quad \begin{aligned} & \mathbf{w}_v = \mathbf{w}_u, b_v = b_u, \quad \forall v \in \mathcal{V}, u \in \mathcal{B}_v; \quad \text{(10a)} \\ & \textstyle\sum_{n=1}^{N_v} \| \delta_{vn} \|^2 \leq C_{v,\delta}, \quad \forall v \in \mathcal{V}_a. \quad \text{(10b)} \end{aligned}
$$

Note that in the last term, l_0 norm $\|x\|_0 := |\{i : x_i \neq 0\}|$ denotes the number of elements which are changed by the attacker, and deleting it captures the attacker's intentions to maximizing the classification errors with changing least number of elements. Constraint (10b) indicates that the sum of modifications in node v are bounded by $C_{v,\delta}$. Following a similar method in training labels attacks, we can construct the iterations of solving Problem (10) as follows [41, 42, 45]:

$$
\delta_v^{(t+1)} \in \arg \max_{\{\delta_v, s_v\}} V_a C_l \mathbf{r}_v^{(t)T} \widehat{\mathbf{I}}_{p \times (p+1)}^T \delta_v - \mathbf{1}_v^T s_v
$$
$$
\text{s.t.} \quad \begin{aligned} & V_a C_a \delta_v \leq s_v, \quad \text{(11a)} \\ & V_a C_a \delta_v \geq -s_v, \quad \text{(11b)} \\ & \| \delta_v \|^2 \leq C_{v,\delta}. \quad \text{(11c)} \end{aligned} \tag{11}
$$

$$
\mathbf{r}_v^{(t+1)} \in \mathbf{DSVM}_{v,D} \left(\mathbf{X}_v, \mathbf{Y}_v, \mathbf{r}_v^{(t)}, \{\mathbf{r}_u^{(t)}\}_{u \in \mathcal{B}_v} \big| \delta_v^{(t+1)} \right) \tag{12}
$$

Note that here δ_{vn} has been summed into δ_v, which captures the modifications in node v. Constraints (11ab) and the last term of the objective function is the relaxation of the l_0 norm. Note that comparing to $\mathbf{DSVM}_v$, $\mathbf{DSVM}_{v,D}$ has $\mathbf{f}_v^{(t+1)} = V_a C_l \delta_v^{(t+1)} + 2\alpha_v^{(t)} - \eta \sum_{u \in \mathcal{U}_v} (\mathbf{r}_v^{(t)} + \mathbf{r}_u^{(t)})$, where $\delta_v^{(t+1)}$ comes from Problem (11).

In this section, we have modeled the conflicting interests of a DSVM learner and an attacker using a game-theoretic framework. The interactions of them can be captured as a zero-sum game where a minimax problem is formulated. The minimization part captures the learner's intentions to minimize classification errors, while the maximization part captures the attacker's intentions to maximize that errors with making less modifications, i.e., flipping labels and modifying data. By constructing the min-problem for the learner and max-problem for the attacker separately, the minimax problem can be solved with the best response dynamics. Furthermore, the min-problem and max-problem can be solved in a distributed way with V_a Sub-Max-Problems (8) and (11), and V Sub-Min-Problems (9) and (12). Combing the iterations of solving these problems, we have the fully distributed iterations of solving the Minimax-Problems (7) and (10). The nature of this iterative operations provides real-time mechanisms for each node to reacts to its neighbors and the attacker. Since each node operates its own sub-max-problem and sub-min-problems, the game between a DSVM learner and an attacker now can be represented by V_a sub-games in compromised nodes. This structure provides us tools to analyze per-node-behaviors of distributed algorithms under adversarial environments. The transmissions of misleading information $\hat{\mathbf{r}}_v$ can be also analyzed via the connections between neighboring games.

5 Impact of Attacks

In this section, we present numerical experiments on DSVM under adversarial environments. We will verify the effects of both the training attacks and the network attacks. The performance of DSVM is measured by both the local and global classification risks. The local risk at node v at step t is defined as follows:

$$R_v^{(t)} := \frac{1}{N_v} \sum_{n=1}^{N_v} \frac{1}{2} \left| y_{vn} - \widetilde{y}_{vn}^{(t)} \right|, \tag{13}$$

where y_{vn} is the true label, $\widetilde{y}_{vn}^{(t)}$ is the predicted label, and N_v represents the number of testing samples in node v. The global risk is defined as follows:

$$R_G^{(t)} := \frac{1}{\sum_{v \in \mathscr{V}} N_v} \sum_{v \in \mathscr{V}} \sum_{n=1}^{N_v} \frac{1}{2} \left| y_{vn} - \widetilde{y}_{vn}^{(t)} \right|, \tag{14}$$

A higher global risk shows that there are more testing samples being misclassified, i.e., a worse performance of DSVM.

We define the degree of a node v as the actual number of neighboring nodes $|\mathscr{B}_v|$ divided by the most achievable number of neighbors $|\mathscr{V}| - 1$. The normalized degree of a node is always larger than 0 and less or equal to 1. A higher degree indicates that the node has more neighbors. We further define the degree of the network as the average degrees of all the nodes.

5.1 DSVM Under Training Attacks

Recall the attacker's constraints $\mathbf{q}_v^T \theta_v \leq Q_v$ in training labels attacks, where $\mathbf{q}_v :=$ $[0, .., 0, q_{v(N_v+1)}, \ldots, q_{v(2N_v)}]^T$ indicates the cost for flipping labels in node v. This constraint indicates that the attacker's modifications in node v are bounded by Q_v. Without loss of generality, we assume that $\mathbf{q}_v := [0, .., 0, 1, \ldots, 1]^T$, and thus, the constraint now indicates that the number of flipped labels in node v are bounded by Q_v. We also assume that the attacker has the same $Q_v = Q$ and $C_{v,\delta} = C_\delta$ in every compromised node $v \in \mathcal{V}_a$. Note that we assume that the learner has $C_l = 1$ and $\eta = 1$ in every experiments.

Figures 3, 4, 5, and 6 show the results when the attacker has different capabilities to flip labels in a fully connected network with 6 nodes [43]. Each node contains 40 training samples and 500 testing samples from the same global training dataset with labels $+1$ and -1. The data are generated from two-dimensional Gaussian

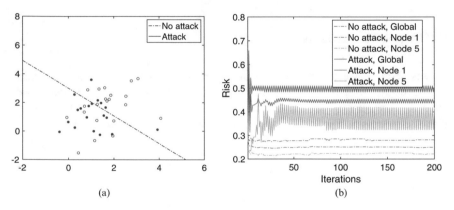

(a) (b)

Fig. 3 ADMM-DSVM under training-label-attacks with $|\mathcal{V}_a| = 4$, $Q = 30$, and $C_a = 0.01$ [43]

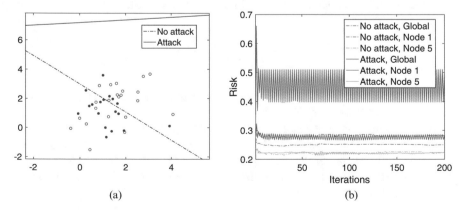

(a) (b)

Fig. 4 ADMM-DSVM under training-label-attacks with $|\mathcal{V}_a| = 1$, $Q = 30$, and $C_a = 0.01$ [43]

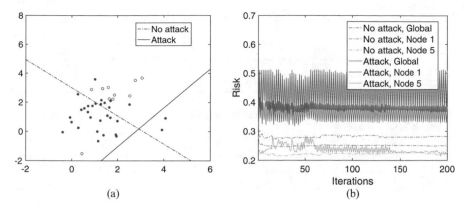

Fig. 5 ADMM-DSVM under training-label-attacks with $|\mathcal{V}_a| = 4$, $Q = 10$, and $C_a = 0.01$ [43]

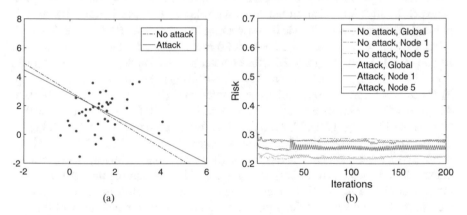

Fig. 6 ADMM-DSVM under training-label-attacks with $|\mathcal{V}_a| = 4$, $Q = 30$, and $C_a = 5$ [43]

distributions with mean vectors $[1, 1]$ and $[2, 2]$, and same covariance matrix $[1, 0; 0, 1]$. $|\mathcal{V}_a|$ indicates the number of compromised nodes. Q indicates the largest number of training samples that can be flipped in each node. C_a indicates the cost parameter. Blue filled circles and red filled circles are the original samples with class $+1$ and -1, respectively. Blue hollow circles and red hollow circles are the flipped samples with class $+1$ and -1, i.e., originally -1 and $+1$ respectively. We can see from the figures that when the attacker attacks more nodes, the equilibrium global risk is higher, and the uncompromised nodes have higher risks (i.e., Figs. 3 and 4). When Q is large, the attacker can flip more labels, and thus the risks are higher (i.e., Figs. 3 and 5). When C_a is large, the cost for the attacker to take an action is too high, and thus there is no impact on the learner (i.e., Figs. 3 and 6). Note that, when the attacker has large capabilities, i.e., larger Q, smaller C_a or larger V_a, even uncompromised nodes, e.g., Node 5, has higher risks.

Tables 1 and 2 show the results when the learner trains on different networks. L and D indicate training labels attacks and training data attacks, respectively.

Table 1 Average equilibrium classification risks (%) of DSVM using Spambase dataset [19] in Network 1 and Network 2

NET	1	1L	1D	2	2L	2D
RISK	11.6	32.3	42.2	10.6	29.4	39.3
STD	1.6	0.6	2.6	0.6	0.3	1.1

Table 2 Average equilibrium classification risks (%) of DSVM using Spambase dataset [19] in Network 3 and Network 4

NET	3	3L$_A$	3L$_B$	3D$_A$	3D$_B$	4	4L	4D
RISK	11.7	29.5	26.9	36.4	34.6	13.5	35.0	47.0
STD	1.5	0.6	1.2	0.9	0.8	1.8	0.9	2.5

Networks 1 , 2 and 3 have 6 nodes, where each node contains 40 training samples. Network 1 and 2 are balanced networks with degree 0.4 and 1, respectively. The normalized degrees of each node in Network 3 are 1, 0.4, 0.4, 0.2, 0.2, 0.2. Network 4 has 12 nodes where each node contains 20 training samples and has 2 neighbors. In $1L$ (resp. $1D$) and $2L$ (resp. $2D$), the attacker attacks 6 nodes with $Q = 20$ (resp. $C_\delta = 10^{10}$). In $3L_A$ (resp. $3D_A$) and $3L_B$ (resp. $3D_B$), the attacker attacks 3 (resp. 2) nodes with higher degrees and lower degrees with $Q = 20$ (resp. $C_\delta = 10^{10}$). In $4L$ (resp. $4D$), the attacker attacks 12 nodes with $Q = 10$ (resp. $C_\delta = 0.5 \times 10^{10}$). Comparing $1L$ (resp. $1D$) with $2L$ (resp. $2D$), we can see that network with higher degree has a lower risk when there is an attacker. From $3L_A$ (resp. $3D_A$) and $3L_B$ (resp. $3D_B$), we can tell that the risks are higher when nodes with higher degrees are under attack. From $1L$ (resp. $1D$) and $4L$ (resp. $4D$), we can see that network with more nodes has a higher risk when it is under attack. Thus, from Tables 1 and 2, we can see that network topology plays an important role in the security of the ML learner.

5.2   DSVM Under Network Attacks

In this subsection, we use numerical experiments to illustrate the impact of network attacks. In node capture attacks, we assume that the attacker controls a set of nodes $\mathcal{V}_a$, and he has the ability to add noise to the decision variables $\mathbf{r}_v$. In Sybil attacks, the attacker can obtain access to compromised node $v \in \mathcal{V}_a$, then he generates another malicious node to exchange information with the compromised node. Instead of sending random information, which can be easily detected, we assume that he sends a perturbed $\mathbf{r}_v$ to make compromised node believe that this is a valid information, where $\mathbf{r}_v$ comes from the compromised node v. In MITM attacks, we assume that the attacker creates adversarial nodes in the middle of a connection, and he receives $\mathbf{r}_v$ from both sides, but he sends a perturbed $\mathbf{r}_v$ to the other sides.

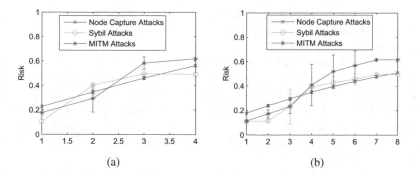

Fig. 7 ADMM-DSVM under network attacks. (**a**) Network 1. (**b**) Network 2

In the experiment in Fig. 7, we assume that the elements of the noise vector are generated by a uniform distribution in $[0, R]$, where R indicates the size of the noise. Network 1 and 2 are fully connected networks with 4 nodes and 8 nodes, respectively. In node capture attacks and Sybil attacks, the x-axis indicates the number of compromised nodes. The attacker has $R = 1, 0.01$ for node capture attacks and Sybil attacks, respectively. In MITM attacks, the x-axis represents the number of compromised connections, especially, 1 indicates only 1 connection has been broken, 4 and 8 for network 1 and 2 indicates that all the connections, i.e., 6 and 28 connections, have been attacked. Note that the attacker has $R = 0.05, 0.02$ for network 1 and 2 in MITM attacks, respectively . From the figure, we can see that when the attacker attacks more nodes or connections, the risk becomes larger. Note that, when more than half of the nodes or connections are compromised, the DSVM will completely fail, i.e, the classifier is the same as the one that randomly labels testing data.

6 Discussions and Future Work

Distributed machine learning (ML) algorithms are ubiquitous but inherently vulnerable to adversaries. This paper has investigated the security issue of distributed machine learning in adversarial environments. Possible attack models have been analyzed and summarized into machine learning type attacks and network type attacks. Their effects on distributed ML have been studied using numerical experiments.

One major contribution of this work is the investigation of the security threats in distributed ML. We have shown that the consequence of both ML-type attacks and Network-type attacks can exacerbate in distributed ML. We have established a game-theoretic framework to capture the strategic interactions between a DSVM learner and an attacker who can modify training data and training labels. By using the technique of ADMM, we have developed a fully distributed iterative algorithms that each node can respond to his neighbors and the adversary in real-time. The developed framework is broadly applicable to a broad range of distributed ML algorithms and attack models.

Our work concludes that network topology plays a significant role in the security of distributed ML. We have recognized that a balanced network with fewer nodes and a higher degree is less vulnerable to the attacker who controls the whole system. We have shown that nodes with higher degrees can cause more severe damages to the system when under attack. Also, network-type attacks can increase the risks of the whole networked systems even though the attacker only add small noise to a small subset of nodes.

Our work is a starting point to explore the security of distributed ML. In the future, we aim to extend the game-theoretic framework to capture various attack models and different distributed ML algorithms. We have proposed four defense methods in [48] to protect DSVM against training data attacks, and we intend to explore other defense strategies for distributed ML by leveraging techniques developed in robust centralized algorithms [4, 20] and detection methods [10, 24]. Furthermore, we could use cyber insurance to mitigate the cyber data risks from attackers [47, 50].

References

1. Barreno, M., Nelson, B., Joseph, A.D., Tygar, J.: The security of machine learning. Mach. Learn. **81**(2), 121–148 (2010)
2. Bekkerman, R., Bilenko, M., Langford, J.: Scaling Up Machine Learning: Parallel and Distributed Approaches. Cambridge University Press, Cambridge (2011)
3. Biggio, B., Corona, I., Fumera, G., Giacinto, G., Roli, F.: Bagging classifiers for fighting poisoning attacks in adversarial classification tasks. In: Multiple Classifier Systems, pp. 350–359. Springer, Berlin (2011)
4. Biggio, B., Nelson, B., Laskov, P.: Support vector machines under adversarial label noise. In: ACML, pp. 97–112 (2011)
5. Biggio, B., Nelson, B., Laskov, P.: Poisoning attacks against support vector machines (2012). Preprint arXiv:1206.6389
6. Biggio, B., Corona, I., Maiorca, D., Nelson, B., Šrndić, N., Laskov, P., Giacinto, G., Roli, F.: Evasion attacks against machine learning at test time. In: Machine Learning and Knowledge Discovery in Databases, pp. 387–402. Springer, Berlin (2013)
7. Boyd, S., Parikh, N., Chu, E., Peleato, B., Eckstein, J.: Distributed optimization and statistical learning via the alternating direction method of multipliers. Found. Trends Mach. Learn. **3**(1), 1–122 (2011)
8. Camponogara, E., Kraus W. Jr.: Distributed learning agents in urban traffic control. In: Progress in Artificial Intelligence, pp. 324–335. Springer, Berlin (2003)
9. Chen, J., Zhu, Q.: Interdependent strategic security risk management with bounded rationality in the internet of things. IEEE Trans. Inf. Forensics Secur. **14**(11), 2958–2971 (2019)
10. Chen, R., Lua, E.K., Crowcroft, J., Guo, W., Tang, L., Chen, Z.: Securing peer-to-peer content sharing service from poisoning attacks. In: Eighth International Conference on Peer-to-Peer Computing, 2008. P2P'08, pp. 22–29. IEEE, Piscataway (2008)
11. Chen, J., Touati, C., Zhu, Q.: A dynamic game approach to strategic design of secure and resilient infrastructure network. IEEE Trans. Inf. Forensics Secur. **15**, 462–474 (2019)

12. Chen, J., Touati, C., Zhu, Q.: Optimal secure two-layer IoT network design. IEEE Trans. Control Netw. Syst. **7**, 398–409 (2019)
13. Chi, S.D., Park, J.S., Jung, K.C., Lee, J.S.: Network security modeling and cyber attack simulation methodology. In: Information Security and Privacy, pp. 320–333. Springer, Berlin (2001)
14. Dalvi, N., Domingos, P., Sanghai, S., Verma, D., et al.: Adversarial classification. In: Proceedings of the Tenth ACM SIGKDD International Conference on Knowledge Discovery and Data Mining, pp. 99–108. ACM, New York (2004)
15. Dekel, O., Shamir, O., Xiao, L.: Learning to classify with missing and corrupted features. Mach. Learn. **81**(2), 149–178 (2010)
16. Desmedt, Y.: Man-in-the-middle attack. In: Encyclopedia of Cryptography and Security, pp. 759–759. Springer, Berlin (2011)
17. Drevin, L., Kruger, H.A., Steyn, T.: Value-focused assessment of ICT security awareness in an academic environment. Comput. Secur. **26**(1), 36–43 (2007)
18. Forero, P.A., Cano, A., Giannakis, G.B.: Consensus-based distributed support vector machines. J. Mach. Learn. Res. **11**, 1663–1707 (2010)
19. Frank, A., Asuncion, A.: UCI machine learning repository. http://archive.ics.uci.edu/ml. University of California, Irvine, CA. School of Information and Computer Science, vol. 213 (2010)
20. Globerson, A., Roweis, S.: Nightmare at test time: robust learning by feature deletion. In: Proceedings of the 23rd International Conference on Machine Learning, pp. 353–360. ACM, New York (2006)
21. Huang, Y., Zhu, Q.: A differential game approach to decentralized virus-resistant weight adaptation policy over complex networks. IEEE Trans. Control Netw. Syst. **7**, 944–955 (2020)
22. Kantarcıoğlu, M., Xi, B., Clifton, C.: Classifier evaluation and attribute selection against active adversaries. Data Min. Knowl. Disc. **22**(1–2), 291–335 (2011)
23. Kohno, E., Ohta, T., Kakuda, Y.: Secure decentralized data transfer against node capture attacks for wireless sensor networks. In: International Symposium on Autonomous Decentralized Systems, 2009. ISADS'09, pp. 1–6. IEEE, Piscataway (2009)
24. Levine, B.N., Shields, C., Margolin, N.B.: A Survey of Solutions to the Sybil Attack. University of Massachusetts Amherst, Amherst (2006)
25. Liu, W., Chawla, S.: A game theoretical model for adversarial learning. In: IEEE International Conference on Data Mining Workshops, 2009. ICDMW'09, pp. 25–30. IEEE, Piscataway (2009)
26. Lu, Y., Roychowdhury, V., Vandenberghe, L.: Distributed parallel support vector machines in strongly connected networks. IEEE Trans. Neural Netw. **19**(7), 1167–1178 (2008)
27. Lye, K.w., Wing, J.M.: Game strategies in network security. Int. J. Inf. Secur. **4**(1), 71–86 (2005)
28. Maaten, L., Chen, M., Tyree, S., Weinberger, K.Q.: Learning with marginalized corrupted features. In: Proceedings of the 30th International Conference on Machine Learning (ICML-13), pp. 410–418 (2013)
29. McCumber, J.: Information systems security: a comprehensive model. In: Proceedings of the 14th National Computer Security Conference (1991)
30. Metzger, J., Schillo, M., Fischer, K.: A multiagent-based peer-to-peer network in java for distributed spam filtering. In: Multi-Agent Systems and Applications III, pp. 616–625. Springer, Berlin (2003)
31. Michiardi, P., Molva, R.: Game theoretic analysis of security in mobile ad hoc networks (2002)
32. Navia-Vázquez, A., Parrado-Hernandez, E.: Distributed support vector machines. IEEE Trans. Neural Netw. **17**(4), 1091–1097 (2006)
33. Nelson, B., Barreno, M., Chi, F.J., Joseph, A.D., Rubinstein, B.I., Saini, U., Sutton, C., Tygar, J., Xia, K.: Misleading learners: co-opting your spam filter. In: Machine Learning in Cyber Trust, pp. 17–51. Springer, Berlin (2009)

34. Newsome, J., Shi, E., Song, D., Perrig, A.: The Sybil attack in sensor networks: analysis & defenses. In: Proceedings of the 3rd International Symposium on Information Processing in Sensor Networks, pp. 259–268. ACM, New York (2004)
35. Nugraha, Y., Hayakawa, T., Cetinkaya, A., Ishii, H., Zhu, Q.: Subgame perfect equilibrium analysis for jamming attacks on resilient graphs. In: 2019 American Control Conference (ACC), pp. 2060–2065. IEEE, Piscataway (2019)
36. Serpanos, D.N., Lipton, R.J.: Defense against man-in-the-middle attack in client-server systems. In: Sixth IEEE Symposium on Computers and Communications, 2001. Proceedings. pp. 9–14. IEEE, Piscataway (2001)
37. Tague, P., Poovendran, R.: Modeling node capture attacks in wireless sensor networks. In: 2008 46th Annual Allerton Conference on Communication, Control, and Computing, pp. 1221–1224. IEEE, Piscataway (2008)
38. Wood, A.D., Stankovic, J., et al.: Denial of service in sensor networks. Computer 35(10), 54–62 (2002)
39. Xiao, H., Xiao, H., Eckert, C.: Adversarial label flips attack on support vector machines. In: ECAI, pp. 870–875 (2012)
40. Zhang, R.: Strategic cyber data risk management over networks: from proactive defense to cyber insurance. Ph.D. thesis, New York University Tandon School of Engineering (2020)
41. Zhang, R., Zhu, Q.: Secure and resilient distributed machine learning under adversarial environments. In: 2015 18th International Conference on Information Fusion (Fusion), pp. 644–651. IEEE, Piscataway (2015)
42. Zhang, R., Zhu, Q.: Student research highlight: secure and resilient distributed machine learning under adversarial environments. IEEE Aerosp. Electron. Syst. Mag. 31(3), 34–36 (2016)
43. Zhang, R., Zhu, Q.: A game-theoretic analysis of label flipping attacks on distributed support vector machines. In: 2017 51st Annual Conference on Information Sciences and Systems (CISS), pp. 1–6. IEEE, Piscataway (2017)
44. Zhang, R., Zhu, Q.: Consensus-based transfer linear support vector machines for decentralized multi-task multi-agent learning. In: 2018 52nd Annual Conference on Information Sciences and Systems (CISS), pp. 1–6. IEEE, Piscataway (2018)
45. Zhang, R., Zhu, Q.: A game-theoretic approach to design secure and resilient distributed support vector machines. IEEE Trans. Neural Netw. Learn. Syst. 29(11), 5512–5527 (2018)
46. Zhang, R., Zhu, Q.: Consensus-based distributed discrete optimal transport for decentralized resource matching. IEEE Trans. Signal Inf. Process. Netw. 5(3), 511–524 (2019)
47. Zhang, R., Zhu, Q.: "FlipIn: a game-theoretic cyber insurance framework for incentive-compatible cyber risk management of internet of things." IEEE Trans. Inf. Forensics Secur. 15, 2026–2041 (2019)
48. Zhang, R., Zhu, Q.: Game-theoretic defense of adversarial distributed support vector machines. J. Adv. Inf. Fusion 14(1), 3–21 (2019)
49. Zhang, L., Yu, S., Wu, D., Watters, P.: A survey on latest botnet attack and defense. In: 2011 IEEE 10th International Conference on Trust, Security and Privacy in Computing and Communications (TrustCom), pp. 53–60. IEEE, Piscataway (2011)
50. Zhang, R., Zhu, Q., Hayel, Y.: A bi-level game approach to attack-aware cyber insurance of computer networks. IEEE J. Sel. Areas Commun. 35(3), 779–794 (2017)

Be Careful When Learning Against Adversaries: Imitative Attacker Deception in Stackelberg Security Games

Haifeng Xu and Thanh H. Nguyen

Abstract One of the key challenges in the influential research field of *Stackelberg security games* (SSG) is to address the challenge of *uncertainty* regarding the *attacker*'s payoffs, capabilities and other characteristics. An extensive line of recent work in SSGs has focused on learning the optimal defense strategy from observed attack data. This however raises the concern that the strategic attacker may mislead the defender by *deceptively* reacting to the learning algorithms, which is particularly nature in such competitive strategic interactions. This paper focuses on understanding how such *attacker deception* affects the equilibrium of the game. We examine a basic deception strategy termed *imitative deception*, in which the attacker simply pretends to have a different payoff given that his *true* payoff is unknown to the defender. We provide a clean characterization about the game equilibrium under unconstrained deception strategy space as well as optimal algorithms to compute the equilibrium in the constrained case. Our numerical experiments illustrate significant defender loss due to imitative attacker deception, suggesting the potential side effect of learning from the attacker.

Keywords Deception · Adversarial learning · Game theory · Stackelberg security game

---

Both the authors "Haifeng Xu and Thanh H. Nguyen" contributed equally to the paper.

H. Xu (✉)
University of Virginia, Charlottesville, VA, USA
e-mail: hx4ad@virginia.edu

T. H. Nguyen
University of Oregon, Eugene, OR, USA
e-mail: thanhhng@cs.uoregon.edu

© Springer Nature Switzerland AG 2021
P. Dasgupta et al. (eds.), *Adversary-Aware Learning Techniques and Trends in Cybersecurity*, https://doi.org/10.1007/978-3-030-55692-1_3

1 Introduction

The past decade has seen significant interest in the application of Stackelberg models in addressing security challenges, also known as *Stackelberg security games* (SSGs). This interest is driven in part by a number of high-impact deployed security applications [28]. An important challenge facing the security agency (the *defender*) in real-world domains is her *uncertainty* about the *attacker*'s capabilities, payoffs, and behavior, etc. To address this challenge, classical SSGs take robust approaches and seek to design defender strategies which optimize the worst-case defender utilities [21, 33]. However, these robust approaches are usually too pessimistic and not able to incorporate past attack data to improve the defender's strategy [4, 23]. To utilize the observed attack data, one natural paradigm that has received significant recent interest is to leverage machine learning techniques to either learn the attacker's characteristics from observed historical attack data [10, 12, 13, 23] or directly learn the defender's optimal strategy via interacting with the attacker (a.k.a., end-to-end learning) [1, 4, 16, 18, 25, 31]. However, a crucial assumption underlying these works is that the attacker always responds *honestly* to the defender's algorithm so that the *true* attacker characteristics or the true defender strategy can be learned. Given the competitive nature of the interaction, this assumption appears problematic in practice—the strategic attacker may manipulate his reactions to mislead the learning algorithm towards an outcome that favors the attacker. Such concern of *attacker deception* motivates the central research question of this paper:

> In Stackelberg security games with a defender learning from an unknown attacker, how would the attacker's deceptive reaction affect the equilibrium of the learning outcome?

This paper initiates the study of attacker deception in SSGs with *unknown attacker payoff*. We investigate a basic deception strategy termed *imitative deception* in which the attacker simply pretends to have some payoff (which may differ from his true one) and always plays *consistently* according to this deceptive payoff. As a result, the defender eventually learns to commit to an optimal defense strategy against the attacker's deceptive payoff. The attacker aims to find an *optimal deceptive payoff* in the sense that it leads to a defender equilibrium strategy that maximizes the attacker's *true utility*. Such deception can happen when, e.g., the defender seeks to learn the optimal strategy against the attacker [4, 10, 25]. Moreover, imitative deception is easy for the attacker to implement and is always effective since imitating his true payoff is at least as good and the optimal imitative payoff should increase the attacker's utility. Thus, we believe imitative deception is natural to study and can serve as an important first step towards a general understanding of attacker deception.

1.1   Results and Implications

We study the attacker's problem of finding the optimal deceptive payoff and the corresponding defender equilibrium strategy that she ends up learning, and refer to this game as the *imitative deception game*. When the attacker's deception is *unconstrained*—i.e., he can choose any deceptive payoff—we provide a clean characterization about the attacker's optimal deception and corresponding optimal defender strategy. Concretely, we prove that the optimal attacker deception in this case is to imitate a (deceptive) payoff such that the resulting optimal strategy for the defender is to play the `Maximin` strategy *regardless of what the attacker's true payoff is*. This result conveys a very interesting conceptual message: in security games, the attacker would always like to pretend to be strictly competitive against the defender regardless of his true payoff. We believe this characterization helps to explain why in many real-world situations the attackers always like to behave completely against the defender regardless of his true preferences. This seemingly irrational behavior is in fact highly strategized and can maximize his true utility. Interestingly, this turns out to be a intriguing special property of security games; We show via an example that it does not hold in general Stackelberg games.

When the attacker's deception is constrained and cannot be arbitrary payoff, it appears challenging to have a clean equilibrium characterization. In this case, we examine the problem *computationally*, and present a general optimization framework to solve the imitative deception game under *constrained attacker deception*. We then show that instantiating our framework for two natural types of constraints results in a compact formulation as a Mixed Integer Linear Program (MILP), which can be solved efficiently as shown by our experiments. Finally, our numerical experiments illustrates significant benefit [loss] of the attacker [defender] in presence of imitative attacker deception. We also demonstrate the efficiency of our MILP formulation for solving the imitative deceptive game.

1.2   Additional Related Work

Secrecy and Deception in Security The study of deception in security domains has a rich literature (we refer curious readers to a recent survey by Fraunholz et al. [8] and references therein). In SSGs, there has been many recent works examining deception from the *defender's side* and study how to mislead the attacker's decision by exploiting the defender's knowledge regarding uncertainties [11, 26, 30, 32, 35]. However, *attacker deception*—the natural counterpart in this line of research—has not been paid much attention. To our knowledge, the only relevant study are the two very recent work by Nguyen et al. [24] and Gan et al. [9]. Nguyen et al. [24] focused on *repeated* games and analyzing Bayesian Nash equilibrium, whereas our game is one-shot and is a Stackelberg model with commitment. Gan et al. [9] considered imitative deception but in general Stackelberg game models where, as will be shown, our characterization result does not hold.

Learning to Play Strategic Games As mentioned previously, there has been significant recent interests in learning to play the Stackelberg security games. However, previous work assumed a *non-deceptive* attacker who always plays truthfully according to his payoff [4, 10, 12, 13, 16, 18, 23]. Balcan et al. [1] and Xu et al. [31] consider learning an optimal defense strategy by taking a regret-minimization approach. Nguyen et al. [24] studies the deception method in which the attacker strategically select non-myopic responses to mislead the defender. Our work focuses on *imitative deception* in which the attacker pretends to have a different payoff and consistently plays a best response accordingly. Beyond security games, there has been many recent works on learning to play other strategic games under uncertainties, particularly in the domain of revenue-maximizing pricing or auction settings [15, 27]. This is another application domain where agents' strategic or deceptive responses are natural. Indeed, in many of these works, such strategic agent responses has been considered under various learning models [7, 19, 20, 29]. This is another motivation for us to study deceptive attacker behaviors in SSGs, which has surprisingly been paid little attention.

Attacks to ML Algorithms Also relevant to our work is the recent explosive research effort on adversarial attacks to machine learning algorithms. Generally, these works focused on designing various types of attacks (such as altering the training process—causative attack) to completely ruin the machine learning algorithms. Our discussion here cannot do justice to the rich literature in this field, we thus only mention those that are closely related to ours. In particular, the attacker deception in our game can be viewed as a *causative attack* [2, 3, 5, 6, 17] to the defender's learning algorithm. However, our models are different from most of the adversarial ML literature and could be more appropriately coined "strategic attacks" to ML algorithms. That is, the attacker in our setting is trying to manipulate the defender's algorithm towards a direction that benefits the attacker, while not to completely ruin the defender's learning algorithm. The ultimate goal of both players is find strategies to maximize their own expected utilities.

2   Preliminaries and Our Model

Basic Setup We consider a standard SSG where a *defender* allocates K *security resources* to protect N *targets* ($K < N$) against an *attacker's* attack. Let $[N] = \{1, 2, \ldots, N\}$ denote the set of targets. A pure strategy of the defender is an assignment of these K resources to an arbitrary subset of K targets (i.e., no scheduling constraints are assumed), and a mixed strategy is thus a probability distribution over these pure strategies. A defender mixed strategy in such a SSG can be equivalently represented as a vector of *marginal coverage* probabilities

$\mathbf{x} = (x_1, x_2, \ldots, x_N)$, where $\sum_j x_j \leq K$ and $x_j \in [0, 1]$ is the probability of protecting target $j \in [N]$ [14]. This is because players' utilities only depend on the protection probabilities of each target in SSGs, as shall be clear when we define player utilities next. Let $\mathbf{X} = \{\mathbf{x} \in [0, 1]^N : \sum_j x_j \leq K\}$ denote the set of all these mixed strategies represented in the form of marginal probabilities. It is easy to see that any marginal coverage probability vector must be in $\mathbf{X}$. Conversely, it can be shown that any marginal probability vector from $\mathbf{X}$ can be written as a distribution over pure strategies as well, e.g., by observing that the vertices of $\mathbf{X}$ are precisely the binary vectors with precisely K entries of 1's, indicating a subset of size K. On the other hand, the attacker's pure strategy is to pick one target $j \in [N]$ to attack. See Example 1 of Sect. 3 for an SSG instance.

Player Payoffs In SSGs, it is assumed that players only derive non-zero utilities from the target that is attacked by the attacker, and receive 0 from all other unattacked targets. If the attacker attacks target j that is not protected by the defender, he obtains a reward of R_j^a while the defender receives a penalty of P_j^d. Conversely, if j is protected, the attacker receives a penalty of $P_j^a(< R_j^a)$ while the defender gets a reward of $R_j^d(> P_j^d)$. For any j, the parameter tuple $(R_j^d, P_j^d, R_j^a, P_j^a)$ captures the two players' payoff on target j. These payoffs are assumed public knowledge. The players' expected utilities at j are thus computed as follows:

$$U_j^d(x_j) = x_j R_j^d + (1 - x_j) P_j^d \tag{1}$$

$$U_j^a(x_j) = x_j P_j^a + (1 - x_j) R_j^a \tag{2}$$

Strong Stackelberg Equilibrium (SSE) Given the payoff structure, for any defense strategy $\mathbf{x} \in \mathbf{X}$, let $\Gamma(\mathbf{x})$ denote the set of targets of the highest expected utility for the attacker. SSG models assume that the attacker can observe the defender's mixed strategy $\mathbf{x}$ (but not the defender's realized pure strategy), and thus the rational attacker will attack some target $j \in \Gamma(\mathbf{x})$ as his best (pure) response [28]. This assumption is due to the fact that in many security applications, the attacker will conduct surveillance to learn the defender's strategy and then best respond. Therefore, it is classical to assume that the attacker observes the defender's strategy, though there is also work addressing potential inaccuracy in attacker's estimations [28]. We call $\Gamma(\mathbf{x})$ the *attack set* with respect to $\mathbf{x}$.

The commonly adopted solution concept in SSGs is the Strong Stackelberg Equilibrium (SSE), which consists of a defender mixed strategy $\mathbf{x}^*$ and an attacker best response $i^* \in \Gamma(\mathbf{x}^*)$. Formally, $(\mathbf{x}^*, i^*)$ is an SSE if:

$$(\mathbf{x}^*, i^*) = \operatorname*{argmax}_{\mathbf{x} \in \mathbf{X}, i \in \Gamma(\mathbf{x})} U_i^d(x_i) \tag{3}$$

That is, in an SSE $(\mathbf{x}^*, i^*)$, defender strategy $vectx^*$ maximizes her utility assuming that the attacker will best respond to $vectx^*$ by attacking a target $i \in \Gamma(\mathbf{x}^*)$ and breaks ties in favor of the defender. Sometimes two action profiles $(\mathbf{x}^*, i^*)$ and $(\mathbf{x}', i')$ are both SSEs of the game. Yet, they must always yield exactly the same utility for both players [34]. In such cases, we say $(\mathbf{x}', i')$ is *reducible* to $(\mathbf{x}^*, i^*)$.

Imitative Attacker Deception Our model assumes that the attacker's true payoff $\{P_j^a, R_j^a\}_{j \in [N]}$ is *unknown* to the defender. The attacker can manipulate his behavior to mislead the defender if that is beneficial. We focus on a basic deception model, which we term *imitative deception*. That is, the attacker simply behaves according to a different payoff $\{\hat{P}_j^a, \hat{R}_j^a\}_{j \in [N]}$, instead of his true payoff, and will do so *consistently throughout the game*. Such deception may happen in many scenarios, especially those where the defender seeks to learn the attacker's payoff. The attacker's goal is to find the optimal *deceptive payoff* so that it leads to an SSE defense strategy that maximizes the attacker's *true utility*.

Remarks on Terminologies Under imitative attacker deception, the SSE is defined in exactly the same way except that the attacker's best response is now with respect to the attacker's *deceptive payoff* whereas his utility is still with respect to his *true payoff*. Yet, to distinguish this deceptive situation from truthful attacker behavior, we call the induced game *imitative deception game* and the corresponding SSE the *deceptive SSE*.

3   Unconstrained Imitative Deception

In this section, we study the case where the attacker's deception is unconstrained. Concretely, the attacker can imitate any payoff values $\{\hat{P}_j^a, \hat{R}_j^a\}_{j \in [N]}$ as long as the following natural constraints are satisfied: $\hat{P}_j^a < \hat{R}_j^a$ for any j. We provide a complete characterization about both players' strategies in this *unconstrained* setting, and prove that the optimal imitative attacker deception is to pretend to have a payoff such that the optimal defender strategy is to play the Maximin strategy. Recall that the defender's Maximin strategy is the defender's optimal strategy assuming that the attacker attacks the worst target for the defender, i.e., $\mathbf{x}^{mm} = \arg\max_{\mathbf{x} \in \mathbf{X}} \min_{j \in [N]} [x_j R_j^d + (1 - x_j) P_j^d]$. The $\mathbf{x}^{mm}$ strategy is the most conservative defender strategy and does not depend on any information about the attacker. Our main theorem is formally stated as follows.

Theorem 1 *For any true attacker payoff* $\{P_j^a, R_j^a\}_{j \in [N]}$, *the deceptive Strong Stackelberg Equilibrium (SSE) under optimal attacker imitative deception is characterized as follows:*

- *The defender's optimal strategy is always the* Maximin *strategy* $\mathbf{x}^{mm}$;
- *The attacker attacks target*

$$i^* = \arg\max_{j \in [N]} \left[x_j^{mm} P_j^a + (1 - x_j^{mm}) R_j^a \right];$$

- *The attacker's optimal imitative payoffs can be constructed as follows (this is just one possible construction; there are many others): (i) For any $j \in [N]$, set $\hat{P}_j^a = -R_j^d$ and $\hat{R}_j^a = -P_j^d$ for all $j \in [N]$; (ii) if $x_{i*}^{mm} = 0$, then re-set $\hat{R}_{i*}^a = -U^{mm}$ and $\hat{P}_{i*}^a = -U^{mm} - 1$ where $U^{mm} = \min_j [x_j^{mm} R_j^d + (1 - x_j^{mm}) P_j^d]$ is the defender's* `Maximin` *utility.*

Remarks Theorem 1 provides a complete characterization about both players' optimal strategies under imitative attacker deception. It also illustrates the usefulness of the `Maximin` strategy in handling attacker deception in security domains. Note that the attacker's optimal deceptive payoffs may *not* be exactly the opposite of the defender's payoffs, i.e., $\hat{P}_j^a = -R_j^d$ and $\hat{R}_j^a = -P_j^d$—sometimes he needs to treat his "favourite" target i^* specially to make sure attacking i^* is indeed his best response (i.e., the "if $x_{i*}^{mm} = 0$" step in Theorem 1). We remark that Theorem 1 relies on the structure of *security* games and does *not* hold for general Stackelberg games. The following corollary shows that the attacker has no incentive for imitative deception in zero-sum SSGs.

Corollary 1 *In zero-sum games, the attacker's optimal imitative deception strategy is to play truthfully.*

Admittedly, Theorem 1 is somewhat counter intuitive since the defender will always be misled to play the same strategy $\mathbf{x}^{mm}$ regardless of the attacker's true payoffs. Before giving the full proof of Theorem 1, we provide an illustrative example and attempt to provide some intuition underlying this result. However, we note that its full proof is more involved.

Example 1 (An Example and Intuitions of Theorem 1) Consider a security game with 3 targets. The defender and attacker payoffs are specified as follows:

	Target 1	Target 2	Target 3
R_i^d	1	3	1
P_i^d	-3	-2	0
R_i^a	2	1	1
P_i^a	-3	-1	-1

The defender only has 1 security guard, which can be allocated to protect any target. We use (x_1, x_2, x_3) to denote a defender mixed strategy where x_i is the probability of allocating the guard to target i. Our model assumes that the attacker payoffs are unknown to the defender, and attacker can imitate any other payoff structure if that is beneficial to him.

If the attacker were honest, then the SSE is $(1/3, 1/3, 1/3)$. The attacker will be induced to attack target 3, resulting in defender utility $1/3$ and attacker utility $1/3$.

According to Theorem 1, under optimal attacker imitative deception, the defender will be misled to play the `Maximin` strategy which is $(2/3, 1/3, 0)$. The attacker will attack target $\arg\max_{j \in [3]} [x_j^{mm} P_j^a + (1 - x_j^{mm}) R_j^a]$, which is target

3 in this example. This results in defender utility 0 and attacker utility 1 (larger than the utility of an honest attacker). The optimal deceptive attacker payoff constructed in Theorem 1 is

$\hat{R}_i^a$	3	2	1/3
$\hat{P}_i^a$	−1	−3	−2/3

It is easy to verify that this deceptive payoff—though make the game non-zero sum at target 3—indeed makes the $\mathtt{Maximin}$ strategy $(2/3, 1/3, 0)$ the SSE.

In this example, through deception, the attacker was able to completely "shift" the defender's resource away from target 3 (i.e., from $x_3 = 1/3$ in honest SSE to $x_3 = 0$ in $\mathbf{x}^{mm}$) and achieve utility 1 by attacking the unprotected target 3. One might wonder whether the attacker can instead completely shift the defender's resource away from target 1 and then attack it, resulting in even higher utility 2. It turns out that this is *not* possible because $(0, x_2, x_3)$ and $i^* = 1$ can never form an SSE since moving some protection from target $2, 3$ to target 1 will surely increase the defender's expected utility.

Intuitions About Why $\mathtt{Maximin}$ Is the Optimal Deception In the proof of Theorem 1, we will give a full characterization about what kind of $(\mathbf{x}, i^*)$ could be a (deceptive) SSE, and identify some "*consistency*" condition. Intuitively, the expected defender utility at i^* should be no worse any other target j with non-zero protection probability (the "$\mathtt{Max}$" part) since otherwise she can move some protection from j to i^* to improve her SSE utility. Now, among all consistent $(\mathbf{x}, i^*)$'s, which is the best for the attacker? It shall be the one minimizing the defender's utility (the "$\mathtt{Min}$" part) since it minimizes x_{i*} and thus maximizes the attacker utility. This is the intuition of why the $\mathtt{Maximin}$ defender strategy shows up at the equilibrium regardless of what the attacker's true payoffs are.

Example 2 (Failure of Theorem 1 in Normal-Form Games) Consider a Stackelberg version of the *battle of the sexes* Game, with payoffs as follows, where row player is the leader.

	Opera	Basketball
Opera	(2, 1)	(0, 0)
Basketball	(0, 0)	(1, 2)

Without deception, the leader should commit to $\mathtt{Opera}$ deterministically, resulting in follower best response $\mathtt{Opera}$ and utility 1. If the leader plays $\mathtt{Maximin}$ strategy $(1/3, 2/3)$, the imitative follower payoff specified by Theorem 1 is to make the game zero-sum in this case. The follower shall take action $\mathtt{Basketball}$, resulting in follower utility 4/3. However, this is not optimal for the follower—at optimal imitative deception, the follower pretends to not "care about" the leader at all, and *always* have utility 2 for `Basketball` and 1 for `Opera`. In this case, the leader will commit to `Basketball`, resulting follower utility 2. In fact, the follower deception essentially served as a way of *commitment*.

3.1 Proof of Theorem 1

The rest of this section is devoted to proving Theorem 1. The main challenge here is that the attacker's deception is to manipulate the space of his payoffs whereas our analysis has to examine the space of (deceptive) SSEs. Unfortunately, the relation between the space of attacker payoffs and the space of SSEs does not admit a clean analytical form. To prove the theorem, we establish various characterizations of SSEs, which we believe might be of independent interest.

Our proofs are divided into three main steps.

3.1.1 Step 1: A Characterization of SSE

As the first step, we provide a characterization of the SSE in security games, which will be crucial for us to analyze what defender mixed strategies can possibly arise in deceptive SSE. Since this characterization may be of independent interest, we state it as Theorem 2. Intuitively, Theorem 2 shows that a strategy profile is an SSE *if and only if* it is reducible to $\{\mathbf{x}^*, i^*\}$ such that: (1) all targets in the attack set have equal attacker utility; (2) i^* has the highest defender utility among all targets in the attack set; (3) any target outside the attack set is covered with a probability of zero; (4) either all the resources are used up or one of the target is covered with a probability of one. We remark that the crucial conditions here are *Condition (3) and (4)*, which are specific to the security game setting, whereas Condition (1) and (2) follow naturally from the definition of SSE.

Theorem 2 *Given any security game, a strategy profile is an SSE if and only if it is reducible to* $\{\mathbf{x}^*, i^*\}$ *s.t.*

1) For any $j \in \Gamma(\mathbf{x}^*)$, $P_{i^*}^a x_{i^*}^* + R_{i^*}^a (1 - x_{i^*}^*) = P_j^a x_j^* + R_j^a (1 - x_j^*)$; *2) For any* $j \in \Gamma(\mathbf{x}^*)$, $R_{i^*}^d x_{i^*}^* + P_{i^*}^d (1 - x_{i^*}^*) \geq R_j^d x_j^* + P_j^d (1 - x_j^*)$; *3) For any* $j \notin \Gamma(\mathbf{x}^*)$, $x_j^* = 0$ *and* $P_{i^*}^a x_{i^*} + R_{i^*}^a (1 - x_{i^*}^*) > R_j^a$; *and 4) either (i)* $\sum_j x_j^* = K$ *or (ii)* $\sum_j x_j^* < K$ *and* $x_k^* = 1$ *for some* $k \in \Gamma(\mathbf{x}^*)$.

Proof Observe that the attacker's [defender's] expected utility at any target i is a strictly decreasing [increasing] function of the coverage probability at that target due to the natural assumption $R_i^d > P_i^d$ and $R_i^a > P_i^a$.

Proof of Necessity Let $(\mathbf{x}^*, i^*)$ be an SSE. Based on the properties of SSE, Condition (1) and (2) always hold. For Condition (3), if there exists some $j \notin \Gamma(\mathbf{x}^*)$ such that $x_j^* > 0$, then we can gradually reduce x_j^* until either $x_j^* = 0$ or $j \in \Gamma(\mathbf{x}^*)$. Note that this will not change the attacker's optimal utility as the attacker's utility on target j increases (as x_j^* decreases) to at most his optimal utility, in which case $j \in \Gamma(\mathbf{x}^*)$. This will not change the defender's utility neither since the attack set $\Gamma(\mathbf{x}^*)$ did not shrink. As a result, the original $\mathbf{x}^*$ is reducible to the one with $x_j^* = 0$ for all $j \notin \Gamma(\mathbf{x}^*)$. In addition, for any $j \notin \Gamma(\mathbf{x}^*)$, based on the definition of the attack set, we have $P_{i^*}^a x_{i^*}^* + R_{i^*}^a (1 - x_{i^*}^*) > P_j^a x_j^* + R_j^a (1 - x_j^*) = R_j^a$. The resulting strategy of the defender and the corresponding attacker best response remains an SSE which satisfies the three conditions (1)–(3).

For Condition (4), let us assume that $\sum_j x_j^* < K$. In this case, there must exist a target $j \in \Gamma(\mathbf{x}^*)$ such that $x_j^* = 1$. Indeed, if $x_j^* < 1$ for all $j \in \Gamma(\mathbf{x}^*)$, then we can strictly increase x_j^* for all $j \in \Gamma(\mathbf{x}^*)$ and thus obtain a strictly higher defender utility, which contradicts the optimality of SSE defined in Eq. (3). Thus, $(\mathbf{x}^*, i^*)$ satisfies Condition (4).

Proof of Sufficiency Consider any $(\mathbf{x}, i)$ satisfying all the four conditions. We first show that $\Gamma(\mathbf{x}^*) = \Gamma(\mathbf{x})$ for any SSE $(\mathbf{x}^*, i^*)$. We denote by w and w^* the attacker's utilities at targets in corresponding attack sets against $\mathbf{x}$ and $\mathbf{x}^*$, respectively. We prove by contradiction.

(i) Assume $\Gamma(\mathbf{x}^*) \nsubseteq \Gamma(\mathbf{x})$, for the sake of contradiction. Then there exists a target $k \in \Gamma(\mathbf{x}^*) \setminus \Gamma(\mathbf{x})$. Thus, the attacker's expected utility at k with respect to $\mathbf{x}$ is R_k^a, satisfying $R_k^a < w$ by Condition (3), whereas his utility with respect to $\mathbf{x}^*$ is $w^* = x_k^* P_k^a + (1 - x_k^*) R_k^a \leq R_k^a$. These together imply $w > w^*$. Note that for all target $j \in \Gamma(\mathbf{x})$, we have $w \leq R_j^a$. This implies $w^* < R_j^a$ and thus j must also belong to $\Gamma(\mathbf{x}^*)$—otherwise, w^* has to be strictly greater than R_j^a due to the above necessity proof and Condition (3). Since $w > w^*$, then $x_j < x_j^*$ for all $j \in \Gamma(\mathbf{x})$, and thus:

$$\sum_j x_j = \sum_{j \in \Gamma(\mathbf{x})} x_j < \sum_{j \in \Gamma(\mathbf{x})} x_j^* \leq K$$

According to Condition (4), there exists some $k \in \Gamma(\mathbf{x})$ such that $x_k = 1$, which means $w = P_k^a > w^*$, contradicting the fact that $w^* \geq P_j^a$ for any target j. Therefore, $\Gamma(\mathbf{x}^*) \subseteq \Gamma(\mathbf{x})$.

(ii) Assume $\Gamma(\mathbf{x}) \nsubseteq \Gamma(\mathbf{x}^*)$ for the sake of contradiction. Similarly, we have $w^* > w$. Since $\Gamma(\mathbf{x}^*) \subseteq \Gamma(\mathbf{x})$ (according to (i)) and $w^* > w$, then $x_j^* < x_j$ for all $j \in \Gamma(\mathbf{x}^*)$. This implies that the defender's utility of playing $\mathbf{x}$ is strictly higher than that of playing $\mathbf{x}^*$, which contradicts the optimality of $(\mathbf{x}^*, i^*)$ as the SSE. Therefore, we must have $\Gamma(\mathbf{x}) \subseteq \Gamma(\mathbf{x}^*)$.

Based on (i) and (ii), we conclude that $\Gamma(\mathbf{x}^*) = \Gamma(\mathbf{x})$. Since $\mathbf{x}^*$ belongs to an SSE, thus $w^* \leq w$. Indeed, if $w^* > w$, then $x_j^* < x_j, \forall j$ which implies that the defender obtains a strictly higher utility for playing $\mathbf{x}$ than for playing $\mathbf{x}^*$ which is contradictory. Therefore, we have $w^* \leq w$, which means $x_j^* \geq x_j, \forall j$. Now, regarding Condition (4), if $\sum_j x_j = K$, then we must have $x_j = x_j^*, \forall j \in \Gamma$ since $\sum_j x_j^* \leq K$ and $x_j^* \geq x_j, \forall j$. If $\sum_j x_j < K$ and $x_k = 1$ for some $k \in \Gamma(\mathbf{x})$, then we must have x_k^* also equal 1 since $1 \geq x_k^* \geq x_k = 1$. Thus, $w^* = w = P_k^a$ and therefore $x_j = x_j^*, \forall j$. □

A useful corollary of Theorem 2 is its instantiation to zero-sum games. In particular, we can view the Maximin strategy as the Stackelberg equilibrium of a zero-sum security game. Therefore, Theorem 2 gives rise to the following characterization of the defender's Maximin strategy, which we denote as $\mathbf{x}^{mm}$. Here, U^{mm} is the defender's Maximin utility and $\Gamma(\mathbf{x}^{mm})$ denotes the attack set of the Maximin strategy.

Lemma 1 *Any* Maximin *defender strategy is reducible to* $\mathbf{x}^{mm}$ *such that: 1) for all* $j \in \Gamma(\mathbf{x}^{mm})$, $x_j^{mm} R_j^d + (1 - x_j^{mm}) P_j^d = U^{mm}$; *2) for all* $j \notin \Gamma(\mathbf{x}^{mm})$, $x_j^{mm} = 0$ *and* $U^{mm} < P_j^d$; *and 3) either (i)* $\sum_j x_j^{mm} = K$ *or (ii)* $\sum_j x_j^{mm} < K$ *and* $x_k^{mm} = 1$ *for some* $k \in \Gamma(\mathbf{x}^{mm})$.

Note that the first two conditions in Theorem 1 are combined as one condition due to $P_j^a = -R_j^d$ and $R_j^a = -P_j^d$.

3.1.2 Step 2: Characterizing the Set of All Deceptive SSE

Our second main step is to characterize the space of all the possible deceptive SSE $\{\mathbf{x}, i^*\}$'s that can possibly arise due to the attacker's imitative deception. Besides revealing useful insights about the SSE, this characterization is also an important step towards analyzing the attacker's imitative deception since the optimal deception strategy is essentially to pick the deceptive SSE that maximizes the attacker's expected utility.

Our characterization of SSE in Theorem 2 will play a key role in this analysis. Naturally, $\mathbf{x}$ must satisfy Condition (4) of Theorem 2 since this condition is out of the attacker's control. Additionally, the i^* cannot be arbitrary. In particular, Condition (3) implies that any j such that $x_j > 0$ must belong to the attack set $\Gamma(\mathbf{x})$. In other words, $\mathbf{supp}(\mathbf{x}) \subseteq \Gamma(\mathbf{x})$ where $\mathbf{supp}$ denotes the support of $\mathbf{x}$. As a result, Condition (2) then implies that $\forall j \in \mathbf{supp}(\mathbf{x})$, we must have $R_{i*}^d x_{i*} + P_{i*}^d (1 - x_{i*}) \geq R_j^d x_j + P_j^d (1 - x_j)$. This leads to the following definition of consistency between $\mathbf{x}$ and i^*.

Definition 1 We say $\{\mathbf{x}, i^*\}$ is consistent if $R_{i*}^d x_{i*} + P_{i*}^d (1 - x_{i*}) \geq R_j^d x_j + P_j^d (1 - x_j)$, $\forall j \in \mathbf{supp}(\mathbf{x})$.

Note that x_{i*} may equal 0 when $\{\mathbf{x}, i^*\}$ is *consistent*. Interestingly, it turns out that consistency is essentially the only requirement to make $\{\mathbf{x}, i^*\}$ a deceptive SSE.

Lemma 2 *For any* $(\mathbf{x}, i^*)$, *there exists* $\{\hat{R}_j^a, \hat{P}_j^a\}_{j=1}^N$ *to make* $\{\mathbf{x}, i^*\}$ *a deceptive SSE if and only if* $\{\mathbf{x}, i^*\}$ *is consistent and* $\mathbf{x}$ *satisfies Condition (4) of Theorem 2.*

Proof We have argued about "only if" direction (i.e., the necessity) previously. Here we prove sufficiency.

Given any consistent $(\mathbf{x}, i^*)$ where $\mathbf{x}$ satisfies Condition (4) of Theorem 2, we construct the following deceptive payoff of the attacker: (i) $\forall j$, if $x_j > 0$, let $\hat{R}_j^a = 2$ and $\hat{P}_j^a = 2 - \frac{1}{x_j}$; (ii) $\forall j$, if $x_j = 0$ and $j \neq i^*$, let $\hat{R}_j^a = 0$ and $\hat{P}_j^a = -1$; and (iii) if $x_{i^*} = 0$, set $\hat{R}_{i^*}^a = 1$ and $\hat{P}_{i^*}^a = -1$.

Therefore, $\forall j \neq i^*$, if $x_j > 0$, the attacker's deceptive utility at target j is $x_j \hat{P}_j^a + (1 - x_j)\hat{R}_j^a = x_j \left(2 - \frac{1}{x_j}\right) + 2(1 - x_j) = 1$; if $x_j = 0$, the attacker's deceptive utility is $\hat{R}_j^a = 0$. For the special target i^*, if $x_{i^*} = 0$, the third step in the above construction sets the deceptive payoff to make the attacker's expected utility at i^* also $1 = \hat{R}_{i^*}^a$. Consequently, we have $\Gamma(\mathbf{x}) = \mathbf{supp}(x) \cup \{i^*\}$. One can easily verify that the constructed $\{\mathbf{x}, i^*\}$ satisfies all the four conditions in Theorem 2: Condition 1 and 2 are satisfied due to the construction of $\{\hat{P}_j^a, \hat{R}_j^a\}_{j=1}^n$ and Condition 3 is satisfied due to consistency assumption. Thus, $\{\mathbf{x}, i^*\}$ is a deceptive SSE. □

3.1.3 Step 3: Completing the Proof

The main part of our final step is to invoke previous characterization results to prove that that under optimal imitative attacker deception, the defender strategy in the deceptive SSE is precisely the Maximin strategy $\mathbf{x}^{\mathrm{mm}}$. As a result, by definition of Maximin, for any target i we have $R_i^d x_i^{\mathrm{mm}} + P_i^d(1 - x_i^{\mathrm{mm}}) \geq R_j^d x_j^{\mathrm{mm}} + P_j^d(1 - x_j^{\mathrm{mm}})$, $\forall j \in \mathbf{supp}(\mathbf{x}^{\mathrm{mm}})$. So $(\mathbf{x}^{\mathrm{mm}}, i)$ is consistent for any $i \in [N]$.

By Lemma 2, $(\mathbf{x}^{\mathrm{mm}}, i)$ can be a deceptive SSE and the optimal target i^* for the attacker is then $i^* = \arg \max_{j \in [N]} \left[x_j^{\mathrm{mm}} P_j^a + (1 - x_j^{\mathrm{mm}})R_j^a\right]$. In this case, the imitative attacker payoff has an even easier construction due to the special property of $\mathbf{x}^{\mathrm{mm}}$. In particular, we simply let $\hat{P}_j^a = -R_j^d$ and $\hat{R}_j^a = -P_j^d$ for all $j \in [N]$. If $x_{i^*}^{\mathrm{mm}} = 0$, re-set $\hat{R}_{i^*}^a = -U^{\mathrm{mm}}$, i.e., the negative of the defender's Maximin utility, and $\hat{P}_{i^*}^a = -U^{\mathrm{mm}} - 1$. It is easy to verify that in this case the attack set is $\tau(\mathbf{x}^{\mathrm{mm}}) \cup \{i^*\}$.

What remains is to argue that the defender strategy is precisely $\mathbf{x}^{\mathrm{mm}}$, as summarized in the following lemma, whose proof is deferred to the full version. These all together concludes the proof of Theorem 1.

Lemma 3 *Let $\mathbf{x}^{\mathrm{mm}}$ be the defender's Maximin strategy. For any $i^* \in [N]$ such that $(\mathbf{x}^{\mathrm{mm}}, i^*)$ is consistent, $(\mathbf{x}^{\mathrm{mm}}, i^*)$ maximizes the attacker's utility among all consistent $(\mathbf{x}, i^*)$'s where $\mathbf{x}$ satisfies Condition (4) of Theorem 2.*

Proof Let $(\mathbf{x}^*, i^*)$ be the optimal deceptive SSE, i.e., maximizing the attacker's true expected utility. We are going to prove $x_{i^*}^{\mathrm{mm}} \leq x_{i^*}^*$. Since $(\mathbf{x}^*, i^*)$ is an SSE, $\mathbf{x}^*$ satisfies Condition (4) of Theorem 2. Our argument follows a case analysis, depending on which of Condition (4) is satisfied.

First, consider $\mathbf{x}^*$ satisfies Condition 4(i) which means $\sum_j x_j^* = K$. Assume, for the sake of contradiction, $x_{i^*}^{\mathrm{mm}} > x_{i^*}^* \geq 0$. Then i^* must be in $\Gamma(\mathbf{x}^{\mathrm{mm}})$ (otherwise, $x_{i^*}^{\mathrm{mm}}$ has to be zero according to Condition (2) of Lemma 1). As a result, the defender's Maximin utility U^{mm} equals $x_{i^*}^{\mathrm{mm}} R_{i^*}^d + (1 - x_{i^*}^{\mathrm{mm}})P_{i^*}^d$ by Condition (1) of Lemma 1, which is strictly greater than $x_{i^*}^* R_{i^*}^d + (1 - x_{i^*}^*)P_{i^*}^d$. In addition, since

i^* is the attacked target with respect to $\mathbf{x}^*$, the defender's expected utility at i^* is the highest among all targets in the attack set $\Gamma(\mathbf{x}^*)$ by Condition (2) of Theorem 2. That is, $x_j^* R_j^d + (1 - x_j^*) P_j^d \leq x_{i^*}^* R_{i^*}^d + (1 - x_{i^*}^*) P_{i^*}^d$ for any $j \in \Gamma(\mathbf{x}^*)$. Therefore, for any target $j \in \Gamma(\mathbf{x}^*)$, we obtain the inequality:

$$x_j^* R_j^d + (1 - x_j^*) P_j^d < U^{\mathrm{mm}} \leq x_j^{\mathrm{mm}} R_j^d + (1 - x_j^{\mathrm{mm}}) P_j^d$$

which implies $x_j^* < x_j^{\mathrm{mm}}$. This inequality leads to

$$\sum_{j \in [N]} x_j^* = \sum_{j \in \Gamma(\mathbf{x}^*)} x_j^* < \sum_{j \in \Gamma(\mathbf{x}^*)} x_j^{\mathrm{mm}} \leq K$$

which contradicts the fact that $\sum_{j \in [N]} x_j^* = K$. Therefore, in this case we must have $x_{i^*}^{\mathrm{mm}} \leq x_{i^*}^*$.

Second, consider $\mathbf{x}^*$ satisfies Condition 4(ii) which means there is some k such that $x_k^* = 1$. We denote by $R_{min}^d = \min_{j \in [N]} R_j^d$. Since the defender's expected utility at i^* is the highest among the set $\Gamma(\mathbf{x}^*)$, we have $(R_{i^*}^d - P_{i^*}^d) x_{i^*}^* + P_{i^*}^d \geq R_k^d \geq R_{min}^d$. In addition, observe that $U^{\mathrm{mm}} \leq R_{min}^d$ because $U^{\mathrm{mm}} \leq x_j^{\mathrm{mm}} R_j^d + (1 - x_j^{\mathrm{mm}}) P_j^d \leq R_j^d, \forall j$. Therefore,

$$x_{i^*}^* \geq \max\left\{0, \frac{R_{min}^d - P_{i^*}^d}{R_{i^*}^d - P_{i^*}^d}\right\} \geq \max\left\{0, \frac{U^{\mathrm{mm}} - P_{i^*}^d}{R_{i^*}^d - P_{i^*}^d}\right\} \geq x_{i^*}^{\mathrm{mm}},$$

The last "$\geq$" based on Conditions (1) and (2) of Lemma 1.

Finally, observe that $(\mathbf{x}^{\mathrm{mm}}, i^*)$ is consistent since the defender's expected utility at i^* for playing $\mathbf{x}^{\mathrm{mm}}$ is no less than U^{mm} which is the defender's expected utility at targets in the attack set $\Gamma(\mathbf{x}^{\mathrm{mm}})$. Additionally, $\mathbf{x}^{\mathrm{mm}}$ satisfies Condition 4 of Lemma 2. According to Lemma 2, there exists a deceptive payoff of the attacker such that $(\mathbf{x}^{\mathrm{mm}}, i^*)$ is the corresponding deceptive SSE. Since the attacker's expected utility at target i^* is a decreasing function of the defender's coverage probability at i^* and $(\mathbf{x}^*, i^*)$ is the optimal deceptive SSE for the attacker, thus we must have $x_{i^*}^* \leq x_{i^*}^{\mathrm{mm}}$.

These imply $x_{i^*}^{\mathrm{mm}} = x_{i^*}^*$, which means $(\mathbf{x}^{\mathrm{mm}}, i^*)$ is an optimal deceptive SSE. This concludes our proof of the lemma. $\square$

4 Constrained Imitative Deception

In the constrained attacker deception scenario, the attacker can pretend his payoff to be different from his true one with some predetermined constraints on his potential lies. For example, the attacker's deceptive rewards and penalties are constrained within some intervals. In this work, we consider two cases: (i) there are value constraints of the attacker's payoff; and (ii) there is a limited number of targets the attacker can report untruthful rewards and penalties.

In value-constrained deception, the attacker can only report its payoff from a *deceptive payoff space* $\Omega \subset \mathbb{R}_+^N \times \mathbb{R}_-^N$ and the defender follows the corresponding deceptive SSE to play. As a corollary of Theorem 1, the following proposition shows that if imitating a strictly competitive opponent is feasible for the attacker, then doing so is always optimal.

Proposition 1 *If the deceptive payoff space Ω includes $\hat{R}_j^a = -P_j^d, \hat{P}_j^a = -R_j^d, \forall j$, then the attacker's optimal deceptive strategy is still to make the deception game* zero-sum *and the defender strategy in the deceptive SSE is* Maximin.

Next we describe a general framework for computing the optimal imitative deception under *arbitrary* value constraints, and then show how to instantiate this framework for two concrete (and natural) types of value constraints.

As stated previously, the utility of the attacker in the SSE is a decreasing function of the defender's coverage probability at the attacked target. Therefore, our idea is to divide the attacker's deceptive payoff space into N sub-spaces such that for all the attacker payoffs from the same sub-space, the attacker attacks the same target in the deceptive SSE. Based on Theorem 2, the problem of computing the optimal deceptive SSE in each sub-space can then be represented as the two Mixed Integer Non-Linear Programs (MINLPs); each corresponds to either Condition 4(i) or 4(ii):

The following MINLP is with respect to the Condition 4(i):

$$\min\ x_i \text{s.t.} \tag{4}$$

$$x_i \hat{P}_i^a + (1 - x_i)\hat{R}_i^a \geq x_j \hat{P}_j^a + (1 - x_j)\hat{R}_j^a, \forall j \tag{5}$$

$$x_i \hat{P}_i^a + (1 - x_i)\hat{R}_i^a \leq x_j \hat{P}_j^a + (1 - x_j)\hat{R}_j^a + (1 - h_j)M, \forall j \tag{6}$$

$$x_i \hat{P}_i^a + (1 - x_i)\hat{R}_i^a \geq \hat{R}_j^a - h_j M + \epsilon, \forall j \tag{7}$$

$$x_i R_i^d + (1 - x_i)P_i^d \geq x_j R_j^d + (1 - x_j)P_j^d - (1 - h_j)M, \forall j \tag{8}$$

$$h_i = 1, h_j \in \{0, 1\}, x_j \leq h_j, \forall j \tag{9}$$

$$\sum_j x_j = K, x_j \in [0, 1], \forall j \tag{10}$$

$$\{\hat{P}_j^a, \hat{R}_j^a\} \in \Omega \tag{11}$$

where $\hat{P}_j^a, \hat{R}_j^a, x_j, h_j$ are variables. This MINLP is non-linear because it has product of variables, i.e., $x_j \hat{P}_j^a$. The MINLP minimizes the defender's coverage probability at the attacked target i, or equivalently, to maximize the attacker's true expected utility. In particular, h_j is a binary variable which indicates if target j belongs to the attack set ($h_j = 1$) or not ($h_j = 0$). Constraint (5) ensures that target i has the highest deceptive expected utility for the attacker. Constraint (8) forces the defender's utility at i to be the highest among targets in the attack set. In other words, constraints (5) and (8) guarantee that i is the attacked target. Constraints (5) and (6) force the deceptive expected utility for the attacker at every target in the attack set to be equal to the one at i. Constraints (7) and (9) force $x_j = 0$ and the attacker deceptive utility at i is strictly greater than R_j^a if $j \notin \Gamma(\mathbf{x})$. Constraint (10) satisfies Condition 4(i) of Theorem 2. In summary, constraints (5)–(10) guarantee that the outcome of this MINLP is a deceptive SSE. Finally, constraint (11) forces the attacker's deceptive payoff to be in the space Ω. Note that, M and ϵ are very large and small constants, respectively.

A similar MINLP with respect to Condition 4(ii) of Theorem 2 can be formulated, simply by substituting Constraint (10) by the following constraints, with additional binary variable q_j indicating whether $x_j = 1$ ($q_j = 1$) or not ($q_j = 0$).

$$\sum_j x_j \leq K, \sum_j q_j = 1, x_j \geq q_j, q_j \in \{0, 1\}, \forall j \tag{12}$$

Value-Bound Constraints We now instantiate the above framework with value-bounded constraints. That is, the space Ω can be represented as a set of separate lower and upper bound constraints on the attacker's rewards and penalties. This is one of the most natural way to model uncertainties in utilities and has been adopted in many previous works [21, 22]. We show that the aforementioned nonlinear optimization problems can be converted into Mixed Integer Linear Programs (MILPs). In particular, assume that Ω can be represented as follows:

$$\Omega_j = \{(\hat{P}_j^a, \hat{R}_j^a) : l_j^p \leq \hat{P}_j^a \leq u_j^p, l_j^r \leq \hat{R}_j^a \leq u_j^r\}, \forall j$$

where $(l_j^r, u_j^r, l_j^p, u_j^p)$ are constants. We introduce new variables $y_j^p = \hat{P}_j^a x_j$ and $y_j^r = \hat{R}_j^a(1 - x_j)$. We now can reformulate the problem (4)–(11) as the following MILP:

$$\min x_i \tag{13}$$

$$\text{s.t.} y_i^p + y_i^r \geq y_j^p + y_j^r, \forall j \tag{14}$$

$$y_i^p + y_i^r \leq y_j^p + y_j^r + (1 - h_j)M \tag{15}$$

$$y_i^p + y_i^r \geq y_j^p + y_j^r - h_j M + \epsilon \tag{16}$$

Constraints (8)–(10)

$$l_j^p x_j \leq y_j^p \leq u_j^p x_j, \forall j \tag{17}$$

$$l_j^r(1 - x_j) \leq y_j^r \leq u_j^r(1 - x_j), \forall j \tag{18}$$

where constraints (14)–(16) correspond to (5)–(7). Constraint (17)–(18) correspond to (11). Similarly, we also obtain a MILP w.r.t. Condition 4(ii). These two MILPs compute the optimal deceptive payoff given that i is the attacked target in the corresponding deceptive SSE. Finally, the best deceptive payoff is chosen as to provide the highest true expected utility for the attacker among all these choices of the attacked target.

Target-Limited Constraints Now we show how the above MILP framework can also be applied to target-limited constraints. That is, the attacker can lie for up to $L < T$ targets. Here, we introduce a binary variable z_j which indicates if the attacker lie at target j ($z_j = 1$) or not ($z_j = 0$). We now can then formulate a new MILP program with the following additional constraints:

$$R_j^a - z_j M \le \hat{R}_j^a \le R_j^a + z_j M, \forall j \tag{19}$$

$$P_j^a - z_j M \le \hat{P}_j^a \le P_j^a + z_j M, \forall j \tag{20}$$

$$\sum_j z_j \le L, z_j \in \{0, 1\} \tag{21}$$

where $\{R_j^a, P_j^a\}_{j \in [N]}$ is the true payoff of the attacker.

When we additionally have value-bound constraints, then the corresponding target-limited constraints for y_j^p and y_j^r are:

$$R_j^a(1 - x_j) - z_j M \le y_j^r \le R_j^a(1 - x_j) + z_j M \tag{22}$$

$$P_j^a x_j - z_j M \le y_j^p \le P_j^a x_j + z_j M \tag{23}$$

5 Experiments

We evaluate the solution quality of our proposed deceptive algorithm. We aim at empirically analyzing the benefit [loss] of the attacker [defender] in terms of expected utility in the presence of the attacker's deception. In our experiments, the players' rewards and penalties are generated in the ranges $[1, 10]$ and $[-10, 1]$ using the covariance game generator, GAMUT (http://gamut.stanford.edu/). The covariance value r governs the correlation between the players' payoffs. If $r = -1.0$, the generated games are zero-sum. Since the attacker always play truthfully in zero-sum games (Corollary 1), we only choose r within $[-0.8, 0.0]$ with a step size of 0.2. Each data point in our results is averaged over 250 different games (50 games per covariance value). Finally, we consider two scenarios: (i) small deceptive payoff space with an interval size of $I = 1.0$; and (ii) large space with $I = 2.0$. Our evaluations are based on various game settings with varying number of deceivable targets, number of targets, and number of defender resources.

In Fig. 1, we evaluate the attacker and the defender's average expected utility in two cases: (i) the attacker plays truthfully; and (ii) the attacker is rationally deceptive. We name the attacker and defender's utilities (trueAttU, trueDefU) and (decAttU, decDefU), respectively. In the deception case, decAttU is computed based on the optimal deceptive SSE and the attacker's true payoff.

In Fig. 1a, d, the x-axis represents the number of targets and the y-axis is the average expected utility of the attacker [defender]. Overall, when the attacker

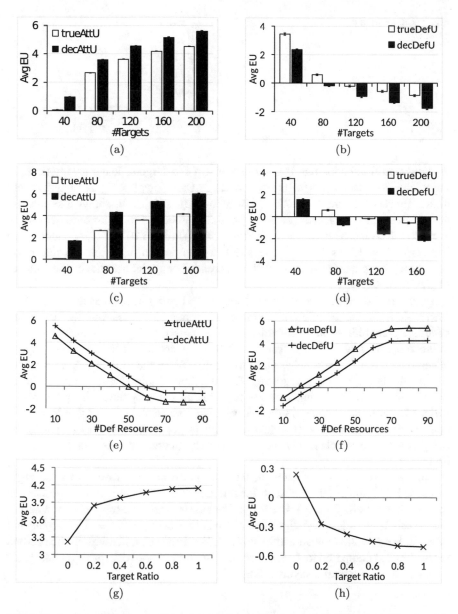

Fig. 1 Evaluation of solution qualities. (**a**) Attacker utility, $I = 1.0$. (**b**) Defender utility, $I = 1.0$. (**c**) Attacker utility, $I = 2.0$. (**d**) Defender utility, $I = 2.0$. (**e**) Attacker utility, $I = 1.0$. (**f**) Defender utility, $I = 1.0$. (**g**) Attacker utility, $I = 1.0$. (**h**) Defender utility, $I = 1.0$

is rationally deceptive, the attacker's [defender's] utility is roughly an increasing concave [decreasing convex] function of the number of targets, which is similar to the case of a truthful attacker. This makes sense, as when the number of target

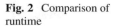

Fig. 2 Comparison of
runtime

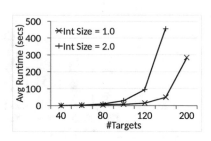

increases, the defender has less protection on the targets, leaving targets more
vulnerable to attacks. Furthermore, the decAttU [decDefU] is quantitatively
higher [lower] than the trueAttU [trueDefU]. This result shows a significant
benefit [loss] of the attacker [defender] in the presence of the attacker's deception.
We also see an increase [decrease] in decAttU [decDefU] when the interval size
increases ($I = 1.0$ vs $I = 2.0$). This reflects the growth in options for deception
(i.e., deceptive payoff space), as well as increased potential benefit for the attacker
to play deceptively.

Figure 1e, f show that the attacker's [defender's] utility in both cases is decreasing
[increasing] in the number of defender resources K, reflecting the increased
coverage probabilities of the defender over the targets. In Fig. 1g, h, the *target ratio*
is the proportion of the target set at which the attacker can lie about his payoff.
When the ratio is 0, the attacker plays truthfully. When the ratio is 1.0, the attacker
can manipulate the whole target set. The attacker's [defender's] utility is shown
to be roughly an increasing concave [decreasing convex] function of the *target
ratio*. Similar to the increase in the interval size, this result reflects the n increasing
concave [decreasing convex] function of the *target ratio*. growth in options for
deception of the attacker, and increased benefit [increased loss] for the attacker
[defender].

Our last experiment evaluates the runtime performance of our proposed algorithm. In Fig. 2, the x-axis represents the number of targets. The y-axis is the average
runtime in seconds. Figure 2 shows that the runtime grows exponentially when N
increases. Nevertheless, the algorithm can easily scale up to $N = 160$ targets and
interval size $I = 2.0$ (solved within $\approx$455 s). We also see an increase in the runtime
when $I = 2.0$ compared to $I = 1.0$, reflecting an increased deceptive payoff space
to search for an optimal deceptive SSE.

6   Conclusions and Future Work

In this paper, we studied a basic attacker deception strategy termed *imitative deception* motivated by security contexts where the defender needs to learn to play against
an unknown attacker by observing attack data or interacting with the attacker. This
is a basic and natural deception strategy, in which the attacker simply behaves

according to a different payoff and will do so consistently. We show that the optimal *unconstrained attacker deception* is to induce the defender to play Maximin in the deceptive game. This interesting result helps in explaining many real-world situations in which the attacker tends to behave completely against the defender regardless of his true preferences. We also present a general optimization framework to solve the game under *constrained deception*. Our experiments illustrate the significant benefit [loss] of the attacker [defender] in the presence of the imitative deception, suggesting potential side effects of learning from the attacker.

Our work leaves many open questions. The most immediate one is probably to understand the computational complexity and to design theoretically efficient algorithms for solving the novel imitative deception game. Though our MILP formulation scales up well in the experiments, it is not guaranteed to be in polynomial time. It is open that whether the new game can be solved in polynomial time or not under different types of deception constraints. Second, imitative deception is a special type of manipulation strategy to learning algorithm. More generally, the attacker does not have to always behave consistently according to certain payoff. That potentially gives him more flexibility to manipulate the defender's learning algorithm. One interesting open question is how powerful is imitative deception. Do there exist natural situations or constraints under which imitative deception is actually the optimal manipulation strategy? Note that one advantage of imitative deception is that it is *oblivious* to the learning algorithm itself as long as the algorithm can effectively learn the optimal defender strategy (thus it will always learn the same strategy under a fixed attacker payoff). One concrete conjecture we have is that imitative deception may be the optimal manipulation strategy among those which are oblivious to the learning algorithm. Finally, a more open-ended direction is to study imitative deception in other application domains, e.g., pricing games or recommender systems, and examine how it affects the players' utilities and the game equilibrium.

References

1. Balcan, M.-F., Blum, A., Haghtalab, N., Procaccia, A.D.: Commitment without regrets: online learning in Stackelberg security games. In: 16th ACM Conference on Economics and Computation, pp. 61–78 (2015)
2. Barreno, M., Nelson, B., Sears, R., Joseph, A.D., Tygar, J.D.: Can machine learning be secure? In: ACM Symposium on Information, Computer and Communications Security (2006)
3. Barreno, M., Nelson, B., Joseph, A.D., Tygar, J.D.: The security of machine learning. Mach. Learn. **81**(2), 121–148 (2010)
4. Blum, A., Haghtalab, N., Procaccia, A.D.: Learning optimal commitment to overcome insecurity. In: Advances in Neural Information Processing Systems, pp. 1826–1834 (2014)
5. Bruckner, M., Scheffer, T.: Stackelberg games for adversarial prediction problems. In: ACM SIGKDD International Conference on Knowledge Discovery and Data Mining (2011)
6. Bruckner, M., Kan-zow, C., Scheffer, T.: Static prediction games for adversarial learning problems. J. Mach. Learn. Res. **13**, 2617–2654 (2012)

7. Drutsa, A.: Weakly consistent optimal pricing algorithms in repeated posted-price auctions with strategic buyer. In: International Conference on Machine Learning, pp. 1319–1328 (2018)
8. Fraunholz, D., Anton, S.D., Lipps, C., Reti, D., Krohmer, D., Pohl, F., Tammen, M., Schotten, H.D.: Demystifying deception technology: a survey (2018). Preprint arXiv:1804.06196
9. Gan, J., Xu, H., Guo, Q., Tran-Thanh, L., Rabinovich, Z., Wooldridge, M.: Imitative follower deception in Stackelberg games. In: Proceedings of the 2019 ACM Conference on Economics and Computation, pp. 639–657 (2019)
10. Gholami, S., Ford, B., Fang, F., Plumptre, A., Tambe, M., Driciru, M., Wanyama, F., Rwetsiba, A., Nsubaga, M., Mabonga, J.: Taking it for a test drive: a hybrid spatio-temporal model for wildlife poaching prediction evaluated through a controlled field test. In: European Conference on Machine Learning (2017)
11. Guo, Q., An, B., Bosan-sky, B., Kiekintveld, C.: Comparing strategic secrecy and Stackelberg commitment in security games. In: 26th International Joint Conference on Artificial Intelligence (2017)
12. Haghtalab, N., Fang, F., Nguyen, T.H., Sinha, A., Procaccia, A.D., Tambe, M.: Three strategies to success: learning adversary models in security games. In: 25th International Joint Conference on Artificial Intelligence, pp. 308–314 (2016)
13. Kar, D., Ford, B., Gholami, S., Fang, F., Plumptre, A., Tambe, M., Driciru, M., Wanyama, F., Rwetsiba, A., Nsubaga, M.: Cloudy with a chance of poaching: adversary behavior modeling and forecasting with real-world poaching data. In: 16th International Conference on Autonomous Agents and Multi-Agent Systems (2017)
14. Kiekintveld, C., Jain, M., Tsai, J., Pita, J., Ordonez, F., Tambe, M.: Computing optimal randomized resource allocations for massive security games. In: 8th International Conference on Autonomous Agents and Multiagent Systems, vol. 1, pp. 689–696 (2009)
15. Kleinberg, R., Leighton, T.: The value of knowing a demand curve: bounds on regret for online posted-price auctions. In: 44th Annual IEEE Symposium on Foundations of Computer Science, pp. 594–605 (2003)
16. Letchford, J., Conitzer, V., Munagala, K.: Learning and approximating the optimal strategy to commit to. In: International Symposium on Algorithmic Game Theory, pp. 250–262 (2009)
17. Lowd, D., Meek, C.: Adversarial learning. In: ACM SIGKDD International Conference on Knowledge Discovery in Data Mining, pp. 641–647 (2005)
18. Marecki, J., Tesauro, G., Segal, R.: Playing repeated Stackelberg games with unknown opponents. In: 11th International Conference on Autonomous Agents and Multiagent Systems (2012)
19. Mohri, M., Medina, A.M.: Optimal regret minimization in posted-price auctions with strategic buyers. In: Advances in Neural Information Processing Systems (NIPS) (2014)
20. Mohri, M., Medina, A.M.: Learning algorithms for second-price auctions with reserve. J. Mach. Learn. Res. **17**, 2632–2656 (2016)
21. Nguyen, T.H., Jiang, A.X., Tambe, M.: Stop the compartmentalization: unified robust algorithms for handling uncertainties in security games. In: Proceedings of the 2014 International Conference on Autonomous Agents and Multi-Agent Systems. International Foundation for Autonomous Agents and Multiagent Systems (2014)
22. Nguyen, T.H., et al.: Regret-based optimization and preference elicitation for Stackelberg security games with uncertainty. In: Twenty-Eighth AAAI Conference on Artificial Intelligence (2014)
23. Nguyen, T.H., Sinha, A., Gho-lami, S., Plumptre, A., Joppa, L., Tambe, M., Driciru, M., Wanyama, F., Rwetsiba, A., Critchlow, R., et al.: Capture: a new predictive anti-poaching tool for wildlife protection. In: 15th International Conference on Autonomous Agents and Multi-Agent Systems, pp. 767–775 (2016)
24. Nguyen, T.H., Wang, Y., Sinha, A., Wellman, M.P.: Deception in finitely repeated security games. In: 33th AAAI Conference on Artificial Intelligence (2019)
25. Peng, B., Shen, W., Tang, P., Zuo, S.: Learning optimal strategies to commit to. In: 33th AAAI Conference on Artificial Intelligence (2019)

26. Rabinovich, Z., Jiang, A.X., Jain, M., Xu, H.: Information disclo- sure as a means to security. In: 14th International Conference on Autonomous Agents and Multi-Agent Systems, pp. 645–653 (2015)
27. Roth, A., Ullman, J., Wu, Z.S.: Watch and learn: optimizing from revealed preferences feedback. In: Proceedings of the Forty-Eighth Annual ACM Symposium on Theory of Computing, pp. 949–962 (2016)
28. Tambe, M.: Security and Game Theory: Algorithms, Deployed Systems, Lessons Learned. Cambridge University Press, Cambridge (2011)
29. Vanunts, A., Drutsa, A.: Optimal pricing in repeated posted-price auctions with different patience of the seller and the buyer. In: Advances in Neural Information Processing Systems, pp. 941–953 (2019)
30. Xu, H., Rabinovich, Z., Dughmi, S., Tambe, M.: Exploring information asymmetry in two-stage security games. In: 29th AAAI Conference on Artificial Intelligence, pp. 1057–1063 (2015)
31. Xu, H., Tran-Thanh, L., Jennings, N.R.: Playing repeated security games with no prior knowledge. In: 15th International Conference on Autonomous Agents and Multi-Agent Systems, pp. 104–112 (2016)
32. Xu, H., Wang, K., Vayanos, P., Tambe, M.: Strategic coordination of human patrollers and mobile sensors with signaling for security games. In: Thirty-Second AAAI Conference on Artificial Intelligence (2018)
33. Yin, Z., Tambe, M.: A unified method for handling discrete and continuous uncertainty in Bayesian stackelberg games. In: Proceedings of the 11th International Conference on Autonomous Agents and Multiagent Systems, pp. 855–862 (2012)
34. Yin, Z., Korzhyk, D., Kiekintveld, C., Conitzer, V., Tambe, M.: Stackelberg vs. Nash in security games: interchangeability, equivalence, and uniqueness. In: 9th International Conference on Autonomous Agents and Multi-Agent Systems, pp. 1139–1146 (2010)
35. Zhuang, J., Bier, V.M., Alagoz, O.: Modeling secrecy and deception in a multi-period attacker-defender signaling game. Eur. J. Oper. Res. **203**, 409–418 (2010)

Part II
Data Modalities and Distributed Architectures for Countering Adversarial Cyber Attacks

Adversarial Machine Learning in Text: A Case Study of Phishing Email Detection with RCNN Model

Daniel Lee and Rakesh M. Verma

Abstract With the exponential increase in processing power and availability of big data, deep learning has pushed the performance of previously considered hard problems. Deep learning refers to the many layers of complex neural networks, where learnable parameters are on the order of millions, sometimes billions. The massive models are trained by leveraging GPUs and large amounts of data.

Studies have shown that these precise models are susceptible to the adversarial environment. This chapter explores the different facets of the adversarial environment and how this further affects the domain of text and natural language processing.

Keywords Adversarial examples · Phishing email · Deep learning · Neural networks · Natural language processing · Machine learning · CNN · RNN · RCNN · Cybersecurity

1 Introduction

Deep neural networks (DNNs) have garnered astonishing interest for many machine learning applications. Alongside this great growth in popularity, researchers started investigating the robustness of DNNs in the presence of adversaries. Models learned on human generated data assume a stochastic nature of that data. However, in an adversarial environment, that assumption becomes a weakness. Attackers can make use of crafted noise and perturbations to wreak havoc on models considered state-of-the-art.

DNNs have achieved superior performance in many domains, e.g., computer vision and natural language processing. The adversarial environment was brought to the forefront for DNNs in [37]. The researchers reveal two weaknesses: (1) DNNs

D. Lee (✉) · R. M. Verma
Department of Computer Science, University of Houston, Houston, TX, USA
e-mail: dljr0122@cs.uh.edu; rmverma@cs.uh.edu

© Springer Nature Switzerland AG 2021
P. Dasgupta et al. (eds.), *Adversary-Aware Learning Techniques and Trends in Cybersecurity*, https://doi.org/10.1007/978-3-030-55692-1_4

are susceptible to crafted perturbations known as adversarial examples, and (2) the same weaknesses can be transferred from a local open model into a remote secure model. Since this pivotal paper, many researchers have investigated this weakness in DNNs. Along with this research have come many defenses as well. Several different frameworks have been proposed to investigate and measure the robustness of DNNs in the presence of adversaries.

Adversarial machine learning is a subset of problems of the greater adversarial environment. It can be defined as the problem of a computer system learning to perform a task in the presence of an active adversary. The adversary can be defined as an actor whose goal is to prevent the proper functioning of the computer system or machine. The adversary can attack during the phase where the machine is training or after the machine's performance meets satisfaction for the task. The former, we refer to an attack at training time and the latter, an attack at testing time.

Much of the research that stems from the seminal paper [37] focuses on attacks at test time. The scope of this chapter is the same, i.e. adversarial examples. However, this chapter shifts the focus from image related tasks to the harder domain of text based adversarial examples. The inherent difficulty of the text domain comes from the nature of the data. Unlike the continuous data of domains like computer vision, the data of text is discrete. Since the adversarial examples are minute perturbations on the input, for images these changes can be many small increments spread across all the pixels of the input. However, for text, a change in a single word can completely change the tone and even meaning of the text. This difficulty will be analyzed in this chapter.

A long studied area of research has been detection of phishing attacks. Phishing emails remain as one of the top attack vectors used by adversaries. The goal of phishing is to steal confidential information through deceptive social engineering. Phishlabs[1] reports that email accounts for 24.1% of all phishing attempts. Phishing emails use urgency and immediacy to lure victims into sharing their personal information, e.g., date of birth or social security number. Unsuspecting victims may also click on a link in the email and unwittingly enter their username and password. Because of this social engineering aspect, research continues in analyzing the body text of the email itself to assist in classification [2, 14, 17, 38, 41]. This chapter will use phishing detection as the running use-case throughout the chapter.

Deep learning has shown great progress in the field of natural language processing. Hard problems like machine translation and sentiment analysis are dominated by solutions that utilize deep learning architectures. Recently, a powerful deep learning architecture has been used to classify emails based on the text only. To detect phishing, some phishing approaches involve feature engineering to identify indicators of phishing intent from email headers, or body text. However, this approach needs much expertise and may not assure success. Deep learning can avoid this cumbersome process, by using as input the email header and body directly. Researchers in [18] employ exactly this approach. The architecture for their deep

---

[1] phishlabs.com.

learning model tries to leverage the benefits of both types of models, a recurrent neural network (RNN) and a convolution neural network (CNN). This is the model we will use in our study in the domain of adversarial text.

1.1 Goals

The aim of this chapter is to compare and contrast the research of adversarial examples in the text domain. One of the main differences that will be explored is the discrete nature of text. Much of the existing research on adversarial examples, in particular deep learning, takes advantage of the continuous nature of the input space (e.g. pixel values of images). We will give a taxonomy of the type of problems machine learning is solving with respect to the input space and output space.

Many attacks have been adapted from the wealth of research on adversarial examples, and we will look at a use case here. Each attack approach will be discussed in detail with running examples for a text-based domain. We will conclude with a statement of current research and some future avenues of discovery.

1.2 Hypothesis

- The discrete nature of text based modeling, makes it inherently more robust against continuous based attacks.
- Adding complexity to the neural network architecture strengthens its robustness against state-of-the-art techniques.

The rest of this chapter is organized as follows. We will begin with some basic background in Sect. 2. Section 3 introduces the model that is trained to classify phishing emails. Attacks against the model are explained in Sect. 4. The experiment and results are discussed in Sects. 5 and 6, respectively. A review of relevant work is in Sect. 7. We end with some concluding remarks in Sect. 8.

2 Background

Although the goal of this chapter is adversarial learning for text, we will use the Recurrent Convolutional Neural Network (RCNN) first introduced in [23]. To this end, some important concepts must be reviewed. We first give a simple taxonomy of the adversarial machine learning environment and then introduce the RCNN model.

2.1 Adversarial Machine Learning

As introduced in [9] and elaborated further in [40], the adversarial machine learning problem can be modelled with five aspects: (1) adversary's goal, (2) adversary's knowledge, (3) adversary's capabilities, (4) attack strategy, and (5) attack timing. These five facets determine the type of attacks the defenders must anticipate and defend against.

2.1.1 Adversary's Goal

The CIA triad of confidentiality, integrity and availability are well known goals in cybersecurity.[2] The adversary seeks to compromise these goals when defended by machine learning. He can try to steal private information through techniques of reverse engineering. He can also attempt to evade detection by compromising the integrity of a machine learning model. To reduce availability of a machine learning model, he could poison data to increase false alarms and thereby inducing a user to ignore the model warning. We will explore different facets in the attacks and defenses discussed in this chapter. Attacker's goal also has error specificity, which ranges from generic to specific. Generic means that the attacker wants a sample misclassified as any class different from the true class, and specific means that the attacker wants a sample misclassified as a specific class different from the true class.

2.1.2 Adversary's Knowledge

Biggio and Roli [9] characterize the knowledge of the attacker into three levels. **Perfect knowledge** means the attacker has complete knowledge of the training datasets, features and the target model. **Limited knowledge** refers to the adversary being placed with constraints. Finally, there is **zero knowledge**, sometimes called "black box," meaning the attacker has only a general knowledge of the goal of the machine learning algorithm, the type of training data and the space of features. This chapter will delve into attacks at all three levels.

2.1.3 Adversary's Capabilities

This refers to how much influence the attacker has on the dataset(s) used by the defender's machine learning algorithm. There may also be constraints on attacker's data manipulation. For example, an attacker cannot control independently installed

---

[2] More goals can be found in [40].

and properly configured/patched SMTP servers for email attacks. In this chapter, we assume that the attacker can manipulate only the email content.

2.1.4 Attack Strategy

Attack strategy refers to the objective function used by the attacker and the optimization technique(s) used. For example, in the case of image recognition, the attacker's objective function could be to maximize the change in the target model's loss function while keeping the change in the input image small.

2.1.5 Attack Timing

The attack timing can be categorized into two: an attack at train time or an attack at decision/test time. In this chapter, we explore mainly test time attacks.

2.2 The Domain of Natural Language

Even for humans, understanding natural language is a difficult task. Children are not expected to speak full sentences until around the age of two. And even then, they may have grammatical errors, e.g., missing function words, and we do not expect them to be able to write novels or give speeches. Yet, we have deep neural network architectures that can mimic styles of important literary figures or translate between languages after training for only a fraction of the time [6, 34]. These human and machine capabilities are still not fully understood and under much research. One of the main difficulties is the discrete nature of text.

2.2.1 WordNet

For computers to understand natural language, we need to organize the basic units of the language. This organization can help guide the learning process. Wordnet is one such lexical resource [27], which organizes nouns, verbs, adjectives and adverbs into synsets, i.e., sets of synonyms and important relations between them, e.g., (hyper/hypo)nymy and meronymy.

WordNet seeks to provide a network between synsets using relationships. In addition to synonyms, our work will also involve the use of hypernyms and hyponyms. Hypernyms can be viewed as words that give a more general sense of the word. For example, "canine" would be a hypernym to "poodle." Hyponyms are simply the opposite direction, i.e., for the "canine" example, "poodle" is the hyponym. We will leverage these relationships to produce adversarial text on the RCNN.

2.2.2   Difficulties of Text Spaces

The immediate problem of text domain is the discrete nature of the data. Adversarial examples are crafted manipulations in the input space such that they produce an unwanted output on the learned machine model. Manipulating the input must be constrained by small changes, otherwise it will be too noticeable and easily detected. Sharing the changes across the high-dimensional continuous space, like that of image pixels, is easy to hide. But this capability is not so easily done in text. Because of its discrete nature, even a single word change is detected and often it can completely change the meaning of the text.

In addition, when the output must be a sequence, the discrete space issue is compounded by searching through an exponential output space. For long sequences like summaries, the exact sequence is an intractable output space. These issues must be tackled to construct adversarial examples.

One could argue that because of the discrete nature of input and sequential nature of output space machine learning models for text data can be more robust than their continuous counterparts. This chapter will delve into that and show that this is not always the case.

2.3   Phishing Detection

As a result of comprehensive literature review on the topic of phishing, Lastdrager [24] gives this definition of phishing:

> Phishing is a scalable act of deception whereby impersonation is used to obtain information from a target.

As of the third quarter of 2019, APWG reports email and SaaS (software-as-a-service) to now hold the top category of phishing attacks since the beginning of 2019 [3–5]. From the viewpoint of machine learning, the task of detecting phishing emails, can be described as a sequence classification, where the email body can be processed as a sequence of tokens, and the machine can classify that email as either "legitimate" or "phishing." Since phishing is a top issue in security and privacy, it is a good choice for the use-case of adversarial machine learning and text.

3   The Recurrent Convolution Neural Network

Two popular deep learning architectures are the recurrent neural network (RNN) and convolutional neural network (CNN). Both are used to automatically detect features from the input in its raw format. In addition, they will also learn dependencies between these identified features. RNNs take as input a sequence of n tokens, $(t_1, \ldots, t_n)$, and produces a hidden state after consuming the input one token at a time. RNNs employ feedback to capture sequential dependence in the input sequence. The hidden state produced is a function of the current input and the previous output. It can be considered a representation of the input which in turn can be the feature for a downstream classifier. Typically for deep learning, this representation is passed to a dense layer of fully connected perceptron units and then passed through a sigmoid unit to produce a probability.

CNNs can also produce a set of features. However, its approach is different. Rather than process the input one token at a time, CNNs instead process the sequence together. First a filter (window) is scanned across the input, and aggregating the data in the window will produce a lower dimensional representation of the original data. Several of these filters are used to produce k equal sized (in dimensions) representations. Then a final pooling layer will gather the data for the respective dimensions across the k representations. This final "pooled" representation is used as the hidden state. At this point, a similar procedure is done (i.e. dense layer with sigmoid activation) to produce a probability. For more details, we refer the reader to [40].

The recurrent neural networks capture text semantics by emphasizing the ordering of words in a sequence [22]. Through the process of consuming tokens in sequence and the feedback mechanism, the RNN can learn context local to each token. These semantics are then used as a hidden state for downstream classification. The convolutional neural network looks at long term dependencies by processing the sequence as a whole as opposed to single tokens in sequence [25]. The RCNN attempts to combine both benefits to produce a superior hidden state (i.e., representation) of the input.

3.1 Sequence Classification

The problem being addressed can be defined as a sequence classification problem. The input will be a sequence of tokens $\mathbf{x} = (x_1, \ldots, x_N)$. In the context of phishing detection, we will be using sequences of tokens that represent the emails. The tokens are extracted using NLTK from the raw email header and email body. Each word is then represented both at the word-level as well as at the char-level. Every word w that is processed is represented by concatenating the word embedding of w ($E(x_i)$) and the words in w's context, before and after. The context is given with two LSTM networks. One makes a forward pass through the sequence, $\mathbf{C}_{pos}$, and the other makes a backward pass, $\mathbf{C}_{neg}$. Specifically, for word x_i, $\mathbf{C}_{neg} = $ LSTM$(x_{i-1}, \ldots, x_1)$ and $\mathbf{C}_{pos} = $ LSTM$(x_{i+1}, \ldots, x_N)$, where LSTM$(\cdot)$ produces a dense representation of given sequence. The final representation of the word is given by the following equation:

$$x_i = \mathbf{C}_{neg} + E(x_i) + \mathbf{C}_{pos} \tag{1}$$

Each word of the sequence is then put through a max pooling layer, that pools at each dimension this context representation across all the words of the sequence.

The RCNN also uses the same procedure to represent a sequence at the character level. These representations of the email text are concatenated and then passed through an attention layer, which then goes through a final dense layer to predict the classification of the email.

3.2 Weaknesses

There are some notable weaknesses of the RCNN model as used in [18]. A limitation of sequence based models is expensive training for longer sequences. This is due to the feedback loop of RNNs. The parameters of an RNN are influenced by each token of the sequence, so values of those parameters must be stored in memory to be correctly updated after processing the complete sequence. To handle this, many recurrent architectures limit the sequence length. Any sequences longer than this limit are simply truncated. In the case of RCNN this truncation is done at the end of the sequence. For a sequence of $\mathbf{x} = (x_1, \ldots, x_n)$ and a truncation at $K < n$, then only the tokens $\mathbf{x}_k = (x_1, \ldots, x_k)$ are used. An easy attack would be to include the adversarial words outside of this truncation limit.

A second weakness is the use of the attention layer. The original intent of the attention layer is to assign importance to certain words in the sequence, i.e., emphasize which word representations are important. However, after going through a max pool convolution, there are only two embeddings: the header representation and the body representation. So essentially the attention layer is comparing the value of the header versus the body. However, in a model that does not use the header, there is no attention, because only the body remains. We will analyze this weakness and explore ways to manage this.

4 Adversarial Text Attacks

We attack the RCNN model with different word based attacks, which are described below.

4.1 Replacement Attack

This attack replaces words with a random synonym. We use the default POS (part-of-speech) tagger of Natural Language Tool Kit. The tagged words are used to lookup Wordnet synsets. Synsets are groups of words or phrases denoting the same concepts. For example, "light" can mean illuminate or it can mean to put on fire.

Table 1 Wordnet lookup of "light"

Sense number	Synonyms	Example
light.v.01	Illume, illuminate	"This lamp lightens the room a bit"
light.v.04	Ignite	"Great heat can ignite almost any dry matter"

Each meaning would be its own synset. Table 1 are the results of a lookup of "light" on the wordnet interface.[3]

We target different POS tags: "NOUN," "VERB," "ADJECTIVE" or "ADVERB". Then all words of that type are replaced by a random synonym. The pool of synonyms is the union of all synsets that match the target word and POS (regardless of the meaning).

4.2 Relationship-Based Attack

WordNet also provides many relationships between synsets. "NOUNS" and "VERBS" are organized into hierarchies based on generality. Hyponyms/Hypernyms designate this relationship. We can replace a word with a hyponym/hypernym, and we use a tunable parameter for the maximum distance up/down the hierarchy.

4.3 Good-Word Attack

We also include a "good word" or "bad word" attack. This attack builds a pool of words that are unique to each class. For example, in phishing email classification, the attack will find a set of words that appear only in legit emails. To attack a model, it will take an example with known class, and inject words that are unique to a different class. A poor model will learn to designate certain words as indicative of a class. When the model sees the presence of these words, the model will raise the probability that a sample is from the class of these words, regardless of the actual sample's class.

We have two versions of Good-word attack. The first version simply looks at all the words in the training set along with their labels. Let V_G and V_B denote the vocabulary of all legitimate and phishing emails, respectively. We then remove $V_G \cap V_B$ from both vocabularies. This creates a vocabulary that is unique to the two classes. In addition, we remove all words that are not found in the English dictionary as compiled by NLTK.[4] Once these sets are computed, they are used to append to the opposite class of emails. To emphasize, given a legit email, we will append words

---

[3]http://wordnetweb.princeton.edu/perl/webwn.
[4]NLTK includes a list of English words.

from V_B and vice versa for phish emails. The intuition is that a model will begin to favor the opposite class as more of these words are added. The choice of the word to append is randomly selected from the respective vocabulary.

In the second version, we improve on the choice, by looking at the most frequent words. Here we append the words that are most frequent for the vocabulary. We also look at the least frequent words and see how this affects the model.

In a third version, we start with the same V_G and V_B. But instead of ranking them based on frequency, we will rank them by the prediction value of the model on just the word.

4.4 Long Email Attack

A common characteristic of RNN based models is the use of truncation for longer sequences. Because longer sequences require more power, often these models enforce sequence truncation. RCNN as used in [18] also follows this rule. So, the truncating nature of the model can be exploited. If the model truncates a sequence after the kth word token, then adding words after that k^{th} will effectively be ignored by the classifier. To exploit this, an adversary trying to evade phishing detection could take a legitimate mail that has k words and begin appending the phishing content afterwards.

A practical use of this attack is to hide the legitimate content using the weakness inherent in human eyes. For example, if all the legitimate words are written in white, the human user would only see the phish content, while a classifier, would "read" the words regardless of their color. A similar tactic can be done, by forcing the font size of the legitimate words to a size imperceivable to human eyes.

4.5 TextBugger Baseline

A current state-of-the-art approach to crafting adversarial text is in [26]. The research provides both a white-box and black-box attack. For our baseline, we used the black-box approach as described in that paper. Essentially the algorithm, ranks each sentence by the confidence of the victim model's prediction. Then in descending order, each word of a sentence is ranked by a decrease in victim model confidence, when that word is removed. The algorithm, then attacks each word (again in descending order) with a 'TextBug' (i.e. adversarial word). If the introduction of the bug exceeds a hyperparameter similarity threshold (it is too different from original email), it will immediately stop the algorithm and report a failure to find adversarial text. On the other hand, if at any time the introduction of the TextBug succeeds in causing a misclassification, the algorithm stops and returns the adversarial text.

4.6   Differential Evolution Attack

We use the genetic algorithm known as differential evolution (DE) [35]. The core of DE revolves around how the potential solutions, chromosomes, are represented. Each full run of DE will produce a population of adversarial examples for a single email. The chromosome $x = (x_1, \ldots, x_n)$ is a sequence of n tokens that represent a whole email. The representation of the token is transformed into a dense embedding with a fixed dimension size, d. As a result the email is now a $x \in \mathbb{R}^n \times \mathbb{R}^d$ matrix.

At initialization of DE, the tokens are randomly swapped using a probability distribution based on the embedding space. For each token, $x_i \in \mathbb{R}^d$, we use cosine similarity to find the k nearest neighbors. We sample from a probability distribution based on how similar each of the k tokens is to the original token.

At each iteration of a generation, words are mutated using the embedding space as well. DE will place each chromosome of the population in a trial against a newly mutated chromosome. DE calls upon the use of vector addition and subtraction to mutate a chromosome:

$$\text{mutate}(A, B, C) = A + (B - C) \tag{2}$$

Here A, B and C are selected randomly from the population of chromosomes. The current trial chromosome is then mixed with this newly mutated chromosome. The mixing algorithm is called crossover, and essentially, for each token of the chromosome there is a 50-50 chance to select the token from the trial chromosome or the mutated chromosome. This final chromosome then competes against the trial chromosome via a fitness function.

$$\text{Fitness}(X) = \text{Similarity}(X) + \text{Confidence}(X) \tag{3}$$

The fitness function measures how similar a chromosome X is to the original email, $O = (o_1, \ldots, o_n)$, and how much the victim model changes in its prediction.

$$\text{Similarity}(X) = \frac{\sum_1^n \cos(x_i, o_i)}{||X||} \tag{4}$$

Cosine similarity is again used for each word, and then summed up (with normalization) for the final similarity score.

$$\text{Confidence}(X) = \text{Prediction}(O) - \text{Prediction}(X) \tag{5}$$

The goal of the Confidence($\cdot$) metric is to measure how much the victim model deteriorates in its confidence. The fitness function will decide the winner between the trial chromosome and mutated chromosome, which will then be put into the next generation.

This whole procedure is repeated for each member of the population. Once a full generation has gone through a trial, DE repeats for the next generation. These new adversarial emails will then be placed in a pool to be used for adversarial training to evaluate their effectiveness.

5 Experiment Design

5.1 IWSPA Dataset

At the 2018 ACM International Workshop on Security and Privacy Analytics [39], a shared task for detecting phishing emails [1] was organized. A unique characteristic of phishing classification is the unbalanced nature of the classes. The dataset includes a version of emails with the header and without the header. The counts can be seen in Table 2. This dataset was improved further as described in [42, 45].

5.2 Evaluation

All attacks are done on the test set. After the model is trained, its parameters are fixed and only modifications to the test set will be allowed. For comparisons, the untouched model is referred to as the "original" model. The attacks are done on every sample of the test set.

The receiver operator characteristic (ROC) curve can be used to measure detection by comparing the false positive rate (FPR) to the true positive rate (TPR) [21]. Measurements of the TPR/FPR are taken at even intervals of different thresholds for the classifier. Then using the x-axis as FPR and y-axis as TPR, the points can be plotted. A perfect ROC curve is a square shape on the graph. And a purely random evaluation is a curve that equates $FPR = TPR$.

$$TPR = \frac{TP}{TP + FN} \tag{6}$$

$$FPR = \frac{FP}{TN + FP} \tag{7}$$

Table 2 IWSPA Dataset counts

Name	Legitimate	Phish	Total
Train (header)	4082	501	4583
Test (header)	3699	496	4195
Train (no-header)	5088	612	5700
Test (no-header)	3825	475	4300

In addition to the ROC, we can compute the area under the ROC curve. This value measures the probability that a randomly chosen positive instance will be ranked higher than a randomly chosen negative instance [19]. This number is always between 0 and 1. Note also that because a purely random classifier will result in a line from (0, 0) to (1, 1) and AUC of 0.5, a classifier with an AUC value below 0.5 is worse than a randomly guessing one.

5.3 Header Usage

We first consider the model based on [18].[5] We first investigate the use of headers for the dataset. Two models are trained using the RCNN: (1) one with the inclusion of headers (M_{full}) and (2) a second model that only trains on the body text of the email (M_{body}).

6 Results

6.1 ROC Curves

The ROC curves of Fig. 1 show clearly that the synonym attack is ineffective M_h. Apart from the curves being nearly identical, the AUC values are 0.9736 and 0.9700 before and after the synonym attack is applied. A possible hypothesis is that the model is depending only on the header. This hypothesis can be tested by performing the same attack on M_b. Figure 2 report the results of this experiment. We see that the AUC drops from 0.9808 to 0.9720. An interesting side effect of training without headers is an increase in the performance of M_{body} (0.9736–0.9808).

When looking at the hypernyms and hyponyms, we see that the effect to the ROC is more dramatic (Fig. 2). The most effective being the hypernym attack with AUC = 0.9560.

In the case of good words attacks, a simple strategy of appending words is not enough to fool the classifier. This can be explained in two parts: first adding single words is not enough to overcome the semantics M_{body} learns from the training set, and second that post-pending will be ignored when the original is longer than the set max-sequence length.

We can see that even focusing on words unique to the opposite class does not reduce the performance of M_{body} in Fig. 3. The most effective attack was the "Forward" frequency based good word attack, with an AUC of 0.9733. "Forward" refers to appending words in order of frequency, where "Backward" would append lowest frequency first.

---

[5]Thanks to the authors for making their code available to us.

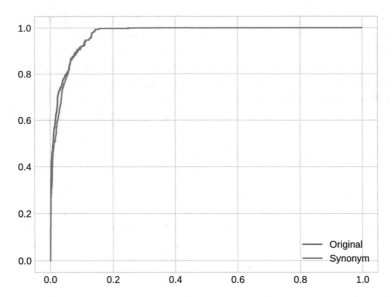

Fig. 1 ROC of Synonym attack on M_{full} (AUC is 0.9736 and 0.9700 before and after attack)

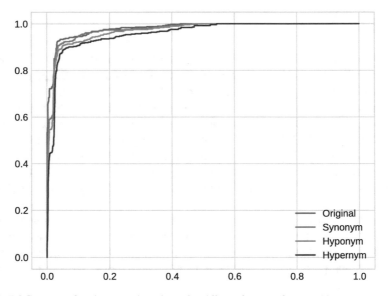

Fig. 2 ROC curves of replacement based attacks. All attacks were done on M_b

In addition to the simple Good Word attack, we also look at one that uses the model to rank the words, instead of by frequency (Fig. 4). The AUCs can be seen in Table 3. It is seen that adding words is not as effective as replacing words.

In fact, if we look at performance for one-sided attacks, we notice something peculiar. When good word attack is only applied to phish emails, the classifier

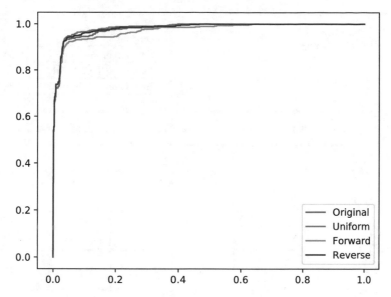

Fig. 3 ROC curves of basic good word attacks

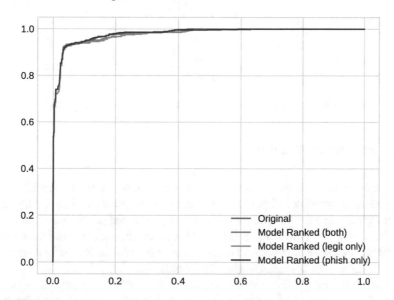

Fig. 4 ROC of Good Word attack where words are ranked by model predictions

begins to perform better. A possible explanation is that M_{body} has learned the semantics of grammatically correct sentences. So, when the model receives a series of grammatically incorrect words (i.e. post-pended good words), it reports higher probabilities of phish emails.

Table 3 Area under ROC
curves for the good word
attack with model ranking

Attack	AUC
Original	0.9808
Target both classes	0.9779
Target only legit emails	0.9778
Target only phish emails	0.9809

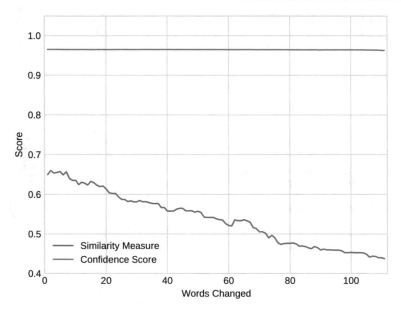

Fig. 5 Similarity score and confidence score vs. number of words changed for TextBugger

6.2   TextBugger Baseline

The results show that even without the header, RCNN remains robust against
the TextBugger baseline. Figure 5 shows the similarity measure as the algorithm
changes words, and the confidence score. For a successful attack, we want to have
a high similarity measure while causing a significant decrease in confidence score.
Intuitively, this means that the semantics of the email remain for the human reader,
but the victim model now fails to classify it correctly.

We see from Fig. 5, that the confidence score barely decreases. The original
paper calls for a similarity measure to remain above 0.8. However, as the figure
reports, TextBugger would immediately fail on changing the first word. In our run,
we ignored the similarity score to measure how well it could find an adversarial text.
The figure shows that at 100 words, the similarity measure is 0.43 and the model
still reports a confidence score of 0.97.

Table 4 Parameter settings of differential evolution

Email ID	Pop.	Gen.	Changeable words	Embedding size	Original prediction	Adversarial prediction
phish-3709	100	500	20	50	0.245	0.004
phish-3723	100	1000	30	50	0.967	0.936
phish-3723	100	1000	30	300	0.967	0.917

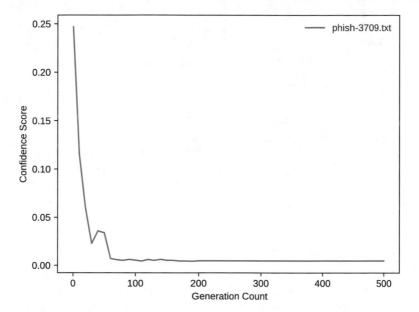

Fig. 6 DE results of phish-3709

6.3 Holistic Approach

Using our novel approach of applying differential evolution we find some slightly more promising results. Table 4 show the parameters used for all runs. Note that 'phish-3709' is already being classified incorrectly. However, we see that the differential evolution can push the wrong classification even further to near 0. Also we see that the difference in embedding dimensions helps to produce strong adversarial examples.

We also see in Figs. 6 and 7 a show stronger impact on the confidence score. However, RCNN remains robust against them, with a loss in confidence score to only 0.917. These tests show the need for more research in adversarial text.

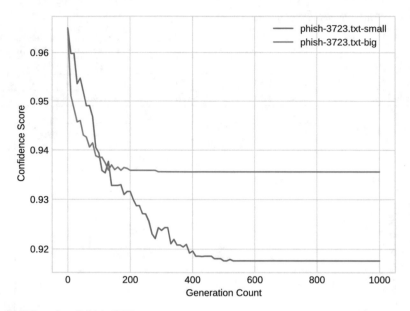

Fig. 7 DE results of phish-3723

7 Related Works

The research community of adversarial text has brought many new ideas. Before, going into those, first we give a brief history of the domain of image processing. Section 7.1 covers this with examples from its research community. Then we return to the domain of NLP in Sect. 7.2 and then look at limitations and why this motivates the holistic approaches in Sect. 7.3.

7.1 Image Processing

Szegedy et al. brought the issue of adversarial examples to the forefront for neural network researchers [37]. Their research revealed two important weaknesses for machine learning models that use neural networks: (1) existence of adversarial examples and (2) the property of transferability. Although the problem of crafting input to manipulate machine learning model was not new at the time, adversarial examples became a serious security concern in neural networks, because of its widespread use (especially in computer vision.

Soon after the publication of [37] many other white-box attacks were developed [7, 11, 20, 28, 29, 31]. White-box refers to the adversary having complete access to the victim model parameters. A quick assumption might be that this kind of access is improbable, however the *transferability* of examples allows white-box threats to be effective. Papernot et al. leverage this property in [30]; they train a local neural network and use white-box attacks on this model. The researchers show that the generated adversarial examples are also effective against black-box (no access) models. Other examples of black-box attacks include [12, 36]. A full review of these attacks and others can be found in [43].

In response to these attacks, many defenses have been proposed. The successful approaches fall into two main categories: (1) adversarial training and (2) adversarial detection. As the name implies *adversarial training* makes use of actual adversarial attacks as a part of the training regime. *Adversarial detection* modifies the target model, by adding a layer of protection through detection. After detection, an approach can choose to discard the adversarial example, or the approach may try to recover from the detected adversarial example.

7.2 Natural Language Processing

Cheng et al. [13] took early steps towards finding attacks against continuous sequence models. Soon after this, research was published that found effective attacks on deep learning text classification models in [16]. In a tangential area of research, studies are looking for more fine-tuned adversarial examples for both continuous and discrete models [33]. Researchers have also started to search for generalized attacks not specific to a dataset or domain [8]. For a good background in adversarial text, a recent survey is [46].

TextBugger This work attacks a text-based DNN classifier with adversarial texts in both white-box and black-box settings [26]. The core of the attack is based on identifying the most "important" words and modifying these words. In the white-box setting they use the Jacobian of the classifier function with respect to the inputs. For the black-box setting, the important sentences are identified by using the confidence value of the classifier on the sentence by itself. Then for each sentence, the words are scored by comparing the confidence value with and without each word. Then the words are modified like in the white-box setting.

Their work also focuses on words and offers five possible "textbugs" that can replace a word in the text: (1) insert a space, (2) delete a random character, (3) swap two random characters, (4) substitute a homograph for a character (e.g. 'a' and '@'), or (5) substitute the word completely.

7.3 Holistic Approach

Limitations A common vein in many state-of-the-art techniques is a greedy approach. They seek to order the words by their influence on the output. They then choose the most influential one and perturb it. This is done one word at a time until the algorithm succeeds, or it runs out of words. We have already seen that greedy approaches won't be enough to make an impact on complex models like RCNN.

Apart from the RCNN, there are several complex transformer based language models, e.g., [15, 32, 44]. These models train on billions of words across millions of documents. The area of embeddings can be promising one for future research.

Metaheuristics An area of research for solving harder discrete based problems is metaheuristics. These are approaches for finding solutions to a group of hard optimization problems as opposed to one specific hard optimization problem [10]. For the case of discrete problems, the metaheuristics can help find optimal solutions across the whole sequence input as opposed to checking one word at a time.

Differential Evolution is a metaheuristic for optimizing function parameters [35].

This, like other evolution strategies (ES), starts with a seed population and uses genetic themes of mutation and crossover to efficiently find optimal solutions. An added benefit is the simplicity of the algorithm. This can be the first next step in exploring adversarial text.

8   Concluding Remarks

In this chapter, we considered adversarial machine learning for text domains. We used phishing email classification as a case study to illustrate our attacks. Literature reveals that text is just as vulnerable to adversarial examples. However, the researchers attack simple neural network architectures. For the task of phishing, a new state-of-the-art deep learning model has been published that can detect phishing with high accuracy and low false positive rate.

We have shown that this model is strong against basic but intuitive attacks. Furthermore, we show that the state-of-the-art techniques for text are relatively ineffective. Only when we look at the sequence as a whole (as the DE algorithm does) are we able to craft adversarial examples against the complex RCNN model.

Ongoing research continues to shed light on this surprising issue. The promise of efficient optimization of metaheuristics may prove to be a fruitful path of exploration for adversarial research in discrete domains like text. In addition, leveraging more semantic based language models will improve the advances of adversarial text, and help to create robust models for NLP.

Acknowledgments We thank NSF for partial support under grants CNS 1319212, DGE 1433817, and DUE 1356705. This material is also based upon work supported in part by the U. S. Army Research Laboratory and the U.S. Army Research Office grant number W911NF-16-1-0422.

References

1. Aassal, A.E., Moraes, L., Baki, S., Das, A., Verma, R.: Anti-phishing pilot at ACM IWSPA 2018 evaluating performance with new metrics for unbalanced datasets. In: Proceedings of IWSPA-AP Anti-Phishing Pilot, CEUR, pp. 2–10 (2018)
2. Aassal, A.E., Baki, S., Das, A., Verma, R.M.: An in-depth benchmarking and evaluation of phishing detection research for security needs. IEEE Access **8**, 22170–22192 (2020)
3. Anti-Phishing Working Group. Phishing Activity Trends Report, 1st quarter 2019. https://docs.apwg.org/reports/apwg_trends_report_q1_2019.pdf (2019)
4. Anti-Phishing Working Group. Phishing Activity Trends Report, 2nd quarter 2019. https://docs.apwg.org/reports/apwg_trends_report_q2_2019.pdf, (2019)
5. Anti-Phishing Working Group. Phishing Activity Trends Report, 3rd quarter 2019. https://docs.apwg.org/reports/apwg_trends_report_q3_2019.pdf (2019)
6. Bahdanau, D., Cho, K., Bengio, Y.: Neural machine translation by jointly learning to align and translate. In: ICLR (2015)
7. Baluja, S., Fischer, I.: Learning to attack: Adversarial transformation networks. In: AAAI, pp. 2687–2695. AAAI Press, Palo Alto (2018)
8. Behjati, M., Moosavi-Dezfooli, S.-M., Baghshah, M.S., Frossard, P.: Universal adversarial attacks on text classifiers. In: ICASSP, pp. 7345–7349. IEEE, New York (2019)
9. Biggio, B., Roli, F.: Wild patterns: Ten years after the rise of adversarial machine learning. Pattern Recognit. **84**, 317–331 (2018)
10. Boussaïd, I., Lepagnot, J., Siarry, P.: A survey on optimization metaheuristics. Inf. Sci. **237**, 82–117 (2013)
11. Carlini, N., Wagner, D.A.: Towards evaluating the robustness of neural networks. In: IEEE Symposium on Security and Privacy, pp. 39–57. IEEE Computer Society, Washington (2017)
12. Chen, P.-Y., Zhang, H., Sharma, Y., Yi, J., Hsieh, C.-J.: ZOO: Zeroth order optimization based black-box attacks to deep neural networks without training substitute models. In: AISec@CCS, pp. 15–26. ACM, New York (2017)
13. Cheng, M., Yi, J., Zhang, H., Chen, P.-Y., Hsieh, C.-J.: Seq2sick: Evaluating the robustness of sequence-to-sequence models with adversarial examples. CoRR, abs/1803.01128 (2018)
14. Das, A., Baki, S., Aassal, A.E., Verma, R.M., Dunbar, A.: Sok: A comprehensive reexamination of phishing research from the security perspective. IEEE Commun. Surv. Tutorials **22**(1), 671–708 (2020)
15. Devlin, J., Chang, M.-W., Lee, K., Toutanova, K.: BERT: Pre-training of deep bidirectional transformers for language understanding. In: NAACL-HLT (1), pp. 4171–4186. Association for Computational Linguistics, Stroudsburg (2019)
16. Ebrahimi, J., Rao, A., Lowd, D., Dou, D.: Hotflip: White-box adversarial examples for text classification. In: ACL (2), pp. 31–36. Association for Computational Linguistics, Stroudsburg (2018)
17. Egozi, G., Verma, R.M.: Phishing email detection using robust NLP techniques. In: Tong, H., Li, Z.J., Zhu, F., Yu, J. (eds.) 2018 IEEE International Conference on Data Mining Workshops, ICDM Workshops, Singapore, November 17–20, 2018, pp. 7–12. IEEE, New York (2018)
18. Fang, Y., Zhang, C., Huang, C., Liu, L., Yang, Y.: Phishing email detection using improved RCNN model with multilevel vectors and attention mechanism. IEEE Access **7**, 56329–56340 (2019)
19. Fawcett, T.: An introduction to ROC analysis. Pattern Recognit. Lett. **27**(8), 861–874 (2006)
20. Goodfellow, I.J., Shlens, J., Szegedy, C.: Explaining and harnessing adversarial examples. In: ICLR (Poster) (2015)
21. Green, D.M., Swets, J.A., et al.: Signal Detection Theory and Psychophysics, vol. 1. Wiley, New York (1966)
22. Hochreiter, S., Schmidhuber, J.: Long short-term memory. Neural Comput. **9**(8), 1735–1780 (1997)

23. Lai, S., Xu, L., Liu, K., Zhao, J.: Recurrent convolutional neural networks for text classification. In: AAAI, pp. 2267–2273. AAAI Press, Palo Alto (2015)
24. Lastdrager, E.E.H.: Achieving a consensual definition of phishing based on a systematic review of the literature. Crime Sci. **3**(1), 9 (2014)
25. LeCun, Y., Haffner, P., Bottou, L., Bengio, Y.: Object recognition with gradient-based learning. In: Shape, Contour and Grouping in Computer Vision, vol. 1681. Lecture Notes in Computer Science, p. 319. Springer, Berlin (1999)
26. Li, J., Ji, S., Du, T., Li, B., Wang, T.: Textbugger: Generating adversarial text against real-world applications. In: NDSS. The Internet Society (2019)
27. Miller, G.A.: WordNet: An Electronic Lexical Database. MIT Press, Cambridge (1998)
28. Moosavi-Dezfooli, S.-M., Fawzi, A., Frossard, P.: Deepfool: A simple and accurate method to fool deep neural networks. In: CVPR, pp. 2574–2582. IEEE Computer Society, Washington (2016)
29. Moosavi-Dezfooli, S.-M., Fawzi, A., Fawzi, O., Frossard, P.: Universal adversarial perturbations. In: CVPR, pp. 86–94. IEEE Computer Society, Washington (2017)
30. Papernot, N., McDaniel, P.D., Goodfellow, I.J., Jha, S., Celik, Z.B., Swami, A.: Practical black-box attacks against deep learning systems using adversarial examples. CoRR, abs/1602.02697 (2016)
31. Papernot, N., McDaniel, P.D., Jha, S., Fredrikson, M., Celik, Z.B., Swami, A.: The limitations of deep learning in adversarial settings. In: EuroS&P, pp. 372–387. IEEE, New York (2016)
32. Radford, A., Wu, J., Child, R., Luan, D., Amodei, D., Sutskever, I.: Language models are unsupervised multitask learners (2019)
33. Ren, S., Deng, Y., He, K., Che, W.: Generating natural language adversarial examples through probability weighted word saliency. In: ACL (1), pp. 1085–1097. Association for Computational Linguistics, Stroudsburg (2019)
34. Shen, T., Lei, T., Barzilay, R., Jaakkola, T.S.: Style transfer from non-parallel text by cross-alignment. In: NIPS, pp. 6830–6841 (2017)
35. Storn, R., Price, K.V.: Differential evolution - a simple and efficient heuristic for global optimization over continuous spaces. J. Glob. Optim. **11**(4), 341–359 (1997)
36. Su, J., Vargas, D.V., Sakurai, K.: One pixel attack for fooling deep neural networks. IEEE Trans. Evol. Comput. **23**, 828–841 (2019)
37. Szegedy, C., Zaremba, W., Sutskever, I., Bruna, J., Erhan, D., Goodfellow, I.J., Fergus, R.: Intriguing properties of neural networks. In: ICLR (Poster) (2014)
38. Verma, R.M., Hossain, N.: Semantic feature selection for text with application to phishing email detection. In: Lee, H.-S., Han, D.-G. (eds.) Information Security and Cryptology - ICISC 2013 - 16th International Conference, Seoul, November 27–29, 2013, Revised Selected Papers, vol. 8565. Lecture Notes in Computer Science, pp. 455–468. Springer, Berlin (2013)
39. Verma, R., Kantarcioglu, M. (eds.): IWSPA '18: Proceedings of the Fourth ACM International Workshop on Security and Privacy Analytics, New York. Association for Computing Machinery, New York (2018)
40. Verma, R.M., Marchette, D.J.: Cybersecurity Analytics. CRC Press, Boca Raton (2019)
41. Verma, R.M., Shashidhar, N., Hossain, N.: Detecting phishing emails the natural language way. In: Foresti, S., Yung, M., Martinelli, F. (eds.) Computer Security - ESORICS 2012 - 17th European Symposium on Research in Computer Security, Pisa, September 10–12, 2012. Proceedings, vol. 7459. Lecture Notes in Computer Science, pp. 824–841. Springer, Berlin (2012)
42. Verma, R.M., Zeng, V., Faridi, H.: Data quality for security challenges: Case studies of phishing, malware and intrusion detection datasets. In: Proceedings of the 2019 ACM SIGSAC Conference on Computer and Communications Security, CCS '19, pp. 2605–2607. Association for Computing Machinery, New York (2019)
43. Wiyatno, R.R., Xu, A., Dia, O., de Berker, A.: Adversarial examples in modern machine learning: A review. CoRR, abs/1911.05268 (2019)
44. Yang, Z., Dai, Z., Yang, Y., Carbonell, J.G., Salakhutdinov, R., Le, Q.V.: XLNet: Generalized autoregressive pretraining for language understanding. CoRR, abs/1906.08237 (2019)

45. Zeng, V., Baki, S., Aassal, A.E., Verma, R., De Moraes, L.F.T., Das, A.: Diverse datasets and a customizable benchmarking framework for phishing. In: Proceedings of the Sixth International Workshop on Security and Privacy Analytics, IWSPA '20, pp. 35–41. Association for Computing Machinery, New York (2020)
46. Zhang, W.E., Sheng, Q.Z., Alhazmi, A.A.F.: Generating textual adversarial examples for deep learning models: a survey. CoRR, abs/1901.06796 (2019)

Overview of GANs for Image Synthesis and Detection Methods

Eric Tjon ⓘ, Melody Moh ⓘ, and Teng-Sheng Moh ⓘ

Abstract This chapter provides an overview of Generative Adversarial Network (GAN) architecture, the use of conditional GAN networks in image synthesis, and detection methods for facial manipulation in images and videos. GANs are a type of neural network architecture that utilize adversarial competition between a generator and discriminator to optimize its output. Recently, conditional GANs have been shown to achieve realistic image synthesis. These computer-generated images are difficult to distinguish from photographic images even for human observers. Effective detection methods are important to combat malicious spread and use of damaging fake media. Among the detection methods, Convolutional Neural Network (CNN) have been adopted to classify images taken from videos and to decide if images are real or fake. The current models are able to detect facial manipulations with acceptable accuracy. The chapter also discusses future research directions including benchmarks, challenges, and competitions in improving detection methods against new attacks.

Keywords GAN · Image synthesis and detection · Fake video detection · Adversarial deep learning

1 Introduction

Computer graphics have traditionally used a rendering pipeline to generate 3D images [12]. These images require a large amount of effort to produce, both in specifying the precise inputs and in the generation techniques to render the image. Manually designed 3d models, lighting conditions, and physical properties all require careful attention to create a realistic appearing image of a scene.

Recent advancements in machine learning techniques provide alternative methods of image generation. Deep neural networks are able to learn image transfor-

E. Tjon · M. Moh (✉) · T.-S. Moh
San Jose State University, San Jose, CA, USA
e-mail: eric.tjon@sjsu.edu; melody.moh@sjsu.edu; teng.moh@sjsu.edu

© Springer Nature Switzerland AG 2021
P. Dasgupta et al. (eds.), *Adversary-Aware Learning Techniques and Trends in Cybersecurity*, https://doi.org/10.1007/978-3-030-55692-1_5

mation techniques and output high quality images [12, 27]. One neural network architecture that has been especially suited for this task is a generative adversarial network or GAN. A GAN contains two models: a generative model and a discriminative model [9, 17]. The generator captures the data distribution from the training data and tries to generate similar input. The discriminator tries to distinguish between training data and generated data. The generator is pitted against the adversarial discriminator. Both the generator and discriminator iteratively improve until the output is indistinguishable from the training data.

In order for useful image synthesis, it is not enough to simply produce a realistic looking image. We must create one that matches a high level description of the desired image. A conditional generative adversarial network or cGAN is able to achieve this goal. A generator for a cGAN takes in a source image, such as a labeled input or a sketch, and outputs a transformed image based on its training data [12, 19]. The discriminator works in the same way and tries to classify between training data and generated data. The end result is a transformed source image that is realistic enough to fool the discriminator.

The ease and availability of image synthesis using deep learning has led to growing concerns about the use of fake videos. There are social concerns in disseminating false information with synthesized public figures, as well as ethical concerns in manipulating the likeliness of unconsenting actors [24]. Image synthesis tools such as DeepFake and FaceSwap are publically available online for anyone to use. Malicious actors can easily acquire and use these tools to produce forged videos.

Identifying these fake videos is necessary to address these social and ethical concerns. High quality image synthesis is too realistic for human observers to distinguish, so we must develop automated detection techniques. Current, state-of-the-art detection relies on tracking the face throughout the video and feeding it into a convolutional neural network (CNN) that will classify it as real or fake [1, 21, 24]. As image synthesis improves, we must also improve these detection techniques.

2 Generative Adversarial Network

Generative adversarial networks are a type of generative model. A generative model is able to take a sample of data and estimate its probability distribution either explicitly with an output of a function, or implicitly with the output of sample data [8]. GANs primarily perform the latter function and generate samples that mimic the training data. Generative models are particularly suited for many tasks including multi-modal output, generating realistic samples, and high resolution image manipulation.

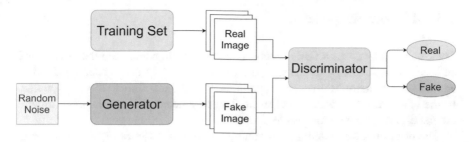

Fig. 1 GAN architecture

GANs overcome many disadvantages of other generative models. Generative stochastic networks and Boltzmann machines require the use of markov chains to sample data that matches the target distribution [2, 8]. These markov chains create a new sample by repeatedly applying transitions based on probabilistic rules to an existing sample. This algorithm is computationally expensive and does not scale well to higher dimensions. GANs are able to represent complex models and can generate a sample in a single step once trained [9]. Compared to variational autoencoders, GANs generally produce higher quality output [8]. Also, GANs are able to produce image transformations more efficiently than other methods [12].

The architecture of a GAN is composed of two parts: a generator and discriminator (Fig. 1). These two parts are implemented as a deep neural network. Typically, the type of neural network is a multilayered perceptron.

2.1 Generator

The generator G is a model that attempts to generate samples of data. The input is a random vector z sampled from a uniform noise distribution [9]. The desired output is a sample of data that mimics the training data set. Using random noise z as the input allows the generator to provide different samples and capture the full distribution of the training set.

2.2 Discriminator

The discriminator is a binary classification model that tries to distinguish between input from a given data set x and input from the generator G(z). The input is a single sample of data. The output is a classification score that is 1 for the training data and 0 for the generated data.

2.3 Adversarial Training

The training process of a GAN involves alternating steps between the generator G
and the discriminator D. In one step, the parameters $\theta^{(G)}$ of the generator are fixed
and the discriminator tries update its parameters $\theta^{(D)}$ according to the cost function.
In the other step, the roles are reversed. The parameters $\theta^{(D)}$ of the discriminator
are fixed, and the generator tries to optimize $\theta^{(G)}$.

The discriminator updating step contains two mini batches of m samples each
to classify. One mini batch contains m samples from the training data set. The
discriminator tries to classify this mini batch as 1, corresponding to the real
classification. The other mini batch consists of the output of the generator when
m random noise samples are inputted. The discriminator tries to classify this batch
as 0, identifying it as generated data. In each step, the model updates its parameters
through gradient ascent [9] using the cost function. The cost of the discriminator
$L^{(D)}$ is always calculated as cross-entropy loss from these two mini batches.

$$L^{(D)}(\theta^{(D)}, \theta^{(G)}) = -\frac{1}{2}\mathbb{E}_{x \sim pdata} log\, D(x) - \frac{1}{2}\mathbb{E}_z log(1 - D(G(z))) \qquad (1)$$

While the discriminator's cost is always the same, the generator's cost may differ.
A natural cost function for the generator would be the inverse of the discriminator,
corresponding to a zerosum, or minimax game [9]. This definition is often used due
to its simplicity and ease of implementation.

$$L^{(G)} = -L^{(D)} \qquad (2)$$

With the two above cost function, the discriminator tries to minimize the cross-
entropy while the generator tries to maximize the same cross-entropy. In other
words, the generator attempts to reduce the correctness of the discriminator. In
practice however, working on the same objective possibly leads to the discriminator
overpowering the generator when it is correct in its binary classification [8]. The
gradient for the generator vanishes, and the discriminator wins the contest.

To solve this problem, we need to carefully change the goal of the generator.
Instead of reducing the correctness of the discriminator, the generator can aim to
increase the amount of mistakes. The result is that the gradient becomes stronger for
each side when it is losing. This game only converges when the generator produces
samples similar to the training data. This change is represented in the cost function
by changing the target of cross entropy.

$$L^{(G)} = -\frac{1}{2}\mathbb{E}_z log\, D(G(z)) \qquad (3)$$

It is important to note that the generator does not learn from the training data
directly. It only updates its parameters based on the discriminator's classification.

This way of indirect learning prevents overfitting, where the generator copies directly from the training set.

2.4 Improving GAN Performance

While GANs are able to avoid the complexities of other generative models, it comes with its own unique obstacles to overcome. The most notable problem is that the GAN may not reach an optimal equilibrium [9]. Some GANs may even diverge, where the generator and discriminator do not converge to an equilibrium. In implementation, there are a number of techniques for improving the quality and convergence of a GAN.

2.4.1 Labeled Training

Introducing labels to the training process increases the subjective quality of the generated images [8, 25]. Using a class-conditional GAN adds label information to both the generator and discriminator input. This improvement also works when the discriminator is also trained to recognize different classes of real objects. The reason for this improvement is not entirely clear. One possible explanation is that labels help the training process. Another is that possibly, labels increase bias towards what humans focus on such as the shape of an image rather than minor details.

2.4.2 One Sided Label Smoothing

Recall that the discriminator outputs a value of 1 for real images and a value of 0 for generated images. Under these conditions, the discriminator has a tendency to produce highly confident decisions that identify the correct class with too high of a probability [8]. One sided label smoothing reduces the target value for a real image from 1 to a lower number such as 0.9 [25]. This change in probability reduces the discriminator's overconfidence and makes it more resilient to adversarial attacks [30]. The negative label is not smoothed as it would encourage the model to generate incorrect samples [8].

2.4.3 Virtual Batch Normalization

Batch normalization is commonly used to improve the training, stability, and performance of deep neural networks [11]. It involves normalizing the input layer based on the mean and variance of the data in the batch. Unfortunately in GANs, the batches are numerous and small. The fluctuation of normalization between batches can overpower individual inputs [8]. A possible remedy is to use reference batch normalization, where the input layer is normalized once based on a chosen reference batch. However, this technique can cause overfitting on the reference batch. Virtual batch normalization is a effective trade off between reference and plain batch normalization [25]. It uses both a reference batch and the current input to normalize the layers. As a result, the normalization is independent of other data in the batch and overfits less on the reference batch.

The internal effects of batch normalization are not well understood. Initially, the improvements made through this technique were attributed to reducing internal covariant shift, defined as the change in distribution of inputs to the internal layers [11]. Subsequent research shows that performance gains are not strongly linked to this reduction, and batch normalization does not always reduce internal covariant shift [26]. One alternative explanation reasons that batch normalization makes loss and optimization functions more smooth. This smoothness results in faster training.

2.4.4 Progressive Growing

Progressive growing of GANs refers to a training technique that gradually increases the layers of the generator and discriminator [13]. Both models begin training using low resolution inputs. During training, higher resolution layers are simultaneously added to the output of the generator and the input of the discriminator. As a result, the majority of learning occurs when working with smaller images than full resolution. This progressive learning vastly improves training speed and stability.

2.5 Variations of GAN Architectures

A GAN is generally made up of a generator, discriminator, and the competition between the two networks. However, the implementation of these networks can vary greatly. Numerous variations of the GAN architecture have been published detailing network architectures that improve the functionality of the system and the stability of training while creating larger images. In this section, we survey a number of notable GAN architectures (Tables 1). Some of these GAN architectures implement one or more of the improvements listed in Sect. 2.4.

2.5.1 Fully Connected GAN (FCGAN)

The first paper that introduced GANs used fully connected neural networks for the generator and the discriminator [9]. This early FCGAN was able to work with low resolution datasets such as MNIST and CIFAR 10. This model does not generalize well and is limited in application, serving more as a proof of concept of a GAN's generative ability.

Table 1 Overview of general GANs

Architecture	Contributions	Data sets	Max resolution
FCGAN [9]	First GAN	MNIST, CIFAR10	32×32
LAPGAN [6]	Lapacian pyramid	CIFAR10, STL, LSUN	96×96
DCGAN [20]	General guidelines	MNIST, CIFAR10, LSUN, Imagenet	64×64
PROGAN [13]	Progressive training	CIFAR10, LSUN, CELEBA	1028×1028
SAGAN [13]	Attention based	ImageNet	128×128
BIGGAN [3]	Larger scale	ImageNet, JFT-300M	512×512

2.5.2 Lapacian Pyramid GAN (LAPGAN)

LAPGAN uses a series of GANs within a Lapacian pyramid to generate a 32×32 or 64×64 output through upsampling [6]. The first GAN in the sequence takes in a random noise vector and generates a coarse image. Each successive GAN takes in the output of the previous GAN as a condition and generates a larger image. This coarse to fine method is able to generate finer details than FCGAN.

2.5.3 Deep Convolutional GAN (DCGAN)

DCGAN provides architectural constraints when using deep convolutional neural networks to create a GAN [20]. These constraints help stabilize training for image generation. The authors have three main recommendations: replacing pooling layers with strided convolutions, using batch normalization layers in both the generator and the discriminator, and removing fully connected layers after convolutions.

The first constraint replaces pooling layers with strided convolutional layers [20]. These types layers serve to upsample or downsample an image. Convolutions allow the model to learn these functions instead of taking the max or average of a group of pixels. Using batch normalization in between layers normalizes the input to each layer which stabilizes training. Lastly, fully connected layers on top of convolutions are removed. One common fully connected layer is global average pooling, which improves stability but worsens convergence speed. Through these improvements, the base DCGAN model is able to create convincing 64×64 images.

2.5.4 Progressive Growing Neural Network GAN (PROGAN)

PROGAN introduces the progressive growing technique outlined in Sect. 2.4.4 to train and generate high resolution images up to 1028×1028 [13]. This GAN is unique in its training process where the GAN starts off training a 4×4 image size. The generator and discriminator progressively increases the image size and trains again. Adding layers one at a time helps stabilize training for large scale images.

2.5.5 Self-Attention GAN (SAGAN)

SAGAN adds a unique self-attention module to a convolutional GAN [33]. The self attention maps combines convolutional feature maps, which represents high level features, with attention maps that indicate the location of those features. SAGAN improves spatial relationships between details and is more flexible in creating diverse images. These advantages noticeably improve modeling the ImageNet data set, which consists of 1000 classes.

2.5.6 Large Scale GAN (BigGAN)

BIGGAN adapts the architecture of SA-GAN and scales up the training set and the batch size [3]. It is known for its high performance on the 128×128 images of the ImageNet dataset and can create images up to 512×512 in size. Its ability to model a diverse dataset is similar to SAGAN, but with increased fidelity.

BigGAN regularizes the input to the generator with a truncation trick, which controls the trade off between quality and variance. Typically, the input of the generator is a random noise vector sampled from a normal or uniform distribution. BigGAN suggests resampling the input if it falls outside a specified range, truncating the range that the random noise vector can fall in. This technique reduces the variation of the generator's outputs and increases image fidelity.

3   Conditional GAN for Image Synthesis

Conditional GANs are an extension of a plain GAN. The generator and discriminator both take in a condition, which represents additional information such as a label, a classification, or an image [19]. The generator creates data from random noise and the condition. The discriminator takes in the input with the condition and makes a classification. This condition is typically encoded as a vector and given into the input layer of the neural networks in the GAN architecture (Fig. 2).

Conditions allow us to specify the type of thing we want the GAN to output. For example, a GAN conditioned on a class label of the number 0 could generate images of 0. This ability combined with the high quality output of GANs make it an ideal choice for manipulating images [12].

In practice, conditions vary greatly between architectures, allowing complex generation of images. Conditional GANs can work with text descriptions, precursor images, and videos. The following sections outline different approaches to image generation (Table 2).

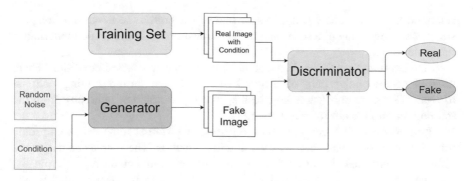

Fig. 2 Conditional GAN architecture

Table 2 Overview of conditional GANs

Architecture	Contribution	Input	Output
pix2pix [12]	Supervised translation framework	Image	Image
UNIT [16]	Unsupervised translation	Image	Image
vid2vid [29]	Video translation	Video	Video
SRGAN [14]	Super resolution GAN	Image	Image
GAN-INT-CLS [23]	Natural text to image	Text	Image
GAWWN [22]	Text with location to image	Text, location	Image
StackGAN [32]	Higher resolution text to image	Text	Image
AttnGAN [31]	Attentional networks with StackGAN	Text	Image
TP-GAN [10]	Generates frontal view of face	Face	Face
DR-GAN [28]	Learns faces and generates poses	Face	Face

3.1 Label to Image

Conditional GANs are able to use a class label y as a condition. This class label y is encoded as a one hot vector and inputted into the generator and discriminator [7, 19]. These labels can force the GAN to produce images such as handwritten numbers and faces with specific emotion. These class labels are integrated into the loss functions as a condition.

$$L^{(D)} = -\frac{1}{2}\mathbb{E}_{x \sim pdata} log D(x|y) - \frac{1}{2}\mathbb{E}_z log(1 - D(G(z|y))) \qquad (4)$$

3.2 Image to Image

Other conditional GAN architecture such as pix2pix can take in an image as the condition and output a similar, transformed image [12]. This architecture can be used for many different image transformations such as black and white to color, semantic labels to image, and edges to photo. Generally, the condition image is some sort of encoding of a scene and the generated image is a realistic rendering of the same scene.

It is important to note that this technique requires a supervised condition. There must be corresponding pairs of encoded and real images in the training set for it to work. The generator learns how to map the transformation indirectly from the training set through adversarial learning.

The direct link between the condition image and target image allows specific improvements to the generator network and loss function. The source and output are different within small details but the overall structure should be the same. Typically, the generator is an encoder decoder pair [12]. The input is downsampled by the encoder layers and then upsampled by the decoder layers. In order to preserve low level details and the similar structure of the source image, we can implement skip connections that directly link channels between the encoder and decoder layers. This architecture is described as a U-Net.

Furthermore, the loss function can take advantage of the fact that there is a specific mapping from the source image to the desired output. If the generator uses an L1 norm as the sole loss function, the image contains the overall structure but the resulting image is blurry.

$$L_{l1}^{(G)} = \mathbb{E}_z \|y - G(z|y)\|_1 \tag{5}$$

Using an adversarial loss, it is possible to achieve finer texture, but it may introduce visual artifacts.

$$L_{GAN}^{(G)} = \frac{1}{2}\mathbb{E}_{x \sim pdata} log D(x|y) + \frac{1}{2}\mathbb{E}_z log(1 - D(G(z|y))) \tag{6}$$

If we combine a traditional L1 loss with adversarial loss, the generator will learn to create realistic images with a reduction in visual artifacts [12].

$$L^{(G)} = L_{GAN}^{(G)} + \lambda L_{l1}^{(G)} \tag{7}$$

Since L1 Loss covers the overall structure, the adversarial loss from the discriminator needs to focus on local textures. Using an algorithm called PatchGAN, the discriminator divides the input into $N \times N$ patches of data [12]. Each patch is classified as real or generated. The final output is the mean of the patches' classifications.

3.3   Unsupervised Image to Image

The previous section involved GANs that had training data with the desired mapping. What if we wanted a GAN to map from one domain to another without having training pairs? For example, what if we wanted to transform a cat image into an equivalent lion image? We have a domain of cat images and a domain of lion images, but we do not have a pair of cat and lion images to train with. This task is referred to as unsupervised image to image translation and can translate between two previously unlinked domains [16].

One proposed architecture called UNIT tackles this problem with Variational Autoencoders (VAE) and coupled GANs [16]. The architecture assumes that a pair of images from two different domains can be mapped into the same representation in a shared latent space. From the same representation, the images can be decoded back into their original form.

The UNIT architecture uses a pair of GANs [16], one for each domain. The encoder-generator pair constitutes a VAE. The pair of VAEs have shared encoder weights so encoding in two different domains leads to the same latent space. Using the encoder from one domain and the generator from the other domain allows image to image translation between the two domains.

3.4 Video to Video

In order to extend image to image translation to video, we need to take into consideration temporal consistency, or how the frames match together. Using previously developed image to image solutions create realistic individual frames. However, these frames do not flow together and video coherency is lost. To produce a realistic video, both the generator and the discriminator consider consecutive frames during training [29]. In implementation, the generator and discriminator are made with residual networks which are able to preserve sequential information. Furthermore, the adversarial loss is carefully constructed to include consecutive frames and optical flow between these frames. As a result, the GAN is able to produce frames in the context of surrounding frames and generate a smooth rendering of the video.

3.5 Super-Resolution

Super Resolution Generative Adversarial Network (SRGAN) is a GAN architecture that takes in a low resolution image and performs $4\times$ upscaling [14]. The architecture uses a deep convolutional neural network with residual blocks. The loss includes both adversarial loss and content loss which preserves the finer details while maintaining realism. SRGAN excels at preserves finer details and sharp edges in the upscaling task.

3.6   Text to Image

GAN-INT-CLS is a proposed architecture that demonstrates generating an image from a text description [23]. First, the text is encoded with a recurrent neural network. This encoding is used as the condition inputted into a conditional GAN. The cGAN architecture is modeled after DCGAN, and produces a 128×128 image.

Generative Adversarial What-Where Network (GAWWN) extends the capabilities of text to image by incorporating locations as well as a text description within the condition [22]. The location is represented as a bounding box or a set of key points. The generator and discriminator each have a local and global branch. The local branch deals with the location specified by the condition. The global branch deals with the background. Combining these two allow the GAN to produce an image of an object at the specified location. GAWWN produces a 128×128 image.

StackGAN is another proposed architecture that aims to improve the resolution of text to image [32]. The GAN is separated into two stages. Stage 1 produces a sketch of a 64×64 image based on the text description. Stage 2 produces a 256×256 image based on the sketch, adding more detail and resolution.

AttnGAN expands on StackGAN by using attentional neural networks in multiple stages for the generator [31]. The word features drive the attentional models, which can focus on the most relevant area. This change allows fine tuned control over the text description.

3.7   Facial Posing

Two-Pathway Generative Adversarial Network (TP-GAN) is a GAN designed to generate a frontal view of a face from a partial profile view of the face [10]. It consists of a local and global branch in both the generator and the discriminator.

Disentangled Representation learning Generative Adversarial Network (DR-GAN) combines the task of learning a pose invariant face representation with generating a certain pose of a face [28]. The generator uses an encoder-decoder architecture which learns an encoding of a face and decodes it into an image of a posed face. The discriminator judges the generated image against real image of the correct pose. Using this adversarial loss, DR-GAN can create a superior image over traditional methods.

4   Detection of Facial Manipulation in Videos

The advancements in deep learning has made video manipulation and synthesis much more accessible than before. Publicly available tools allow users to create their own forgeries and distribute them. It is especially concerning when these tools are uses to change the facial expressions or identity in a video [5, 24]. Since these manipulated faces are not immediately discernible to a human observer, detection methods must be developed to identify these fake videos. The major concern is that these synthetic videos can spread false information easily over social media. These videos can misrepresent political figures and even influence the outcome of an election. Because of these concerns, detecting forged videos is both an academic and mainstream research interest.

4.1 DeepFake Manipulation

The DeepFake algorithm was originally dedicated to creating adult content where an actress's face is inserted into a pornographic video [1, 24]. These unethically produced videos received strong public backlash and brought attention to AI-manipulated videos. While the original creator is no longer active, community developed implementations of the algorithm exist online.

DeepFake aims to replace the face in one source video with the face of another person. The architecture of the DeepFake algorithm is loosely based on the unsupervised image to image solution, with two faces as the two domains. It contains a pair of autoencoders that are trained simultaneously [1], The encoders from both networks share weights, so that they encode into the same latent space. The decoders learn to generate their respective faces. Manipulation takes place by encoding the source face image and decoding into the target face image.

4.2 Challenges and Dataset

The task of detecting forged videos comes with many challenges. Online videos are often compressed from the original source. This compression removes fine details that could distinguish between real or fake videos [24]. These videos also have varying resolutions so any detection method must have flexible sized input. Furthermore, since the area of interest is the facial region, a reliable face cropping method needs to be used [1].

In order to compare different detection method and encourage research, a consistent and available set of data is needed. Standard image datasets such as ImageNet, CIFAR10, and MNIST exist for image recognition tasks. These data sets allow reliable and consistent benchmarks for tasks such as adversarial defense [18]. However, the availability of forged videos remains limited and hard to collect. One suggested dataset is FaceForensics++ [24]. This set of data is specially designed to combat fake videos. It includes 1.6 million images from more than 1000 videos. These videos are manipulated by four different facial manipulation techniques including DeepFake and Face2Face. Furthermore, the authors of the data set include a public benchmark to test detection solutions against other algorithms.

4.3   Detection Methods

Detection methods for forged videos often use a convolutional neural network (CNN) approach due to their state of the art performance in image recognition tasks. There are numerous proposed models aimed at detecting manipulated images. This section contains selected recent methods for forgery detection (Table 3).

4.3.1   Long-Term Recurrent Convolutional Networks (LRCN)

Long-term Recurrent Convolutional Networks is designed to detect blinking in videos [15]. Forged videos commonly do not have the correct amount of generated blinking. A recurrent neural network such as LRCN is able to detect blinking or the lack of it within the context of the previous frames in a given video.

4.3.2   MesoNet

MesoNet is a CNN based detection method designed for detecting DeepFake and Face2Face manipulations. The design of MesoNet comes from analyzing mid-level features [1]. Small details of the forged video may be lost in compression while high level features will generally be correct even after manipulation. The architecture uses a deep neural network with a small number of layers to focus on the right level of detail. The loss used in this network is mean squared error between predicted and true labels [5].

4.3.3   XceptionNet

XceptionNet uses depth-wise separable convolutional layers with residual connections [4]. This architecture was originally designed for general image classification, showing strong results on the ImageNet data set. XceptionNet pretrained on the ImageNet data is adapted through transfer learning. The final fully connected layer with 1000 class output is replaced with a layer that has a 2 class output. This model is then trained on the FaceForensics++ data set. The video is preprocessed into facial

Table 3 Overview of selected forgery detection

Architecture	Mechanism	Contribution
LRCN [15]	Detect eye blinking	Feature detection over time
Mesonet [1]	CNN classification	Specially designed for forgery detection
Xception [4]	CNN classification	ImageNet transfer learning
ForensicTransfer [5]	Autoencoder embedding	High generalization for unseen domains

images. This network has promising performance compared to specially designed networks [24].

4.3.4 ForensicTransfer

ForensicTransfer uses an autoencoder based architecture to distinguish between real and manipulated images [5]. The autoencoder learns an embedding of an image and marks an image as fake if it is sufficiently distant from the cluster of real images. This architecture is designed to improve generalization, or the ability to transfer learning between different domains. Compared to CNN based methods, Forensic Transfer performs comparably when trained and tested on data from the same domain. However when tested on data from an unseen domain, Forensic Transfer has a noticeable advantage. This ability can be useful when detecting images manipulated through an unknown method.

5 Conclusion and Future Work

Generative adversarial networks are generative models that utilize deep learning methods. These GANs are able to simplify loss functions and generative methods as a competition between two networks. The generator network creates samples of data. The discriminator network classifies input as real or generated. These two networks run simultaneously and iteratively improve until the generated data resembles the target data set.

Conditional generative adversarial networks allow specification of the desired generated data through a condition, which is extra information supplied to the generator and discriminator. These modified GANs have found great use in image to image translations and video synthesis. They especially excel at producing realistic textures in rendering images over traditional methods.

Facial manipulation methods such as DeepFake utilize similar deep learning methods to change the facial identity of people in videos. This technology may possibly be used for malicious intent such as misrepresenting a political figure. Current manipulation techniques are difficult for humans to identify, so automated detection methods are needed to identify fake videos. Currently, convolutional neural network based classification models are able to identify facial manipulation with reasonable accuracy.

Future research is needed to create reliable methods to detect forged videos. Classification models exist for known manipulation methods, but these models are vulnerable to newer attacks. Models need to detect a wide range of facial manipulation techniques to implement effective detection. Benchmarks and challenges such as FaceForensics++ and the DeepFake Detection Challenge promote competition and stimulate research into this field. Improvements to detection methods may include specialized neural network architecture to analyze faces and better facial extraction.

References

1. Afchar, D., Nozick, V., Yamagishi, J., Echizen, I.: Mesonet: a compact facial video forgery detection network. In: 2018 IEEE International Workshop on Information Forensics and Security (WIFS), pp. 1–7. IEEE, New York (2018)
2. Bengio, Y., Thibodeau-Laufer, E.R., Alain, G., Yosinski, J.: Deep generative stochastic networks trainable by backprop. In: Proceedings of the 31st International Conference on International Conference on Machine Learning - Volume 32, ICML'14, p. II-226–II-234. JMLR.org (2014)
3. Brock, A., Donahue, J., Simonyan, K.: Large scale GAN training for high fidelity natural image synthesis (2018). CoRR abs/1809.11096. http://arxiv.org/abs/1809.11096
4. Chollet, F.: Xception: deep learning with depthwise separable convolutions (2016). CoRR abs/1610.02357. http://arxiv.org/abs/1610.02357
5. Cozzolino, D., Thies, J., Rössler, A., Riess, C., Nießner, M., Verdoliva, L.: Forensictransfer: weakly-supervised domain adaptation for forgery detection (2018). CoRR abs/1812.02510. http://arxiv.org/abs/1812.02510
6. Denton, E.L., Chintala, S., Szlam, A., Fergus, R.: Deep generative image models using a laplacian pyramid of adversarial networks (2015). CoRR abs/1506.05751. http://arxiv.org/abs/1506.05751
7. Gauthier, J.: Conditional generative adversarial nets for convolutional face generation. Class Project for Stanford CS231N: Convolutional Neural Networks for Visual Recognition, Winter semester, vol. 2014(5), p. 2 (2014)
8. Goodfellow, I.: NIPS 2016 tutorial: generative adversarial networks (2016). Preprint. arXiv:1701.00160
9. Goodfellow, I., Pouget-Abadie, J., Mirza, M., Xu, B., Warde-Farley, D., Ozair, S., Courville, A., Bengio, Y.: Generative adversarial nets. In: Advances in Neural Information Processing Systems, pp. 2672–2680 (2014)
10. Huang, R., Zhang, S., Li, T., He, R.: Beyond face rotation: global and local perception GAN for photorealistic and identity preserving frontal view synthesis (2017). CoRR abs/1704.04086. http://arxiv.org/abs/1704.04086
11. Ioffe, S., Szegedy, C.: Batch normalization: accelerating deep network training by reducing internal covariate shift (2015). CoRR abs/1502.03167. http://arxiv.org/abs/1502.03167
12. Isola, P., Zhu, J.Y., Zhou, T., Efros, A.A.: Image-to-image translation with conditional adversarial networks. In: Proceedings of the IEEE conference on computer vision and pattern recognition, pp. 1125–1134 (2017)
13. Karras, T., Aila, T., Laine, S., Lehtinen, J.: Progressive growing of gans for improved quality, stability, and variation (2017). Preprint. arXiv:1710.10196
14. Ledig, C., Theis, L., Huszar, F., Caballero, J., Aitken, A.P., Tejani, A., Totz, J., Wang, Z., Shi, W.: Photo-realistic single image super-resolution using a generative adversarial network. CoRR abs/1609.04802 (2016). http://arxiv.org/abs/1609.04802
15. Li, Y., Chang, M., Lyu, S.: In Ictu Oculi: exposing AI generated fake face videos by detecting eye blinking(2018). CoRR abs/1806.02877. http://arxiv.org/abs/1806.02877
16. Liu, M., Breuel, T., Kautz, J.: Unsupervised image-to-image translation networks (2017). CoRR abs/1703.00848. http://arxiv.org/abs/1703.00848
17. Mani, N., Moh, M.: Adversarial attacks and defense on deep learning models for big data and IoT. In: Handbook of Research on Cloud Computing and Big Data Applications in IoT, pp. 39–66. IGI Global, Hershey, PA (2019)
18. Mani, N., Moh, M., Moh, T.S.: Towards robust ensemble defense against adversarial examples attack. In: IEEE GLOBECOM 2019, Waikoloa, HI, December 2019. IEEE, New York (2019)
19. Mirza, M., Osindero, S.: Conditional generative adversarial nets (2014). Preprint. arXiv:1411.1784
20. Radford, A., Metz, L., Chintala, S.: Unsupervised representation learning with deep convolutional generative adversarial networks (2015). CoRR abs/1511.06434

21. Rahmouni, N., Nozick, V., Yamagishi, J., Echizen, I.: Distinguishing computer graphics from natural images using convolution neural networks. In: 2017 IEEE Workshop on Information Forensics and Security (WIFS), pp. 1–6 (2017). https://doi.org/10.1109/WIFS.2017.8267647

22. Reed, S.E., Akata, Z., Mohan, S., Tenka, S., Schiele, B., Lee, H.: Learning what and where to draw. CoRR abs/1610.02454 (2016). http://arxiv.org/abs/1610.02454

23. Reed, S.E., Akata, Z., Yan, X., Logeswaran, L., Schiele, B., Lee, H.: Generative adversarial text to image synthesis (2016). CoRR abs/1605.05396. http://arxiv.org/abs/1605.05396

24. Rössler, A., Cozzolino, D., Verdoliva, L., Riess, C., Thies, J., Nießner, M.: Faceforensics++: Learning to detect manipulated facial images (2019). CoRR abs/1901.08971. http://arxiv.org/abs/1901.08971

25. Salimans, T., Goodfellow, I., Zaremba, W., Cheung, V., Radford, A., Chen, X.: Improved techniques for training gans. In: Advances in Neural Information Processing Systems, pp. 2234–2242 (2016)

26. Santurkar, S., Tsipras, D., Ilyas, A., Madry, A.: How does batch normalization help optimization? In: Bengio, S., Wallach, H., Larochelle, H., Grauman, K., Cesa-Bianchi, N., Garnett, R. (eds.) Advances in Neural Information Processing Systems, vol. 31, pp. 2483–2493. Curran Associates, Inc., Red Hook, NY (2018). http://papers.nips.cc/paper/7515-how-does-batch-normalization-help-optimization.pdf

27. Thies, J., Zollhöfer, M., Nießner, M.: Deferred neural rendering: image synthesis using neural textures (2019). Preprint. arXiv:1904.12356

28. Tran, L., Yin, X., Liu, X.: Representation learning by rotating your faces (2017). CoRR abs/1705.11136. http://arxiv.org/abs/1705.11136

29. Wang, T.C., Liu, M.Y., Zhu, J.Y., Yakovenko, N., Tao, A., Kautz, J., Catanzaro, B.: Video-to-video synthesis. In: NeurIPS (2018)

30. Warde-Farley, D., Goodfellow, I.: 11 adversarial perturbations of deep neural networks. In: Perturbations, Optimization, and Statistics, vol. 311. The MIT Press, Cambridge, MA (2016)

31. Xu, T., Zhang, P., Huang, Q., Zhang, H., Gan, Z., Huang, X., He, X.: AttnGAN: fine-grained text to image generation with attentional generative adversarial networks (2017). CoRR abs/1711.10485. http://arxiv.org/abs/1711.10485

32. Zhang, H., Xu, T., Li, H., Zhang, S., Huang, X., Wang, X., Metaxas, D.N.: Stackgan: text to photo-realistic image synthesis with stacked generative adversarial networks (2016). CoRR abs/1612.03242. http://arxiv.org/abs/1612.03242

33. Zhang, H., Goodfellow, I., Metaxas, D., Odena, A.: Self-attention generative adversarial networks. In: K. Chaudhuri, R. Salakhutdinov (eds.) Proceedings of the 36th International Conference on Machine Learning, Proceedings of Machine Learning Research, vol. 97, pp. 7354–7363. PMLR, Long Beach, CA (2019). http://proceedings.mlr.press/v97/zhang19d.html

Robust Machine Learning Using Diversity and Blockchain

Raj Mani Shukla, Shahriar Badsha, Deepak Tosh, and Shamik Sengupta

Abstract Machine Learning (ML) algorithms are used in several smart city-based applications. However, ML is vulnerable to adversarial examples that significantly alter its desired output. Therefore, making ML safe and secure is an important research problem to enable smart city-based applications. In this chapter, a mechanism to make ML robust against adversarial examples for predictive analytics-based applications is described. The chapter introduces the concept of diversity where a single predictive analytic task is separately performed using heterogeneous datasets, or ML algorithms, or both. The given diversity components are implemented in distributed platforms using federated learning and edge computing. The diversity components use blockchain to ensure that the data is transferred safely and securely between distributed components such that edge and federated learning devices. The chapter also describes some of the challenges that should be met while adopting diversity mechanism, distributed computation, and blockchain to secure ML.

Keywords Diversity · Adversarial learning · Ensemble learning · Blockchain · IoT · Edge computing · Federated services

1 Introduction

Machine Learning (ML) is frequently used in efficient provisioning of several smart city-based services like traffic management, smart farming, parking space allocation, and Electric Vehicle (EV) charging [25]. Many of these services use data-analytics to forecast certain parameter and based on the predicted value better optimization decisions are made. For example, advance traffic prediction near an

R. M. Shukla (✉) · S. Badsha · S. Sengupta
University of Nevada, Reno, Reno, NV, USA
e-mail: rshukla@unr.edu; sbadsha@unr.edu; ssengupta@unr.edu

D. Tosh
University of Texas, El Paso, El Paso, TX, USA
e-mail: dktosh@utep.edu

© Springer Nature Switzerland AG 2021
P. Dasgupta et al. (eds.), *Adversary-Aware Learning Techniques and Trends in Cybersecurity*, https://doi.org/10.1007/978-3-030-55692-1_6

Electric Vehicle (EV) charging station assists in deciding whether to schedule an EV for charging near that station [24]. However, it is no secret that ML algorithms are prone to adversarial attacks [19]. In adversarial attacks, a well-crafted noise is added to the input feature vector. The perturbed input affects the outcome of the ML algorithm significantly. The adversarial examples, that are quite popular for image processing applications, maliciously affect the time-series data too [14]. Therefore, the mitigation of these attacks is an important field in ML that needs to be studied.

There have been different approaches researched out to detect adversarial examples. For instance, a subsidiary Neural Network (NN) can be used to classify the adversarial examples [17], [11]. In this strategy, the base NN model is augmented so that it has an additional output that classifies the example as adversarial. Principal Component Analysis (PCA) has often been used for the adversarial example detection. PCA is used for the dimensionality reduction of the data [4, 12]. Dimensional reduction of input feature vector results in noise removal from it. Thus, the effect of noise in the input perturbation is minimized. This makes the generation of adversarial examples difficult and hence the effectiveness of PCA in detecting adversarial examples. Input randomization and blurring are also used for adversarial example detection [10]. However, it has been found that most of these methods fail to detect adversarial examples if attacker has priori knowledge of the detection mechanism [7]. Thus, the defense mechanisms fail against the white box attacks when an attacker knows the defense strategy and tailors the attack accordingly. Since existing mechanisms are not efficient, a robust adversarial example detection method still needs to be explored. Moreover, the strategies to mitigate the effect of adversarial examples is also required to be studied.

This chapter presents a discussion on mitigating the effects of the adversarial examples for predictive analytics applications using heterogeneous datasets and different ML algorithms. We introduce the concept of *diversity* that utilizes either heterogeneous datasets or different ML algorithms. We show that the proposed diversity can be used for mitigating the effects of the adversarial examples. In the proposed diversity-based method, a certain predictive analytic task is performed using different methods. Subsequently, a consensus is built on the obtained results from those methods. For example, the snow condition at a certain location can be predicted using image analysis from cameras located in a region. However, the snow condition can also be determined by analyzing the weather monitoring system. Comparison between results obtained using two methods validates the information about snow condition at a certain location. If results are similar, the information about snow conditions can be relied with confidence. On the other hand, a significant variation in predicted value from a certain method lead to the plausibility of the adversarial perturbation.

Therefore, in the proposed method, obtained results from diverse platforms are compared to build a consensus on the predicted output. Any significant variation in prediction level of a certain component may lead to suspect that given output. To find the nodes that introduce adversarial attacks, we propose to use anomaly detection technique [13, 15, 16]. Henceforth, we bring out the idea that the heterogeneous datasets and ML algorithms have the potential to bring diversity that mitigate the effects of the adversarial attacks.

However, the proposed diversity requires computational resources for its implementation. In this regard, the chapter discusses the use of Federated Learning (FL) and edge computing-based infrastructure to execute diversity components. Federated learning is a paradigm where ML models are trained in a distributed manner [31]. Edge computing provides cloud computing like distributed storage and computational resources [20]. The two distributed platforms provide computational resources for implementing diversity.

Also, one of the other challenge in implementing diversity in federated learning devices and edge computing infrastructure is that the information needs to be shared in a secure manner between distributed nodes. Therefore, an efficient data transfer model needs to be developed. Blockchain provides an efficient method to share or store data in a distributed platform. Blockchain technology effectively stores, validates, and distributes transactions among the distributed nodes. Although blockchain was developed for the Bitcoin crypto-currency, it is used in various other platforms like Internet of Things (IoT), communication networks, and smart contracts [27, 37]. Since blockchain is a popular and secure method to store and distribute data, it is used in the given mechanism that uses data from different sources and disparate ML algorithms.

Thus, the major contributions of this work are as follows:

- This chapter introduces the concept of diversity that uses data from different sources, different ML algorithms, or both to mitigate the effect of the adversarial examples for predictive analytics applications.
- The chapter portrays the use of federated learning devices and edge computing infrastructure for implementing diversity components.
- The chapter discusses the use of blockchain to efficiently share information between distributed federated learning and edge devices in a secure manner.

2   Introducing Diversity

This section explains the concept of diversity for the predictive analytics application. We describe the use of diversity in making reliable prediction in the presence of an adversary. Before proceeding further, a formal definition of the diversity, in the context of ML-based prediction, is provided below.

Diversity Diversity is a mechanism where a predictive analytics task is separately performed using different ML methods, different data-sets, or both, often in a distributed manner, to make the prediction mechanism robust.

To explain diversity, consider that the prediction of a parameter p is required at some time t_i. Then, different diversity components $d_1, d_2, d_3 \ldots, d_n$ are used to make a prediction of the quantity p. Here, diversity components $d_1, d_2, d_3 \ldots, d_n$ are trained ML models that employ either different ML methods, different datasets,

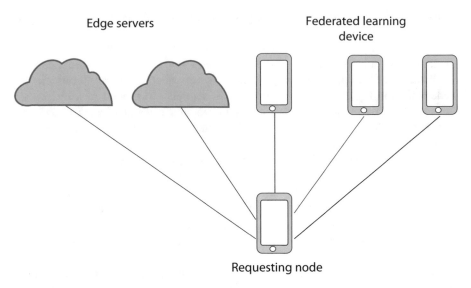

Fig. 1 Overview of the proposed architecture

or both. The diverse components make predictions $\hat{p}_1, \hat{p}_2, \hat{p}_3, \ldots, \hat{p}_n$ and the results are compared. If the predictions made by different components are close to each other, the predicted values are combined using some statistical function (e.g. mean). On the other hand, if prediction from a certain component significantly varies from others then it can be suspected that the input feature vector for the component has been modified. The obtained abnormal component is discarded, and similar predictions are used to deduce the result.

The diverse component $d_1, d_2, d_3 \ldots, d_n$ are implemented in distributed manner in federated learning devices and edge servers. A basic overview of the proposed architecture, implementing diversity, is provided in Fig. 1. The proposed architecture consists of the federated devices, edge devices, and requesting nodes. Federated learning devices and Edge servers provide a pool of distributed computing resources and are explained in brief as follows:

Federated Learning The federated learning is a platform for ML training. In federated learning, the ML algorithms are trained in a distributed manner using mobile devices. The ML training is distributed among different devices and thus it reduces computation burden on a single server [31].

Edge Servers Edge servers provide cloud computing type resources near the user. They facilitate *edge computing*. In edge computing, a computation task is performed using edge devices that are close to the data source [20].

As shown in the figure, these different units are connected to requesting node through a network and can share information. Requesting node transmits the prediction service requirement to the other nodes through the blockchain. The other nodes (federated learning and edge devices), once they got the information, will figure out whether they can perform prediction task. If they can make prediction, will inform to the requesting node about this. The requesting node will select some of these nodes to perform prediction. The distributed nodes will predict the quantity and send the information to the requesting node. The requesting nodes then verify the prediction results and based on that decides a final predicted value and any anomalous node. It discards the suspected anomalous predictions and combines the similar prediction using statistical method. The information is shared between requesting node, federated learning devices, and edge servers through the blockchain.

In subsequent sections, we describe these different components in more detail. First, we explain the two diversity mechanisms. Then, we proceed to explain in detail the use of federated learning and edge devices. Subsequently, we describe the use of blockchain in information sharing process.

3   Diversity Types

In this section, we describe the use of heterogeneous datasets and disparate ML algorithms in making reliable prediction of a certain parameter. In our discussion, we will show that heterogeneous datasets and ML algorithms can be used for making predictions that are like each other. Subsequent comparison of similar predicted values makes ML robust in the presence of an adversary.

3.1   Diversity Using Heterogeneous Datasets

In smart city, presence of a large number of sensors enables measurement of different environmental parameters. Often there exists a correlation between hetero-geneous datasets, obtained from different sensors, as values of one dataset affects the values of other. For example, the environmental pollutant level at a certain location depends upon the wind speed at same location [2]. Thus, it is possible to estimate pollutant level by analyzing wind speed. Similarly, the humidity and temperature are correlated and one can be predicted using other [8]. The noise pollution at a certain point and traffic density at same location are correlated [22]. An unusual event, like traffic crash, may affect the frequency of social media posts at a certain location [35]. Since various heterogeneous datasets in smart city are correlated, it is possible to predict the values of one dataset using another dataset. Often certain parameter can be separately predicted using multiple different datasets. For example, the vehicular traffic at a particular location can be separately predicted either using spatio-temporal traffic patterns, noise data, or pollutant levels [16, 22]. These separate predictions can be compared to ensure the trust in the predicted values.

In traditional predictive analytic applications, the spatio-temporal characteristic of a certain dataset is used to predict the values of the same parameter. For example, the vehicular traffic at a certain location is predicted using the spatio-temporal values of the vehicular traffic [16]. However, the strategy is vulnerable to adversarial examples as the input feature vector is known to the attacker. Thus, any malicious perturbation in input feature vector may affect the prediction result significantly.

However, separate prediction using heterogeneous datasets has potential to mitigate the effects of the adversarial examples. This is because several prediction results are compared and then based on that a consensus is made. A significant variation in the predicted value by a certain diverse component may be discarded. For example, the parameter p can be independently determined using the values from sensor data q, r, and s. Subsequently, these separate predictions are combined to verify the correctness of the predicted values of p. Thus, for implementing diversity, using heterogeneous datasets, separate prediction models can be developed to estimate the values of p using the data from sensors q, r, and s as given in Eq. (1).

$$\hat{p}_1 = f_1(q), \tag{1}$$

$$\hat{p}_2 = f_2(r), \tag{2}$$

$$\hat{p}_3 = f_3(s), \tag{3}$$

Here, f_1, f_2, and f_3 are ML models developed and trained on different datasets but same ML algorithm. If $\hat{p}_1 \sim \hat{p}_2 \sim \hat{p}_3$, it can be inferred that the models are making correct prediction. If one of them varies significantly then it may be prone to adversarial attack. Thus, in general, if n models are used to make prediction, the adversary must target at-least $n/2$ of them to affect the prediction result. The similar results are combined using certain statistical function, like averaging of individual results.

To verify the use of heterogeneous datasets in implementing diversity, we performed experiments using Convolution Neural Network (CNN). In our experiments, we used different air pollutant data to predict vehicular traffic. The data for our experiments is obtained from California Air Resource Board (ARB) and Performance Measurement Systems (PeMS) [6, 29]. The air pollutant data contains the information about different pollutant levels. The PeMS provides the number of vehicles passing near a certain location in every 5 min. The input feature-vector to the CNN includes a pollutant level combined with the wind speed and temperature.

Our CNN architecture consists of two convolution layers, a max-pooling layer, two more convolution layer, and a global-average pooling layer. First two CNN layers used a filter size of 64 and kernel size of 3. In next two layers filter size and kernel size are selected as 128 and 3 respectively. The *relu* activation is employed in hidden layers. A dense layer consisting of a single neuron is added to the CNN. For dense layer, *softmax* activation function is used. The dropout of 50% is used after global-average pooling layer. For CNN training, we use *rmsprop* optimizer. The 80% of data is used for training and 20% for testing purpose. Table 1 shows the Mean Average Error (MAE) and Mean Square Error (MSE) between actual and

Table 1 Prediction performance using same ML algorithm but different datasets

Pollutant	MAE	RMSE
CO	0.17	0.04
BC	0.17	0.05
NO2	0.15	0.03
NOX	0.16	0.04
PM25HR	0.16	0.04

predicted values using CNN for different pollutant datasets. As we can see from the table, using the different datasets, the accuracy level is almost equivalent. Thus, a certain predictive analytics task can be performed using different datasets with comparable accuracy.

Therefore, the availability of the heterogeneous datasets in smart city can be leveraged to perform prediction using different methods (datasets). Subsequent analysis of prediction results, obtained using different methods, may help to discard the anomalous values. Next, it is described the use of various ML algorithms to bring diversity.

3.2 Diversity Using Machine Learning Models

Diversity can also be implemented using different ML models. In this type of diversity, different ML models are trained on the similar dataset for performing predictive-analytics task. The similar strategy is used in the ensemble learning to develop a generalized ML models [33]. In contrast to ordinary ML methods, that trains a single model to get an optimal parameter, ensemble learning combines different models to get a better generalized result. In ensemble learning, a set of hypotheses are trained and then combined to estimate the result. The ensemble learning is efficient because it boosts the multiple weak learners to get a strong learner for better accuracy. To obtain the final prediction, either majority voting or weighted averaging is used. For ensembles to produce a better prediction, the base-learners should be accurate and diverse in nature [39]. However, one of the problem with ensemble learning is that it is implemented in the same node. Since adversarial examples are transferable, an example generated against one ML model can be used for another. Therefore, the ensemble learning is prone to the malicious perturbations as the different base-learners use same input data. However, if different ML models are implemented in distributed nodes, the vulnerability against the adversarial examples can be mitigated. This is because in different nodes ML model will use different input for prediction. It is possible for an adversary to maliciously change input data in some nodes but not all of them.

Therefore, like ensemble learning, diversity can be introduced using different ML model. However, in contrast to ensemble learning, we propose to train and store different ML models in distributed servers. Implementation of ML models

Table 2 Prediction performance using different ML algorithms but same dataset

Pollutant 1	MAE	MSE
MLP	0.13	0.03
LSTM	0.22	0.07
CNN	0.17	0.04
CNN_LSTM	0.15	0.04

in distributed servers is possible because similar data is often available at spatially distributed locations. For example, sensors measuring pollutant level are spatially distributed but they measure similar data. This data may be stored in the server located close to a sensor. The different such servers may use disparate ML methods for the predictive analytics. For example, one such server may use Support Vector Machine (SVM) and another may use Long-Short Term Memory (LSTM) neural network [16, 34]. Thus, ML implemented at a certain node uses the localized data near that node and different such nodes may use different ML models.

To further explain the use of diversity in ML, we performed experiments using different NN algorithms for predicting vehicular traffic. The data used for the experiment is obtained from PeMS and CRA websites as explained earlier in Sect. 3.1. The input to the model consists of the feature vector formed using air pollutant (CO) data, wind speed, and temperature. We used Fully Connected Network (FCN), Long-short Term Memory (LSTM), Convolution Neural Network (CNN), and CNN connected in series with LSTM as our ML models. The obtained MAE and MSE using the given models are shown in Table 2.

The maximum difference in MAE and MSE, using different methods is 0.009 and 0.04 respectively. Thus, the different ML methods provide prediction at same confidence level. Therefore, diversity using ML methods can be used for making ML secure. The prediction results can be compared and if they are similar the predicted value can be inferred as correct.

The two different diversity methods can also be mutually combined to predict the same quantity. For example, different ML models may be trained on different datasets to perform a single prediction task. Further, the use of diversity requires computation resources for data storage, ML training, and prediction. Federated learning (FL) devices and edge computing servers have potential to provide computational resources for implementing given diversity mechanism. In the following section, we present an overview of FL and edge computing and will describe their use in implementing diversity.

4   Computing Model

To enable diversity, such that different ML models to be trained on different datasets the FL devices and edge computing servers can be potentially used. The trained ML models can be stored in distributed manner in those FL devices and edge computing servers. We explain below how the FL devices and edge computing resources provide distributed pool of computational resources for ML training and storage.

4.1 Federated Learning devices

To explain the use of Federated Learning (FL) devices in ML training and storage, the concept of FL for developing ML model is described below.

In a standard ML model, the data from sensors and devices is transferred to the centralized cloud. In cloud, the ML models are trained on the collected data. In this process, a huge amount of data is transferred to the cloud. This consumes network bandwidth and is an inefficient technique. The security and privacy of the data may be compromised because the data is being transferred and stored remotely. FL is a new framework for ML model development that employs distributed mobile or IoT devices. In FL rather than data being transferred to the cloud, the ML models are brought near the data source (mobile/IoT devices). Thus, federated learning avoids the data transfer by training ML models in device itself. This is possible due to the advance computation capabilities of the mobile devices, equipped with Artificial Intelligence (AI) chips. AI chips are the processors that are designed to perform AI tasks faster while consuming less power [26].

In federated learning, the parameters of a ML algorithm are set with the initial value at the centralized cloud. The ML model, with initial parameters set, is distributed to the different mobile and IoT device. The distributed devices run the ML model locally and improves it by learning on their stored data. Subsequently, the devices summarize the learning process in the form of updates in the model parameter. The updated parameters are transferred to the centralized cloud using a secure communication network [31]. Thus, the training process happens in the device, not in the cloud.

At the centralized cloud, the updated parameters obtained from the distributed nodes are combined. The updated model is again sent to the distributed devices where they improve the model by training on their stored data. This process continuously updates the model in a distributed manner [5]. Most importantly, in this process, the data is not transferred to the cloud. The model parameters are fused at the centralized cloud [31]. FL models are smarter, have low latency, and consume less power.

The FL infrastructure has potential to provide computing resources to the propose diversity mechanism. Since a large number of mobile/IoT devices have stored ML models, they can be potentially used for prediction. Thus, we propose that mobile/IoT devices not only train a model but can also perform the prediction task. Since, the devices are distributed the prediction task is performed separately by different devices. The devices will use their sensed data to perform the prediction. As our diversity mechanism uses either heterogeneous datasets or ML algorithms, both the techniques can be used in FL infrastructure. For heterogeneous datasets, the different devices may use ML models trained on different datasets but predicting same quantity. For disparate ML-based diversity, the devices may use similar data but use different ML models.

Thus, our diversity mechanisms can be implemented in FL-based infrastructure leveraging the computing power of distributed devices. However, this also brings out the security challenges as the predicted results need to be transferred between distributed devices. Therefore, efficient use of federated learning requires the predicted results at different devices need to be shared safely and securely. We discuss in this chapter how blockchain can contribute in solving such vulnerabilities while using federated learning for predictive analytics applications. However, before addressing this issue we describe the benefits of the edge computing, another pool of computing resources, that can be used in the proposed diversity mechanism.

4.2   Edge Computing

The growing data in IoT puts pressure on the cloud computing facilities. The clouds are also located far-away from the devices. Therefore, data processing done at the cloud imposes communication delay as data have to travel from the device to the cloud. The edge computing paradigm brings cloud computing like facilities near the user. Edge computing contains the servers located near the data source to perform computational task. Thus, data analysis need not be all done at the centralized cloud and can be distributed to a local region. Edge computing enables the data to be processed near its source such that closer to the sensor or device where it is created. Therefore, it assists in faster data processing and analysis. Edge computing has capability to transform the way data is handled, processed, and stored. There are several advantages of edge computing [25]. For example, computation using edge server has lower latency because of its proximity to the user. Due to low latency, data can be processed in real-time. In edge computing, the information from a local area can be processed based on a local context and location-sensitive applications can be developed [20]. For example, edge computing enables location-based advertisement services [20]. In edge computing, as all data is not transmitted to the cloud, the communication bandwidth is efficiently used. Edge computing provides an infrastructure to store huge amount of sensor data. Hardware parameters of edge devices can be tuned to meet requirements of an application. For example, the frequency tuning can be used to save the power requirements of a device and enable meeting real-time requirements of an application [23].

In edge computing, the information from a group of localized sensors is transferred to a certain edge server. For example, the data from weather monitoring station at a location is transferred to an edge server located near that station. The traffic data from sensors that are spatially close to each other is stored in a nearby edge server. Thus, different edge servers collect and store specific dataset. This data is processed and used for decision making. In the given context, edge computing provides us a distributed pool of resources where ML models are trained and stored.

Edge computing has potential to implement the two types of diversity presented in this chapter. Since distributed edge servers store either similar or heterogeneous data, the ML models can be trained using the data stored in those servers. For ML diversity, edge servers having similar dataset can be used for training different ML algorithms. If the edge servers have heterogeneous dataset, the same ML algorithm can be used for training and model development. Thus, edge computing facilitates diversity because it provides resources where ML models are trained for the prediction process. The trained models are stored at the edge servers. If some node makes prediction request, the edge server uses the trained ML model.

Both the federated learning and edge computing provide computing platforms for data and ML diversity. The prediction results obtained from the different nodes are gathered and analyzed. Based on that, the final predicted value can be deduced. It is possible that a device participating in the federated learning process or an edge device is compromised. In that case, the device will not produce correct prediction result. To ensure the correctness, obtained prediction results are compared for any anomaly or outliers. The anomalous values are not used for final prediction output.

As it is described earlier, the given diversity implementation requires data to be transferred in a safe and secure manner. The blockchain is employed to implement the data transfer model. In following section, the chapter describes the basic overview of the blockchains and then it proceeds to explain how blockchain can be used in the given approach.

5 Blockchain for Imparting Security

In this section, it is described how blockchain can be used to provide security in the data transfer process while implementing proposed diversity mechanism.

5.1 Blockchain Overview

Blockchain technology is a paradigm to store the data or record in a distributed manner in a set of many clusters of computers. In a traditional system of record storage or transaction, a centralized system has the sole responsibility of data management. However, any vulnerability in a centralized system may result in the whole dataset to get corrupt. The reliability of the centralized system is often not guaranteed. In a blockchain, the transactions are stored in a series of blocks that are distributed throughout the different computers. The blocks are time-stamped and immutable. Thus, the time at which data or transactions in the blockchain is generated is stored in the block along with the associated data. It is very difficult to make any alteration or add a new malicious block. The information in the block is stored in a cryptographically manner so that the privacy of the transactions is preserved. As the blockchain system of storing data has no central authority, a single node is not responsible for data management. Blockchain technology has attracted the attention of many academic researchers or industry in recent years. It was originally designed for the crypto currency. However, in recent years it has found several applications in IoT, networking, real estate, government agencies, share markets, and legal systems for storing records in a secured manner [30, 38].

The blocks contain the data or transactions in the blockchain. Each block contains data, the hash of the block, and the hash of the previous block in the chain. Hash is a cryptographic method that maps the data of arbitrary size to fix size. Hash functions are easy to compute. However, decoding hash to get the original message is difficult. In a hash function, even a minor change in input message results in a major change in the output of the hash function [21]. The transaction can be in various form that depends on the application. For blockchain using money exchange between two entities, the transaction is when someone initiates a money transfer. For an application involving sensor data, the transaction is the sensor data obtained after a certain time interval.

The hash of the block is a unique value that identifies the block and its content. Since a block also stores the hash of the previous block a chain of blocks is formed and thus, we have blockchain. This form of connection between different blocks in a chain makes it very secure. The first block is called as the genesis block as it cannot point to any previous block. If the content of a block is maliciously changed then it will result in the hash of the block to change. Since the blocks are connected in a chain, and as the next block contains the hash of the previous block, the two hashes will be different and thus next and following blocks will become invalid. However, this is not enough to make them secure as the hash function can be computed very fast. Thus, it may be possible that a malicious adversary changes a block and recalculates the hash of the following blocks and alters all of them.

To get rid of this, the blockchain uses a consensus algorithm to decide if a new block should be added to it [3]. In consensus building, blockchain uses a Peer-to-Peer (P2P) network. In blockchain-based P2P network, anyone can participate in the blockchain and allowed to add a valid block. Every node in the distributed system has a copy of the blockchain. If a node creates a new block, then the copy of the block is sent to every node in the blockchain. Each node verifies the block and if the block is not tampered, it is added to the blockchain. This process is called as the consensus where every node agrees whether the block should be added to the blockchain or not. The agreement between different nodes is based on a consensus algorithm. For example, in one of the consensus algorithm Proof of Work (PoW), a certain node must solve a complex mathematical puzzle. The consensus algorithms ensure the reliability and trust between different unknown nodes. The consensus mechanisms ensure that every node contains the authentic copy of the new block being added. There are various consensus algorithms other than PoW like Practical Byzantine Fault Tolerance (PBFT), Proof of Stake (PoS), Proof of Capacity, Proof of Elapsed Time (PoET) [36].

To maliciously change a block, an adversary must tamper with all the blocks in the chain. Then, it must re-calculate consensus for every block and take control of at-least 50% of nodes in the distributed system. This process is very difficult and hence it is considered as blockchain is a very safe way of securing transactions. Since it provides a decentralized infrastructure, the two nodes can share the information without the requirement of a central authority. As a centralized server is not needed to authenticate the transaction, the server cost can be greatly reduced. Because every transaction is distributed throughout every node it is very difficult to make any unintentional changes in the block. Also, as any new transactions need to be confirmed by every node, it is practically impractical to insert malicious information in the blockchain. Since the transactions in a blockchain are recorded with a timestamp, any previous transactions stored in the blocks can be traced easily. This improves the transparency in the data stored in the blockchain.

5.2   Blockchain for Securing Diversity Components

In this section, the use of blockchain to secure data transfer between distributed FL devices and edge servers is described.

Using traditional ML models, if a node needs to perform some predictive analytics it has two options. It may upload the data to the cloud where the trained models are present. The cloud has trained ML algorithms stored in it. At the cloud, the prediction is performed, and the results are sent to the user. It is also possible that rather than sending the prediction task to cloud the node uses the model trained using its computing resources. For these two cases, the input feature set and ML models for training and prediction are generally well defined. Thus, a malicious attacker only has to craft an input feature vector to make the prediction result vary. Therefore, the above approaches are vulnerable to the adversarial examples due to the use of their well-defined feature vector.

The proposed method makes ML algorithms robust as the predictive analytics is made at different diverse components and subsequently the results are compared. Thus, a single node and input dataset are not responsible for a prediction task and results are combined from different sources. The diverse components use different feature-vectors for training and prediction. Therefore, diversity makes it secure as the malicious attacker may target one or few nodes but not all of them. A malicious attacker needs to control over 50% of diverse components that take participate in the prediction process to cause any significant effect. Therefore, predictive analytics becomes robust against adversarial attacks due to added diversity. Since different diverse components are implemented in distributed nodes, the prediction task and results need to be transferred in a safe and secure way to prevent information leakage to an intruder. The blockchain, as explained earlier, provides a safe way to secure information in a distributed node and thus it is used in the data sharing process [28].

In the given architecture, consisting of the blockchain, the different diverse components or nodes are present in a distributed system. The nodes are devices participating in a federated learning process, edge servers, or a device that may request a predictive analytics task. The devices participating in the federated learning process and edge servers contain the trained ML models. The different models are trained on different datasets and may use different ML algorithms.

The flow diagram depicting the detailed prediction process is shown in Fig. 2. Initially, a node (requesting node) in the distributed system requests forecasting the value of a certain parameter.

The node adds a transaction to the blockchain, specifying its meta-data. The data may contain the value that needs to be predicted, the timeframe for which predicted values are required, a bid, available cost, and the number of diverse components it requires. The requesting node must pay to nodes providing prediction service to it. The payment can be directly in form of crypto-currency or indirectly in the form of computing resource. Hence, if a node needs more diverse elements, it must spend more cost. If the number of diverse elements is less, the cost is less, but the confidence in accuracy level may be compromised.

The block is transmitted throughout the distributed system. The distributed nodes verify the authenticity of the block and it is permanently added to the blockchain. If distributed nodes find that the block is malicious then it is discarded. Once the block is added to the blockchain, distributed nodes may participate in the bidding process. In bidding process, the nodes providing prediction service specifies the cost of the service, accuracy level of the prediction, and specification about the diversity components. The information from different nodes participating in bid process is added to the blocks. The information is important for requesting node as it must decide, based on the submitted bids, which nodes should participate in prediction process. The new blocks are verified by distributed nodes and added if found authentic. The requesting node waits until the enough blocks participating in the bidding process are added.

After nodes add their blocks to the chain, it is time for the requesting node to decide on the bidding process. For this purpose, the requesting node traces down previously added blocks. The decision of the requesting node may depend upon the diverse components of the nodes providing service, bidding cost, and model accuracy of the diverse components. The requesting node selects some nodes among many nodes that participate in bidding process. The requesting node decides this on factors like its available cost. If some nodes, providing prediction service, demands high cost, that requesting node cannot afford, it may not select particular node. So, it is up to the requesting node to decide who should participate in prediction process. Based on the results of the bidding process, the new block is generated specifying the nodes that should perform the prediction process. The requesting node adds the information in the block, and it is distributed throughout the system.

After bidding process, the nodes that won the bid starts making predictions based on their trained ML models. Once a node makes prediction it adds the result to a new block, that is added to the blockchain. The process repeats for all the nodes that won the bidding process. During this time, the requesting nodes wait for all nodes to make predictions.

It is also possible that some nodes that have won the bidding process fail to make predictions or back-up during the process. In such a case, the information is added to the blockchain and the requesting node may put some penalty on it. In the case

Fig. 2 Flow diagram
depicting prediction process

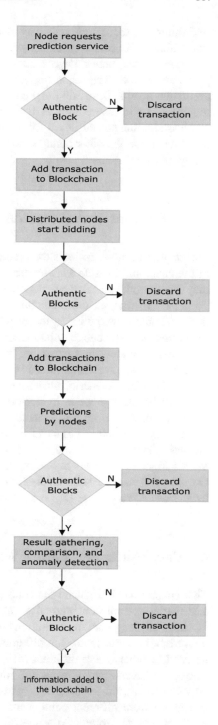

of failures, the requesting node may also decide to select the nodes that have failed in the bidding process in prior steps.

After all the nodes have made predictions, requesting node compares the prediction results. The requesting node verifies all the prior blocks containing the prediction results. Based on the prediction results, it calculates the final value. The requesting node also compares the different prediction results and if a model's result is significantly different from the others then the rating of that model may be lowered. On the other hand, if two models show very similar results then their rating may be increased.

5.3   Malicious Node Detection

The requesting node collects the prediction information from all the prior blocks in the chain and then decides on the final predicted values. However, some nodes may have produced false prediction results due to compromised feature vector. To get rid of this, all the prediction results need to be compared to find if there is any anomaly or outlier in the results. These anomalies can be discarded, and the corresponding node may be marked as the malicious node. There are different statistical techniques and clustering-based anomaly detection methods that can be used for finding anomalous values [1, 9].

For the given scenario, clustering methods may be most appropriate for the anomaly detection process. In clustering-based anomaly detection mechanism, the different points are verified whether they are close to each other. If some point is far-away from other points then that is classified as anomaly. Many different clustering methods exist and can be used for anomaly detection purpose. Support Vector Machines (SVM) is one of the popular supervised learning method [32]. On the other hand, Hierarchical clustering is an unsupervised and parameter-free technique and can be used for the anomaly detection process [18].

6   Conclusions and Future Work

This chapter has introduced the concept of diversity to mitigate the effects of the adversarial example for predictive analytics applications. The diversity can be in the form of using data from different sources but the same ML algorithm or using data from the same source but different algorithms. The two kinds of diversity can be used together where different ML algorithms are trained on different datasets. The given diverse components are implemented in FL devices or edge servers. Blockchain is used to share data between the distributed platforms. The obtained prediction from different components is combined to obtain the final prediction level. If a certain predicted value differs significantly then it can be discarded. The method also detects the malicious nodes by analyzing the predicted values and performing an anomaly test. Since the input feature-vector is not fixed in different diverse components, the malicious adversary must target at-least 50% of nodes to alter the prediction results. Therefore, the given method makes the ML algorithms robust against the adversarial examples. In future, many aspects of the current architecture can be explored in more detail. Some of them are described below.

- **Consensus Algorithm:** The blockchain requires a consensus algorithm for agreement between nodes. For the current application, the feasibility of the existing mechanisms like Proof of Work (PoW), Practical Byzantine Fault Tolerance (PFBT), Proof of Stake (PoS), Proof of Capacity, and Proof of Elapsed Time (PoET) need to be examined [36]. The new consensus mechanism that may reduce the time taken to build consensus need to be explored.
- **Bidding Process:** The bidding process selects the nodes that should provide prediction service to requesting node. This requires optimization technique that maximizes the user profit and minimizes the required error level. Also, it should select the components that are diverse, as more diverse the different components are the more robust is the prediction. Thus, optimization strategies to get the suitable cost benefit is required to be developed.
- **Consensus among Diverse Components:** The nodes making predictions use different data and different ML algorithms. Therefore, ML methods should be optimized in such a way so that the accuracy of the different models are similar. For this, the diverse components using different datasets or ML methods should be designed and trained so that they make similar predictions.
- **Final Prediction:** The final predicted value is determined by comparing different results. There may be different techniques to determine the final output. For example, a simple or weighted mean with weights depending upon accuracy can be used as the final value. Thus, a statistical technique that deduces the final predicted value based on the obtained predictions from different components need to be explored.

References

1. Amer, M., Goldstein, M.: Nearest-neighbor and clustering based anomaly detection algorithms for rapidminer. In: Proceedings of the 3rd RapidMiner Community Meeting and Conference (RCOMM 2012), pp. 1–12 (2012)
2. Ayanlade, A., Oyegbade, E.F.: Influences of wind speed and direction on atmospheric particle concentrations and industrially induced noise. SpringerPlus 5(1), 1898 (2016). https://doi.org/10.1186/s40064-016-3553-y
3. Bach, L.M., Mihaljevic, B., Zagar, M.: Comparative analysis of blockchain consensus algorithms. In: International Convention on Information and Communication Technology, Electronics and Microelectronics (MIPRO), pp. 1545–1550 (2018). https://doi.org/10.23919/MIPRO.2018.8400278
4. Bhagoji, A.N., Cullina, D., Sitawarin, C., Mittal, P.: Enhancing robustness of machine learning systems via data transformations. In: 2018 52nd Annual Conference on Information Sciences and Systems (CISS), pp. 1–5. IEEE, New York (2018)

5. Bonawitz, K., Eichner, H., Grieskamp, W., Huba, D., Ingerman, A., Ivanov, V., Kiddon, C., Konecný, J., Mazzocchi, S., McMahan, H.B., Overveldt, T.V., Petrou, D., Ramage, D., Roselander, J.: Towards federated learning at scale: System design (2019). CoRR abs/1902.01046. http://arxiv.org/abs/1902.01046
6. California air resource board (2020). https://ww2.arb.ca.gov
7. Carlini, N., Wagner, D.: Adversarial examples are not easily detected: bypassing ten detection methods. In: Proceedings of the 10th ACM Workshop on Artificial Intelligence and Security, AISec '17, pp. 3–14. ACM, New York, NY, (2017). http://doi.acm.org/10.1145/3128572. 3140444
8. De Bruin, H., Van Den Hurk, B., Kroon, L.: On the temperature-humidity correlation and similarity. Boundary-Layer Meteorol. **93**(3), 453–468 (1999)
9. Erfani, S.M., Rajasegarar, S., Karunasekera, S., Leckie, C.: High-dimensional and large-scale anomaly detection using a linear one-class svm with deep learning. Patt. Recogn. **58**, 121–134 (2016)
10. Feinman, R., Curtin, R.R., Shintre, S., Gardner, A.B.: Detecting adversarial samples from artifacts (2017). Preprint. arXiv:1703.00410
11. Gong, Z., Wang, W., Ku, W.S.: Adversarial and clean data are not twins (2017). Preprint. arXiv:1704.04960
12. Hendrycks, D., Gimpel, K.: Early methods for detecting adversarial images (2016). Preprint
13. Hochenbaum, J., Vallis, O.S., Kejariwal, A.: Automatic anomaly detection in the cloud via statistical learning (2017). CoRR abs/1704.07706. http://arxiv.org/abs/1704.07706
14. Ismail Fawaz, H., Forestier, G., Weber, J., Idoumghar, L., Muller, P.: Adversarial attacks on deep neural networks for time series classification (2019). Preprint. arXiv:1903.07054
15. Jia, W., Shukla, R.M., Sengupta, S.: Anomaly detection using supervised learning and multiple statistical methods. In: IEEE International Conference On Machine Learning and Applications (ICMLA), pp. 1291–1297 (2019)
16. Malhotra, P., Vig, L., Shroff, G., Agarwal, P.: Long short term memory networks for anomaly detection in time series. In: Proceedings, p. 89. Presses Universitaires de Louvain, Louvain-la-Neuve (2015)
17. Metzen, J.H., Genewein, T., Fischer, V., Bischoff, B.: On detecting adversarial perturbations (2017). Preprint. arXiv:1702.04267
18. Murtagh, F.: A survey of recent advances in hierarchical clustering algorithms. Comput. J. **26**(4), 354–359 (1983)
19. Papernot, N., McDaniel, P., Goodfellow, I., Jha, S., Celik, Z.B., Swami, A.: Practical black-box attacks against machine learning. In: Proceedings of ACM on Asia conference on Computer and Communications Security, pp. 506–519. ACM, New York (2017)
20. Patel, M., Hu, Y., Hédé, P., Joubert, J., Thornton, C., Naughton, B., Ramos, J.R., Chan, C., Young, V., Tan, S.J., Lynch, D., Sprecher, N., Musiol, T., Manzanares, C., Rauschenbach, U., Abeta, S., Chen, L., Shimizu, K., Neal, A., Cosimini, P., Pollard, A., Klas, G.: Mobile-edge computing. In: ETSI White Paper (2014)
21. Preneel, B.: Cryptographic hash functions: theory and practice. In: Gong, G., Gupta, K.C. (eds.) Progress in Cryptology - INDOCRYPT 2010, pp. 115–117. Springer, Berlin, Heidelberg (2010)
22. Ross, Z., Kheirbek, I., Clougherty, J.E., Ito, K., Matte, T., Markowitz, S., Eisl, H.: Noise, air pollutants and traffic: continuous measurement and correlation at a high-traffic location in New York city. Environ. Res. **111**(8), 1054 – 1063 (2011). https://doi.org/10.1016/j.envres.2011.09. 004. http://www.sciencedirect.com/science/article/pii/S0013935111002167
23. Shukla, R.M., Munir, A.: A computation offloading scheme leveraging parameter tuning for real-time iot devices. In: Proceedings of the IEEE International Symposium on Nanoelectronic and Information Systems (iNIS), pp. 208–209 (2016). https://doi.org/10.1109/iNIS.2016.055
24. Shukla, R.M., Sengupta, S.: Cop: an integrated communication, optimization, and prediction unit for smart plug-in electric vehicle charging. Internet of Things **9**, 100148 (2020). https://doi.org/10.1016/j.iot.2019.100148. http://www.sciencedirect.com/ science/article/pii/S2542660519301398

25. Shukla, R., Sengupta, S., Chatterjee, M.: Software-defined network and cloud-edge collaboration for smart and connected vehicles. In: Proceedings of the Workshop Program of the International Conference on Distributed Computing and Networking, pp. 6:1–6:6 (2018)
26. The future of ai chips, they will be in everything (2019). https://interestingengineering.com/the-future-of-ai-chips-they-will-be-in-everything
27. Vakilinia, I., Badsha, S., Sengupta, S.: Crowdfunding the insurance of a cyber-product using blockchain. In: IEEE Annual Ubiquitous Computing, Electronics Mobile Communication Conference (UEMCON), pp. 964–970 (2018). https://doi.org/10.1109/UEMCON.2018.8796515
28. Vakilinia, I., Vakilinia, S., Badsha, S., Arslan, E., Sengupta, S.: Pooling approach for task allocation in the blockchain based decentralized storage network. In: International Conference on Network and Service Management (CNSM), pp. 1–6 (2019). https://doi.org/10.23919/CNSM46954.2019.9012719
29. Varaiya, P.P.: Freeway performance measurement system. Citeseer (2001)
30. Wang, X., Zha, X., Ni, W., Liu, R.P., Guo, Y.J., Niu, X., Zheng, K.: Survey on blockchain for internet of things. Comput. Commun. **136**, 10–29 (2019). https://doi.org/10.1016/j.comcom.2019.01.006. http://www.sciencedirect.com/science/article/pii/S0140366418306881
31. Yang, Q., Liu, Y., Chen, T., Tong, Y.: Federated machine learning: Concept and applications. ACM Trans. Intell. Syst. Technol. **10**(2), 12:1–12:19 (2019). http://doi.acm.org/10.1145/3298981
32. Zhang, X.: Support Vector Machines, pp. 941–946. Springer US, Boston, MA (2010)
33. Zhang, C., Ma, Y.: Ensemble Machine Learning: Methods and Applications. Springer, New York (2012)
34. Zhang, H., Moura, S., Hu, Z., Song, Y.: PEV fast-charging station siting and sizing on coupled transportation and power networks. IEEE Trans. Smart Grid **PP**(99), 1–1 (2017)
35. Zheng, Y., Zhang, H., Yu, Y.: Detecting collective anomalies from multiple spatio-temporal datasets across different domains. In: SIGSPATIAL International Conference on Advances in Geographic Information Systems, SIGSPATIAL '15. Association for Computing Machinery, New York, NY (2015). https://doi.org/10.1145/2820783.2820813
36. Zheng, Z., Xie, S., Dai, H., Chen, X., Wang, H.: An overview of blockchain technology: architecture, consensus, and future trends. In: IEEE International Congress on Big Data (BigData Congress), pp. 557–564 (2017). https://doi.org/10.1109/BigDataCongress.2017.85
37. Zheng, Z., Xie, S., Dai, H.N., Chen, X., Wang, H.: Blockchain challenges and opportunities: a survey. Int. J. Web Grid Serv. **14**(4), 352–375 (2018)
38. Zheng, Z., Xie, S., Dai, H.N., Chen, X., Wang, H.: Blockchain challenges and opportunities: a survey. Int. J. Web Grid Serv. **14**(4), 352–375 (2018)
39. Zhou, Z.H.: Ensemble Methods: Foundations and Algorithms, 1st edn. Chapman & Hall/CRC, Boca Raton, FL (2012)

Part III
Human Machine Interactions and Roles in Automated Cyber Defenses

Automating the Investigation of Sophisticated Cyber Threats with Cognitive Agents

Steven Meckl, Gheorghe Tecuci, Dorin Marcu, and Mihai Boicu

Abstract This chapter presents an approach to orchestrating security incident response investigations using cognitive agents trained to detect sophisticated cyber threats and integrated into cybersecurity operations centers. After briefly introducing advanced persistent threats (APTs), it overviews the APT detection model and how agents are trained. It then describes how hypotheses that may explain security alerts are generated using collected data and threat intelligence, how the analyses of these hypotheses guide the collection of additional evidence, the design of the Collection Manager software, used to integrate cognitive agents with selected collection agents, how results of searches are added to the knowledge base as evidence, and how the generated hypotheses are tested using this evidence. These concepts are illustrated with an example of detecting an APT attack. We finally overview our experimental method and results.

Keywords Intrusion detection · Advanced persistent threats · Cognitive agents · Evidence-based reasoning · Hypothesis generation and testing · Learning

1 Introduction

While the state of the art in cybersecurity has seen steady progress, the volume and sophistication of attacks have out-paced the rate at which network defenses have evolved [1]. What was once the realm of criminals with a small collection of easily discovered automated tools is now ruled by well-funded and highly sophisticated sets of hackers carefully orchestrating intrusions as a means to advance their criminal enterprises or intelligence collection missions. State-sponsored attack groups such as the People's Republic of China's APT1 have demonstrated that

S. Meckl (✉) · G. Tecuci · D. Marcu · M. Boicu
Learning Agents Center, Volgenau School of Engineering, George Mason University, Fairfax, VA, USA
e-mail: smeckl@gmu.edu; tecuci@gmu.edu; dmarcu@gmu.edu; mboicu@gmu.edu

© Springer Nature Switzerland AG 2021
P. Dasgupta et al. (eds.), *Adversary-Aware Learning Techniques and Trends in Cybersecurity*, https://doi.org/10.1007/978-3-030-55692-1_7

organization, funding, and lack of consequences can be more effective than the use of sophisticated intrusion tools [2].

Commercial intrusion detection tools have not adapted well to this shift in attacker methodology. For example, in 2013, the attacker's time to compromise was measured in days over 90% of the time while the defender's time to detection was measured in days less than 25% of the time, leaving large windows of time for attackers to operate undetected [1]. What's worse is that the attackers' time to compromise is shrinking at a faster rate than defenders' time to detection. Technological advances are necessary to shrink the gap between the two.

Well-organized cybersecurity operations centers (CSOCs) leverage analysts with a wide variety of skills to constantly monitor and adjust their security infrastructure to adapt to intrusion methodology changes. However, even advanced CSOCs, leveraging state-of-the-art intrusion detection system (IDS) technology, receive too many alerts for their analysts to handle. Investigation of each alert has a cost to the organization, measured in time, man-hours, and infrastructure expenses. While many simple network compromises are routine and easy to overcome, the average cost of a data breach has risen to nearly $4 million in recent years [3]. False positives are also expensive [4], as network defenders waste time investigating incorrectly identified security incidents. In large enterprises, that see thousands of network events per day, even a 1% false positive rate can be unmanageable.

One approach to increasing CSOC efficiency is to employ cognitive agents able to capture and automatically apply the expertise of cybersecurity analysts, to automate detection of APTs and other sophisticated threats [5, 6]. A significant architectural challenge to this approach is integration of the agents into real-world CSOCs which have a wide variety of security infrastructure. There are thousands of commercial and open source security products available for CSOC managers to choose from. For this approach to be successful, cognitive agents must be able to seamlessly interact with security sensors in place in the CSOC with minimal re-architecture of the system. This chapter focuses on how the cognitive agents we are researching interact with real-world security infrastructure to detect attacks, and is organized as follows. Section 2 provides an overview of our approach to teaching the agents how to detect APTs. Then, Sect. 3 presents the integrated architecture of the Cognitive Agents for APT Detection (CAAPT). Section 4 presents how hypotheses that may explain a cybersecurity alert are generated. Then Sect. 5 presents how these hypotheses are used to search for evidence, and Sect. 6 presents how the search results are represented as evidence in the knowledge base of CAAPT. Section 7 presents the architecture of the Collection Manager that integrates the cognitive agents with the search/collection agents. Section 8 discusses our selection of collection agents from the many available ones. Section 9 presents how the evidence returned by the collection agents is used to synthesize a conclusion on whether an intrusion is being made. Section 10 presents the process used to evaluate CAAPT and the evaluation results. Finally, Sect. 11 presents our conclusions and future research directions.

2   APT Detection: Teaching and Learning

We have created the Disciple theory, methodology, and tools for the development of knowledge-based cognitive agents that: (1) can learn complex problem-solving expertise directly from subject matter experts; (2) can support experts and non-experts in problem solving; (3) can autonomously perform the learned tasks; and can teach their problem-solving expertise to students [7–15].

In the following we summarize how the Disciple learning agent shell for evidence-based reasoning (Disciple-EBR) is taught to detect APT intrusions. In essence, an expert cybersecurity analyst teaches Disciple-EBR in a way that is similar to how the expert would teach a student or an apprentice, by explaining APT detection examples to it. The agent learns general ontology-based rules from these examples and applies them to new situations. Then the expert critiques the attempted reasoning of the agent, and the agent improves its learned rules and its ontology, to more accurately simulate the detection activity of the expert. Figure 1 is an abstract illustration of this process.

First, the expert specifies an event of interest, or alert (A_1 in Fig. 1), that should alert the agent of a potential intrusion, for example, an alert generated by the BRO IDS [16] in the case of an intrusion by the Auriga malware of APT1. The problem is that such an alert may be generated by BRO also in cases when there is no intrusion, called false positives. Thus, once such an event is generated by BRO in a real situation, the expert's question is: *What hypotheses would explain it?* Therefore, the next step in the teaching process is to specify the abductive steps of generating alternative hypotheses that may explain this alert, as abstractly shown in the left

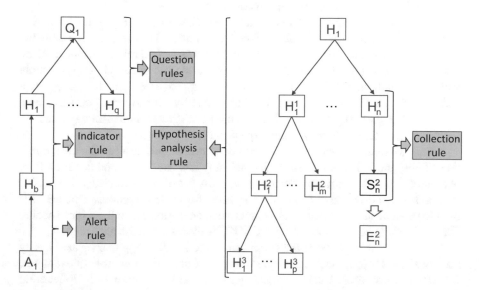

Fig. 1 Agent teaching and learning

part of Fig. 1. Some of these hypotheses are APT1 intrusion hypotheses (e.g., H_1), but others are false positive hypotheses (e.g., H_q). From these abductive reasoning steps, the agent will learn alert, indicator, and question rules. These rules will enable the agent to automatically generate alternative hypotheses that could explain similar alerts.

Abduction was first defined by Peirce [17] as being the following type of inference: *The surprising fact, C, is observed; But if A were true, C would be a matter of course. Hence, there is reason to suspect that A is true.*

Automatic hypothesis generation through abductive reasoning is computationally-intensive because there are numerous hypotheses that can be abduced from an observation [18, 19]. In our approach, however, this process is much more efficient because CAAPT learns rules as ontology-based generalizations of the abductions performed by the teaching expert and then simply applies these rules.

Once the hypotheses that can explain the alert are generated, the expert would need to assess which of them is most likely, and thus to determine whether there is an intrusion or not. For this, however, the expert would need more evidence. The expert will put each hypothesis to work to guide him/her in the process of collecting this evidence, as abstractly illustrated in the right-hand side of Fig. 1. In particular, the expert will decompose H_1 into simpler and simpler hypotheses, down to the level of hypotheses that show very clearly what evidence is needed to prove them. For example, H_1 would be true if H_1^1 and ... and H_n^1 would be true. Then, to determine whether H_n^1 is true, one would need to invoke a search procedure S_n^2 that may return evidence E_n^2, if present. If E_n^2 is found, its credibility and relevance determine the probability of H_n^1 [20]. Once the probabilities of the sub-hypotheses are assessed, the probabilities of the upper-level hypotheses are determined, and one may conclude whether there is an intrusion or not.

From a decomposition tree like that in the right-hand side of Fig. 1, the agent will learn both hypothesis analysis rules and collection rules. These rules will enable the agent to automatically decompose similar hypotheses and search for evidence. Each rule is initially partially learned as an ontology-based generalization of one example and its explanation. They are then used in reasoning to discover additional positive and negative examples and are further incrementally refined based on these new examples and their explanations. This approach integrates multi-strategy machine learning [9, 15, 21] with knowledge acquisition [22].

Agent teaching and learning is a continuous process resulting in the customization of Disciple-EBR into an agent that not only has reasoning modules for all the phases of the APT1 intrusion detection process, but also a knowledge base (KB) with a developed ontology and reasoning rules for all these phases. This agent is used to generate several autonomous cognitive agents, each specialized for a specific phase of APT intrusion detection in a CSOC, as discussed in the next section.

While the vast majority of the current machine learning approaches are heavily statistical and focus on learning single functions from a large number of examples, CAAPT employs an instructable agent approach based on apprenticeship learning from examples demonstrated by the instructor. However, as opposed to other instructable agent approaches, such as those employed by PLOW [23] or LIA [24] that rely on inductive learning and natural language processing, CAAPT uses a multistrategy learning approach that synergistically integrates inductive learning from examples, learning from explanations, by analogy and through experimentation, in the context of a multi-agent architecture.

3   Cognitive Agents for APT Detection

Figure 2 shows an overview of the architecture of the Cognitive Agents for APT Detection (CAAPT). The *Alert Agent* receives alerts from a variety of sources, such as network IDSs or endpoint protection systems, uses a matching alert rule to represent the alert in ontological form in a knowledge base (KB), and places that KB into the *Hypotheses generation queue* from which KBs are extracted by the Hypotheses Generation Agent. The *Hypotheses Generation Agent* uses indicator and question rules to generate alternative hypotheses that could explain the alert and places the KB into the *Hypotheses analyses queue* from which KBs are extracted by the Automatic Analysis Agents. The *Automatic Analysis Agents* use hypothesis analysis rules to decompose the hypotheses from such a KB, as much as possible, down to the level of evidence collection requests. Then they place the KB into the *Evidence collection queue* from where each KB is extracted by the Collection

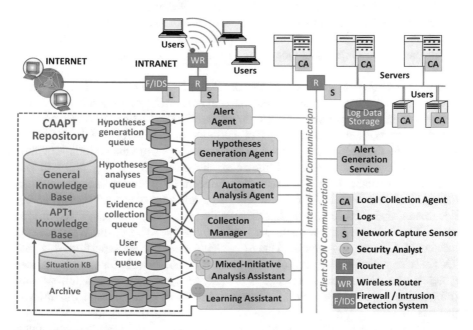

Fig. 2 CAAPT architecture overview

Manager. The *Collection Manager* uses collection rules to generate search requests and invokes specialized collection agents to search for evidence on the network in response to these requests. Then it uses matching collection rules to represent the retrieved evidence into the corresponding KB that is placed back into the Hypotheses analyses queue for further analysis (if needed), until the hypothesis with the highest probability is determined.

4 Generating Hypotheses that May Explain a Security Alert

The cognitive agents in CAAPT respond to and investigate security alerts generated by a CSOC's security infrastructure, where an analyst is typically required to conduct follow-on analysis to determine whether a threat was accurately identified. The first step in this process is to use available detection technologies to identify potential threats based on threat intelligence and use the resulting security alerts to generate competing hypotheses that may explain them. Security alerts are created by applying threat intelligence to data collected by security sensors, which include endpoint security such as anti-virus software or network-based firewalls and intrusion detection systems. Threat intelligence data is distributed in the form of *indicators of compromise* (IOCs), which include file hashes, anti-virus signatures, and the fully-qualified domain names (FQDNs) or IP addresses of known malicious servers. Security alerts come in a variety of formats but are normalized and sent to the Security Information and Event Management (SIEM) system. Modern SIEMs are often based on an unstructured database system such as Elasticsearch [25], which is open source database software that stores unstructured data, formatted in the JavaScript Object Notation (JSON) format, and indexes it to support fast searches.

Figure 3 shows an overview of the process by which a BRO alert log entry becomes an alert message sent to the Alert Agent. BRO was chosen as the IDS because it easily consumes network threat intelligence, efficiently applies it to identify threats, and generates logs of network metadata for use in follow-on analysis. The first step in this process is to convert logs from the comma-separated value (CSV) format to a JSON message and transport the log entry to our Elasticsearch database. This is done using Filebeat [26], an open source program designed to monitor CSV-formatted log files, reformat new log lines as JSON documents, and send them to an Elasticsearch server. Next, a process is required to search Elasticsearch for new alerts and send them to the Alert Agent. We developed a custom Windows program called the *Alert Generation Service* to perform this task. This service polls Elasticsearch on a specified interval, looking for alert log entries generated by BRO. A new message is created for each new alert, using relevant information from the BRO alert, and sent to the Alert Agent to start the analytic process.

In the example in Fig. 3, an alert was generated by BRO because a computer it was monitoring made a DNS request to resolve a domain known, via threat

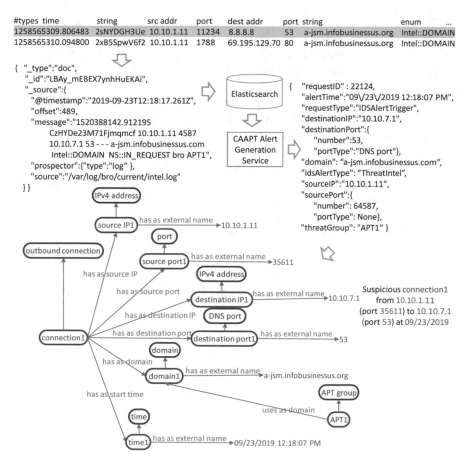

Fig. 3 How security alerts become abductive alerts

intelligence, to be associated with APT1. The message sent to Elasticsearch contains several extemporaneous data elements added by Filebeat. For the purposes of threat detection, the system is primarily concerned with the information contained in the *message* data element. The Alert Generation Service parses that field, converting the relevant data fields into appropriate data elements required for the JSON message on the right. When the Alert Agent receives this message it generates both its natural language representation and its ontological representation in a knowledge base, as shown at the bottom of Fig. 3. In this example, knowledge of the connection (source and destination IPs and ports) is captured directly from the BRO alert. The Alert Agent can further specify, based on a learned rule, that the destination port is for DNS because it uses the standard port 53. The domain a-jsm.infobusinessus.org is associated with the connection. Because the knowledge base includes modeled knowledge of adversary TTPs, the domain's association with APT1 is automatically recognized.

When the process illustrated in Fig. 3 is complete, the Alert Agent places the knowledge base into the hypotheses generation queue, to be used for further analysis by the Hypotheses Generation Agent. This agent uses abductive reasoning to generate a set of competing hypotheses that could explain why the alert was generated, as illustrated in Fig. 4. First, an indicator rule is matched, which generates a hypothesis from the suspicious connection that there is an active APT1 intrusion on the network. Then a question rule is matched, to generate a question that the previously generated hypothesis could answer. The other possible answers to this question are the competing hypotheses. The first hypothesis is that the connection is part of the APT1 intrusion. The second hypothesis is that connection was generated as part of security intelligence gathering. Security operations or research personnel often accidentally trigger security alerts while performing their duties. The third hypothesis is that a trusted application made the connection. Security tools often perform DNS lookups to enrich data, enhancing their detection features. Unless

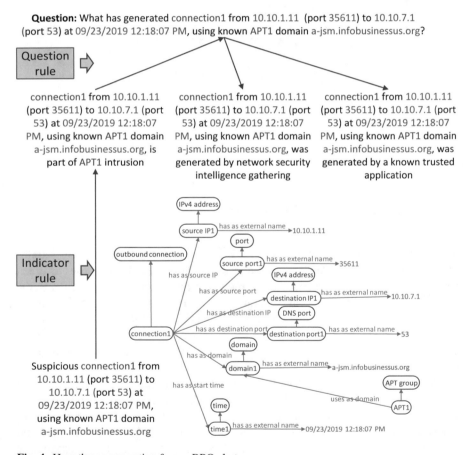

Fig. 4 Hypotheses generation from a BRO alert

the IDS is configured to exclude applications performing this type of activity, false positive alerts can be generated. It should be noted both of these two types of false positives were accidentally triggered during the course of this research.

5 Hypothesis-Driven Search for Evidence

As illustrated in the previous section, three hypotheses may explain the alert generated by the BRO IDS, an intrusion hypothesis and two false positive hypotheses. One would need additional evidence to assess the probability of each of these hypotheses, and thus determine whether there is an intrusion or not. We are employing an exhaustive knowledge-based search strategy where each generated hypothesis guides the search for evidence that would support its truthfulness. The Automatic Analysis Agent uses all applicable hypothesis analysis rules in a depth-first fashion to decompose the hypothesis into simpler and simpler hypotheses, down to the level of elementary hypotheses that reveal what evidence would favor them. Then requests to search for this evidence are generated.

Figure 5 illustrates this process for the intrusion hypothesis. There are two main indicators of this hypothesis. The left branch investigates the first indicator, whether connection1 involves an active command-and-control (C2) server. This hypothesis is further broken down to its two components: the domain a-jsm.infobusinessus.org was active at the time of the connection and was registered using a dynamic DNS provider. These are typically true when there is an active APT1 attack. The right

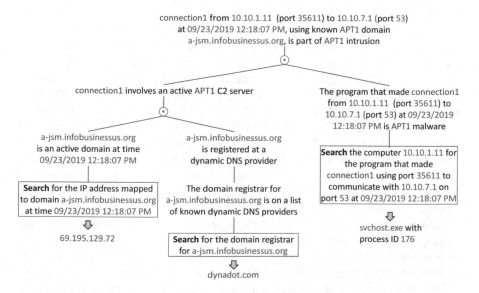

Fig. 5 Hypothesis-driven search for evidence

branch of the decomposition in Fig. 5 investigates the other indicator, whether the program that made connection1 is an APT1 malware.

The leaf nodes of the decomposition tree result in three different searches for evidence. All three searches will eventually lead to evidence being added to the KB for this security alert investigation. The search for the program that made the network connection will result in that branch of the decomposition tree being further decomposed, asking more detailed questions about the behavior of the malware.

6   Using Search Results as Evidence

The abstract searches from Fig. 5 must be turned into concrete searches for real evidence on the network. The Collection Manager is responsible for that process. Let us consider, for example, the left-most search from Fig. 5, which is looking for the IP address to which a domain was mapped at a specific point in time. Using the JSON request template associated with the collection rule that generated that leaf, the JSON-formatted search message at the top-right of Fig. 6 is created and sent to the Collection Manager. When the Collection Manager receives this message, it will call the function GetDomainIPResolution, which is one of the programmed search functions supported by the Collection Manager, mapping data elements from the search into function parameters. GetDomainIPResolution uses a passive DNS database, such as the one maintained by VirusTotal, to determine the IP address mapped to APT1 domain a-jsm.infobusinessus.org at the time specified in the *timeStamp* field in the JSON request.

When the Collection Manager completes the GetDomainIPResolution search, it will respond to the calling agent with the JSON-formatted response from the middle part of Fig. 6. The response message contains the input parameters from the search request, a *requestID* used by the Collection Manager and calling agent to map response messages to the corresponding request messages, and the output parameters. In this example, it was determined, based on passive DNS data, that the domain a-jsm.infobusinessus.org was mapped to the IP address 69.195.129.72 at time 09/23/2019 12:18:07 PM because that IP address was assigned to the domain at the time in *mappingStartTime* (08/15/2019 11:11 GMT) and it is still assigned (*mappingEndTime* is set to "present"). The response message also includes a human-readable description of what the found evidence means (*evidenceDescription*), and the value denoted in the *evidenceCredibility*, which is a value on a linear probability scale ranging from L0 (lacking support) to L11 (certain). In this case, the Collection Manager is certain the returned evidence is credible.

The response is matched with the JSON response template associated with the corresponding collection rule, and the ontology actions associated with the same rule are used to generate the ontology fragments corresponding to the data elements in the response message and store them in the knowledge base as evidence as shown at the bottom of Fig. 6. This evidence can now be used by automatic analysis agents to decide on the likelihood of an actual APT1 attack present on the network, or to request additional evidence, if needed.

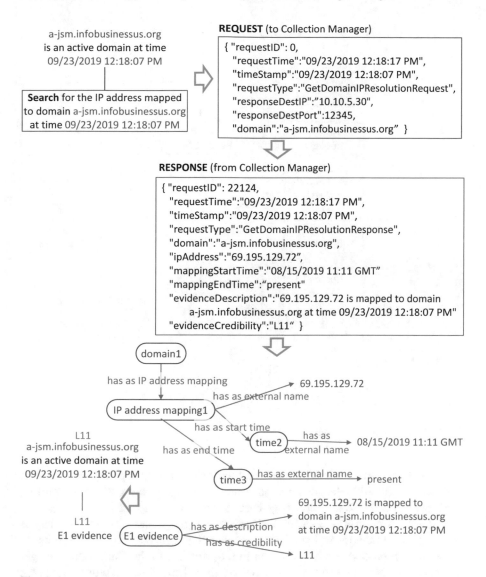

Fig. 6 Automatic evidence collection and use

7 Collection Manager Architecture

The Collection Manager is the main integration point between the cognitive agents and CSOC infrastructure. The analysis agents know what information is needed to expand their analyses, but the search requests are in abstract form. The primary function of the Collection Manager is translating high-level (abstract) search instructions into specific API calls to host and network agents, determining which

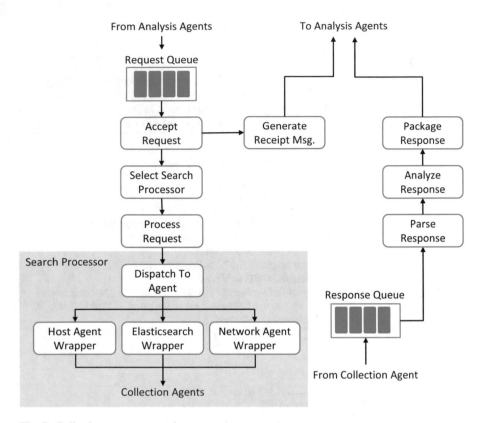

Fig. 7 Collection manager overview

such agent to send search requests to, and wrapping calls to specific search agents with a RESTful API. Results returned from search agents are then converted into evidence and added to the knowledge bases of the analysis agents.

Figure 7 is an overview of the Collection Manger process. When the analysis agents analyze competing hypotheses, the searches generated by the hypothesis-driven search process (such as those in Fig. 5) are sent to the Collection Manager and added to the request queue. Requests are then dispatched for processing and a receipt message is sent back to the caller. The receipt includes the *requestID* so the response can be matched to the search.

Abstract searches requested by analysis agents require evidence from multiple types of data sources available to the CSOC. In order for the analysis agents to integrate with real networks, the Collection Manager uses a plugin architecture for search agent wrappers, allowing it to easily translate abstract search requests into requests for information from real search agents. Depending on the amount of time required to complete a search, requests to a search agent can be either synchronous or asynchronous. From the perspective of analysis agents, all requests are asynchronous, but internally, the Collection Manager supports both call models.

In the *synchronous* call model, there is a single thread responsible for dequeuing abstract search requests from the Request Queue, formatting a concrete search for a specific search agent and dispatching the request to the appropriate search agent. It then waits on the TCP connection for a synchronous response. When it is received, the thread is responsible for parsing the response to extract digital artifacts, formatting it as evidence, and sending it to the caller. In the *asynchronous* call model, the call happens in two threads. In one thread, the abstract search request is received from the Request Queue. The request is parsed, and a concrete search request is prepared and sent to the intended search target. A second thread is responsible for polling the search target on an interval for the response. When it is available, the response data is parsed, artifacts are extracted, and a response is prepared and sent to the Response Queue.

The Collection Manager has robust exception handling built into the software. In the case that it encounters an error while processing either a synchronous or asynchronous search request, it will send a special error message to the requesting agent, notifying it of the exception. The requesting agent will then notify an analyst of the issue so he/she can troubleshoot it and restart the processing of the incident analysis.

The Collection Manager's flexible architecture and support of multiple call models allows it to easily integrate with a wide variety of security infrastructure, making the process of porting CAAPT to a new CSOC straightforward.

8   Selection and Integration of Collection Agents

Abstract searches requested by the analysis agents require evidence from multiple types of data sources available on a typical network. There are hundreds of security appliances, log source, and data store combinations in real-world networks. Therefore, a comprehensive set of corresponding collection agents is required. Industry research has determined that the most critical security technologies are a SIEM system, a network detection/collection solution, and a host detection and query solution [27], so our selection of agents focused on those areas. We have chosen to use those critical technologies, as well as others, as needed, broken down into the following categories from the taxonomy in Fig. 8.

Passive network monitors are responsible for passively watching data as it moves across the network and either recording it in full or recording metadata in the form of logs. *Passive host monitors* watch operating system and application activity on a host computer and record metadata as logs. *On-demand host agents* allow for collection and analysis of raw forensic artifacts, including disk and memory data, from workstations and servers. They can also be used to retrieve log data generated by *passive host monitors* in an on-demand fashion.

For CAAPT, collection agents were chosen based primarily on their ability to collect and query data required for detecting sophisticated attacks. Based on the requirements for modeling detection for APT1 malware, we chose a collection of

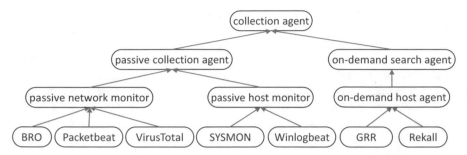

Fig. 8 Ontology of search and collection agents

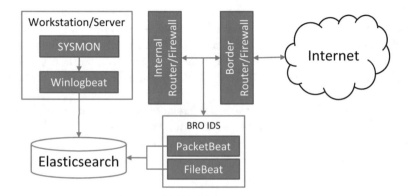

Fig. 9 Passive collector integration architecture

agents for network connection data, full packet capture, DNS logs, volatile memory artifacts, Windows Registry keys and values, file-based artifacts, endpoint logs, domain controller logs, EDR logs, and passive DNS data. Next, free or open source solutions were prioritized to eliminate cost as a barrier to adoption. Lastly, we chose tools supporting a RESTful API [28] for uniformity of integration.

GRR [29] is used as our sole on-demand host agent and is comprised of an agent which must be run on each host computer on the network and a server responsible for managing search requests. GRR allows for on-demand searches for file system and memory-resident digital forensic artifacts, which are often required to perform detailed incident analysis. Its collection functions can be managed using its RESTful API. The output of passive collection agents is log data which must be stored in a SIEM based on tools such as Elasticsearch or Splunk [30]. For CAAPT, we use Elasticsearch. As shown in Fig. 9, all passive collectors used by the system send log data, in the form of JSON documents, to Elasticsearch for storage and indexing. For collection agents having a non-JSON log format (such as SYSMON and BRO) Elasticsearch Beats [31] are used to convert the logs to JSON before sending them to Elasticsearch. This includes Filebeat for collecting BRO logs, Winlogbeat for collecting SYSMON and Windows system logs, and Packetbeat for collecting raw network data. VirusTotal provides a free passive DNS database which is used for historical domain/IP resolution queries.

9   Evidence-Based Assessment of Hypotheses

Figure 10 shows how the analysis in Fig. 5 was refined after the automatic analysis agent has received the results of the three search requests from the bottom of Fig. 5. This is a Wigmorean probabilistic inference network [32] where the probabilities of the bottom hypotheses are determined based on the credibility and relevance of the discovered evidence, and the probabilities of the upper-level hypotheses are determined based on the probabilities of their sub-hypotheses [15, 20]. Our agents employ an intuitive system of Baconian probabilities [33] with Fuzzy qualifiers [34] which are shown at the upper left of Fig. 10. Note that some of the probability intervals are associated with familiar names, such as likely (60–65%) or almost certain (95–99%).

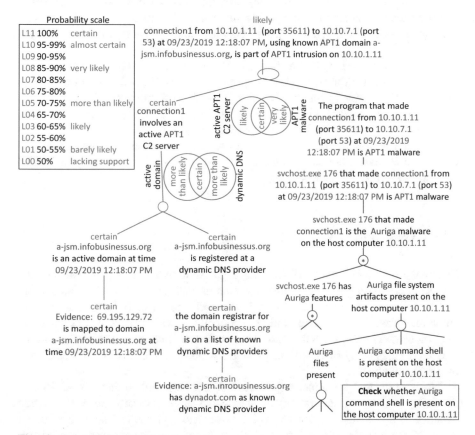

Fig. 10 Automatic hypothesis analysis

Let us first consider the left branch of the Wigmorean argumentation from Fig. 5. Note in Fig. 10 that the search nodes were replaced by the corresponding evidence items returned. In this case, the credibility of each evidence item is certain. As a result, the analysis agent infers that the following two indicators of the sub-hypothesis "connection1 involves an active APT1 C2 server" are also certain:

1. a-jsm.infobusinessus.org is an active domain at time 09/23/2019 16:23 GMT
2. a-jsm.infobusinessus.org is registered at a dynamic DNS provider

Because the combined relevance of these two indicators is certain, the agent concludes that the sub-hypothesis "connection1 involves an active APT1 C2 server" is certain. If only one of these two indicators would have been detected, the inferred probability would have been more than likely (70–75%). In general, the probability of a hypothesis that has n indicators, is computed based on the combined relevance of the detected indicators, and the probabilities of these indicators.

Consider now the right branch of the argumentation from Fig. 5. In this case the result of the search was the identification of the program that has made the suspicious connection1 (i.e., svchost.exe 176). This enables the automatic analysis agent to further investigate whether this program is APT1 malware by considering various possible indicators for specific malware, such as Auriga. This leads to additional evidence collection requests, such as the one shown at the bottom right of Fig. 10.

However, at this point in time, the automatic analysis cannot infer the presence of the second indicator for the top level hypothesis in Fig. 10, and it has to determine the probability of this hypothesis based only on the left indicator which is certain. Because the relevance of this indicator alone is only likely, the automatic analysis agent infers that the top-level hypothesis is, at this point, likely.

After the results of the new evidence collection requests are returned by the Collection Manager, the automatic analysis agent will refine the analysis, and so on, until no further refinements are possible.

10   Evaluation of CAAPT

Evaluating a system like CAAPT is challenging due to a lack of standardized data for use in comparing it against other systems or approaches. It is also challenging due to a lack of similar systems. It is a novel approach, both with respect to autonomous evidence-based reasoning in general and with respect to APT detection in particular. As such, the only reasonable approach to compare CAAPT would be to manual analysis by an expert, but even this is problematic because of lack of data on manual analysis.

We designed and performed experiments to test both the training of CAAPT and its ability to detect configuration changes in the same malware and new malware versions as the attackers' tool set evolved over time. The experiment simulated a subset of the historical evolution of APT1 malware: Auriga → Auriga variants →

Bangat → Bangat variants → Seasalt → Seasalt variants → Kurton → Kurton variants. This enabled us to test five claims:

1. *Ability to automatically detect the training malware:* Once trained with a malware, CAAPT can automatically detect it. This creates a baseline for the evaluation.
2. *Ability to detect variants of the training malware:* Once trained with a malware (e.g., Auriga) CAAPT can automatically detect new variants of it (i.e., versions of Auriga containing configuration changes).
3. *Some ability to detect evolved malware:* Once trained with some members of a malware family (e.g., Auriga and Bangat of APT1), it may be able to detect an intrusion by a new member of the (APT1) family (e.g., Seasalt).
4. *Limited incremental training needed to detect a new malware from the same family* (e.g., to detect Bangat after it was trained to detect Auriga).
5. *Efficient and high quality analysis:* It can rapidly detect APT1 intrusions through a rigorous and transparent analysis, as judged by the training expert.

We started the evaluation experiment with developing a cyber ontology and with training CAAPT to analyze the Auriga malware of APT1. After that we tested CAAPT's detection capabilities in three scenarios:

1. With the Auriga intrusion used in training, to create the evaluation baseline.
2. With an intrusion by a variant of Auriga. This variant used a different APT1 domain to trigger the security alert, and the malware process %SYSTEM-ROOT%\Temp\svchost.exe did not contain unique strings.
3. With a Bangat intrusion. Bangat does not have the library files riodrv32.sys and netui.dll, uses a different regular expression for its temporary file names, stores its data files in different folders, and uses different Windows Service names for its persistence mechanisms.

In the second phase of the experiment we extended the ontology and trained CAAPT to detect the Bangat malware used in the testing of the first phase. This process was repeated with Seasalt (third phase) and Kurton (fourth phase). The main results are summarized in Table 1, phase by phase, and discussed in the following with respect to the above five claims.

The first column of Table 1 lists the malware detected by CAAPT in each phase of the experiment, when the intrusion was made by the malware shown in the leading row of the other columns. Consider, for example, the second row in Table 1. CAAPT detected an Auriga intrusion with probability L08 when the intrusion was made by the Auriga used in training, with the same probability of L08 when the intrusion was made by the variant of the Auriga used in training, and with probability of L06 when the intrusion was made by Bangat.

Ability to automatically detect the training malware. As shown in column 2 of the table, CAAPT detected the intrusion with the malware used in training with probability L08 (85–90%) for Auriga, Bangat and Seasalt, and with probability L07 (80–85%) for Kurton.

Table 1 Summary of the CAAPT experimental results

1.Intrusion Detection	Intrusion by the Auriga used in training	Intrusion by variant of Auriga used in training	Intrusion by Bangat
Auriga	L08 (85-90%) very likely	L08 (85-90%) very likely	L06 (75-80%)
APT1	L08 (85-90%) very likely	L08 (85-90%) very likely	L08 (85-90%) very likely
Duration	143 seconds	121 seconds	119 seconds
2.Intrusion Detection	Intrusion by the Bangat used in training	Intrusion by variant of Bangat used in training	Intrusion by Seasalt
Auriga	L06 (75-80%)	L06 (75-80%)	L01 (50-55%) barely likely
Bangat	L08 (85-90%) very likely	L08 (85-90%) very likely	L01 (50-55%) barely likely
APT1	L08 (85-90%) very likely	L08 (85-90%) very likely	L08 (85-90%) very likely
Duration	265 seconds	228 seconds	274 seconds
3.Intrusion Detection	Intrusion by the Seasalt used in training	Intrusion by variant of Seasalt used in training	Intrusion by Kurton
Auriga	L01 (50-55%) barely likely	L01 (50-55%) barely likely	L01 (50-55%) barely likely
Bangat	L01 (50-55%) barely likely	L01 (50-55%) barely likely	L03 (60-65%) likely
Seasalt	L08 (85-90%) very likely	L08 (85-90%) very likely	L00 (0-50%) lacking support
APT1	L08 (85-90%) very likely	L08 (85-90%) very likely	L08 (85-90%) very likely
Duration	382 seconds	406 seconds	344 seconds
4.Intrusion Detection	Intrusion by the Kurton used in training	Intrusion by variant of Kurton used in training	
Auriga	L01 (50-55%) barely likely	L01 (50-55%) barely likely	
Bangat	L03 (60-65%) likely	L03 (60-65%) likely	
Seasalt	L00 (0-50%) lacking support	L00 (0-50%) lacking support	
Kurton	L07 (80-85%)	L07 (80-85%)	
APT1	L08 (85-90%) very likely	L08 (85-90%) very likely	
Duration	587 seconds	631 seconds	

Ability to detect variants of the training malware. As shown in column 3 of the table, CAAPT detected the intrusion with a variant of the malware used in training with the probability of L08 for the Auriga, Bangat, and Seasalt variants, and with probability of L07 for the Kurton variant.

Some ability to detect evolved malware. As shown in column 4, after being trained to detect Auriga and invoked to analyze an intrusion using Bangat, CAAPT still reported an APT1 intrusion with probability L08 (85–90%), but the probability of being Auriga was lower L06 (75–80%). In the case of analyzing Seasalt after being trained on Auriga and Bangat, CAAPT still detected an APT1 intrusion with probability L08 (85–90%), but the probability of being Auriga or Bangat was only L01 (50–55%). A similar result was obtained in when analyzing Kurton: After being trained on Auriga, Bangat, and Seasalt, CAAPT still detected an APT1 intrusion with probability L08 (85–90%), but the probability of being Auriga was L01 (50–55%), of being Bangat was L03 (60–65%), and of being Seasalt was L00 (0–50%).

Several remarks about the estimated probabilities are appropriate. Notice that, in the first phase of the experiment (first four rows in Table 1), the sum of the probabilities of "Auriga intrusion" and "APT1 intrusion" is over 100%. This is because these two hypotheses are not disjoint. Indeed, "APT1 intrusion" means any intrusion performed by the APT1 attacker group, using any of their malware tools, including Auriga. Notice also that, as expected, in each of the four phases of

Table 2 The evolution of the ontology during agent training

	Initial KB	+ Auriga	+ Bangat	+ Seasalt	+ Kurton	Total
Concepts	72	48	0	0	0	120
Instances	76	27	3	4	0	110
Features	17	13	10	10	7	57
Facts	32	47	40	40	32	191
Total	197	135	53	54	39	478

the experiment, the probability of "APT1 intrusion" is greater than or equal to the probability of the intrusion with any of the considered members of the APT1 family (i.e., Auriga, Bangat, Seasalt, and Kurton).

Let us now consider the results of the second phase of the experiment, shown in rows 5–9 of Table 1. Notice in column 2 that the probability of "Auriga intrusion" is L06 (75–80%) and the probability of "Bangat intrusion" is L08 (85–90%). This is not a contradiction because these two hypotheses are not disjoint. The Bangat malware is an evolution of the Auriga malware and therefore it has many features in common with Auriga. When checking for an intrusion with Auriga, the system looks for the presence of the features of the Auriga malware on the infected computer, but some of these features are also the features of Bangat, so it is possible that the computer is infected by both Auriga and Bangat. Therefore, Auriga intrusion with probability L06 (75–80%) covers the case where the Auriga intrusion is accompanied by a Bangat intrusion. Similarly, Bangat intrusion with probability L08 (85–90%) is based on the detected Bangat features on the host computer which also includes some Auriga features. Thus, this probability also covers the case when there is both a Bangat an Auriga and intrusion.

Limited incremental training needed to detect a new malware from the same family. Table 2 shows the evolution of the ontology during agent training. Column 2 shows the number of domain-independent ontological elements present in the initial knowledge base. To model the detection of the Auriga malware, the ontology was extended with 48 concepts, 27 instances, 13 feature definitions, and 47 facts, for a total of 135 new elements. However, modeling the Bangat malware required only 53 additional elements (no new concepts, three new instances, ten new feature definitions, and 40 new facts). Similarly, modelling Seasalt and Kurton required the extension of the ontology with only 54 and 39 new elements, respectively. After training, the final ontology contained only 478 elements, with over 40% of them being part of the initial knowledge base.

Table 3 shows the number of new knowledge elements learned during each phase of the experiment. As a result of the initial training of CAAPT to detect Auriga, it learned 28 context-independent hypotheses patterns, two alert rules, two abductive rules, 13 hypotheses analysis rules, 15 collection tasks, and 15 collection rules, for a total of 75 learned elements. Eight collection agents were also defined. However, further training of CAAPT to detect Bangat resulted in only one new context-independent hypothesis pattern, one hypotheses analysis rule, one collection task, and one collection rule. Thus, a total of only four new elements needed to be learned

Table 3 The evolution of the rules during agent training

	Auriga	+ Bangat	+ Seasalt	+ Kurton	Total
Hypothesis patterns	28	1	10	1	40
Alert rules	2	0	0	0	2
Abductive rules	2	0	0	0	2
Hypothesis analysis rules	13	1	7	2	23
Collection tasks	15	1	5	0	21
Collection rules	15	1	5	0	21
Collection agents	8	0	1	0	9
Total elements	83	4	28	3	118

to detect Bangat. For Seasalt, which is a more significant evolution of Bangat, a total of 27 new elements needed to be learned and one new collection agent defined. Finally, for Kurton however, only three new elements needed to be learned. Overall, CAAPT had to learn only 40 context-independent hypotheses patterns, two alert rules, two abductive rules, 23 hypotheses analysis rules, 21 collection tasks, and 21 collection rules, in order to detect intrusions from the four families of the APT1 malware discussed above: Auriga, Bangat, Seasalt, and Kurton (nine collection agents were also defined).

Efficient and high quality analysis. The Duration rows in Table 1 provide the total run times to detect an intrusion. This time increased from around two minutes, when CAAPT was checking for Auriga intrusions only, to around ten minutes when CAAPT was checking for Auriga, Bangat, Seasalt, and Kurton intrusions. However, most of this time was spent by waiting for the Collection Manager to return the results requested from the collection agents. The actual run time for the development and evaluation of the reasoning trees only increased from around two seconds, when CAAPT was checking for Auriga intrusions only, to around 6 s when CAAPT was checking for all four types of intrusions. Additionally, the training expert judged the generated reasoning trees as correct, rigorous and very clear.

11   Conclusions and Future Research

The research described in this chapter is a novel approach to the problem of detecting sophisticated cyber attacks by using cognitive agents trained by expert analysts to orchestrate the evidence collection and analysis typically performed by a human analyst. While the research proved successful in detecting sophisticated APT attacks, in a simulated CSOC environment, by searching for and analyzing evidence related to weak IOCs, we envision future research in this space focusing on detection based on attacker behavior instead of or in combination with detection based on IOCs. The security industry is filled with products capable of detecting the presence of IOCs, which are very good at detecting threats that network defenders are aware of, but are generally not capable of detecting novel threats. CAAPT was successful in detecting novel APT attacks based on insights about how APT attacks evolve over time. However, to increase the ability to detect truly new attacks, detection based on attacker techniques is likely to yield better results. It is relatively easy to change the IOCs present during an attack, but it is much more difficult to execute an attack without performing activities such as executing your malware, performing reconnaissance on the target network and moving laterally within it, and elevating privileges. Our future research will focus on learning generalized detection models based on the detection of such actions.

Acknowledgements This research was sponsored by Air Force Research Laboratory under contract number FA8750-17-C-0002 and by George Mason University. The views and conclusions contained in this document are those of the authors and should not be interpreted as necessarily representing the official policies or endorsements, either expressed or implied, of the U.S. Government.

References

1. Verizon: Learn from Verizon's 2014 data breach investigations report. http://www.verizonenterprise.com/DBIR/2014/ (2014). Accessed 9 Mar 2015
2. Mandiant: APT1 - exposing one of China's cyber espionage units. https://www.fireeye.com/content/dam/fireeye-www/services/pdfs/mandiant-apt1-report.pdf (2013)
3. Ponemon Institute: The cost of insecure endpoints. https://datasecurity.dell.com/wp-content/uploads/2017/09/ponemon-cost-of-insecure-endpoints.pdf (2017)
4. Zimmerman, C.: Ten strategies of a world-class cybersecurity operations center. MITRE Press, London (2014)
5. Meckl, S., Tecuci, G., Marcu, D., Boicu, M., Bin Zaman, A.: Collaborative cognitive assistants for advanced persistent threat detection. In Proceedings of the 2017 AAAI Fall Symposium Cognitive Assistance in Government and Public Sector Applications, AAAI Technical Report FS-17-02, Arlington, VA, pp. 171–178. AAAI Press, Palo Alto, CA (2017)
6. Tecuci, G., Marcu, D., Meckl, S., Boicu, M.: Evidence-based detection of advanced persistent threats. Comput. Sci. Eng. **20**(6), 54–65 (2018)
7. Boicu, M., Tecuci, G., Marcu, D., Bowman, M., Shyr, P., Ciucu, F., Levcovici, C.: Disciple-COA: From agent programming to agent teaching. Proceedings of the 27th International Conference on Machine Learning (ICML), Morgan Kaufman, Stanford, CA (2000)
8. Boicu, M., Tecuci, G., Stanescu, B, Marcu D., Cascaval C.E.: Automatic knowledge acquisition from subject matter experts. In: Proceedings of the Thirteenth International Conference on Tools with Artificial Intelligence (ICTAI), pp. 69–78. 7–9 Nov Dallas, TX. IEEE Computer Society, Los Alamitos, CA (2001)
9. Tecuci, G.: Disciple: A theory, methodology and system for learning expert knowledge. Thése de Docteur en Science, University of Paris South (1988)
10. Tecuci, G.: Building intelligent agents: An apprenticeship multistrategy learning theory, methodology, tool and case studies. Academic Press, San Diego, CA (1998)
11. Tecuci, G., Boicu, M., Bowman, M., Marcu, D., Shyr, P., Cascaval, C.: An experiment in agent teaching by subject matter experts. Int. J. Hum. Comput. Stud. **53**, 583–610 (2000)
12. Tecuci, G., Boicu, M., Marcu, D., Stanescu, B., Boicu, C., Comello, J., Lopez, A., Donlon, J., Cleckner W.: Development and deployment of a Disciple agent for center of gravity analysis. Proceedings of the Eighteenth National Conference of Artificial Intelligence and the Fourteenth Conference on Innovative Applications of Artificial Intelligence, pp. 853–860. AAAI Press, Edmonton, AB (2002).

13. Tecuci, G., Boicu, M., Boicu, C., Marcu, D., Stanescu, B., Barbulescu, M.: The Disciple-RKF learning and reasoning agent. Comput. Intell. **21**(4), 462–479 (2005)
14. Tecuci, G., Boicu, M., Marcu, D., Boicu, C., Barbulescu, M., Ayers, C., Cammons, D.: Cognitive assistants for analysts. In: John Auger, J., Wimbish, W. (eds.) Proteus Futures Digest: a Compilation of Selected Works Derived from the 2006 Proteus Workshop, pp. 303–329. Office of the Director of National Intelligence, and U.S. Army War College Center for Strategic Leadership, Joint publication of the National Intelligence University (2007)
15. Tecuci, G., Marcu, D., Boicu, M., Schum, D.A.: Knowledge engineering: Building cognitive assistants for evidence-based reasoning. Cambridge University Press, Cambridge, UK (2016)
16. Paxson, V.: Bro: A system for detecting network intruders in real-time. Computer Networks. **31**, 23–24 (1999). https://doi.org/10.1016/S1389-1286(99)00112-7
17. Peirce, C.S.: Abduction and induction. In: Buchler, J. (ed.) Philosophical writings of Peirce, pp. 150–156. Dover, New York (1901)
18. Josephson, J.R., Josephson, S.G.: Abductive inference: Computation, philosophy, technology. Cambridge University Press, Cambridge, UK (1994)
19. Schum, D.A.: Species of abductive reasoning in fact investigation in law. Cardozo Law Review. **22**(5–6), 1645–1681 (2001)
20. Tecuci, G., Schum, D.A., Marcu, D., Boicu, M.: Intelligence analysis as discovery of evidence, hypotheses, and arguments: Connecting the dots. Cambridge University Press, Cambridge, UK (2016)
21. Tecuci, G.: Plausible justification trees: A framework for deep and dynamic integration of learning strategies. Machine Learning. **11**(2–3), 237–261 (1993)
22. Tecuci, G., Kodratoff, Y. (eds.): Machine learning and knowledge acquisition: Integrated approaches. Academic Press, Cambridge, MA (1995)
23. Allen, J. F., Chambers, N., Ferguson, G., Galescu, L., Jung, H., Swift M., Taysom W.: PLOW: A collaborative task learning agent. In: Proceedings of the AAAI Conference on Artificial Intelligence (AAAI) (2007)
24. Azaria, A., Krishnamurthy, J., Mitchell, T.M.: Instructable intelligent personal agent. In: Proceedings of the AAAI Conference on Artificial Intelligence (AAAI), Phoenix, AZ, USA, February 12–17, 2016, AAAI Press (2016)
25. Elasticsearch: Elasticsearch: Restful, distributed search & analytics. https://www.elastic.co/products/elasticsearch (2015)
26. Filebeat: Filebeat. https://www.elastic.co/products/beats/filebeat (2018). Accessed 4 July 2018
27. Chuvakin, A.: The best starting technology for detection? https://blogs.gartner.com/anton-chuvakin/2018/03/06/the-best-starting-technology-for-detection/ (2018)
28. MuleSoft: What is rest API design?. https://www.mulesoft.com/resources/api/what-is-rest-api-design (2016)
29. GRR: GRR rapid response: Remote live forensics for incident response. https://github.com/google/grr (2013)
30. Splunk: Operational intelligence, log management, application management, enterprise security and compliance. http://www.splunk.com/ (2015)
31. Beats: Beats. https://www.elastic.co/products/beats (2017)
32. Wigmore, J.H.: The problem of proof. Illinois Law Rev. **8**, 77–103 (1913)
33. Cohen, L.J.: *The probable and the provable*. Clarendon Press, Oxford, UK (1977)
34. Zadeh, L.: The role of fuzzy logic in the management of uncertainty in expert systems. Fuzzy Sets Syst. *11*, 199–227 (1983)

Integrating Human Reasoning and Machine Learning to Classify Cyber Attacks

Ying Zhao and Lauren Jones

Abstract The US Department of Defense (DoD) computer networks, like many other enterprise computer networks, require strong cyber security because adversaries deploy increasingly sophisticated malicious activities against the networks. Human cyber analysts currently have to sift through the big data manually to look for the suspicious activities. New big data analytical tools and technologies bring fresh hope to help human analysts to automate the data analysis. The authors presented a use case and process that integrates human reasoning and domain knowledge to identify critical effects of cyber attacks to effectively narrow down and isolate infected computers. The authors first applied exploratory visualization to view big cyber event data. The authors then applied an unsupervised learning method, i.e., lexical link analysis (LLA), to compute the associations, statistics, and centrality measures for nodes (computers) and derived metrics to predict hacked or hacking nodes. The human reasoning and LLA allowed us to identify a single best metric that identifies the top 14% of the sorted nodes (computers) attributed to 62% hacked or hacking nodes, while the bottom 40% of the nodes (computers) are 100% normal, and can be eliminated from examination. Human reasoning and machine learning need to be integrated systematically to handle cyber security and rapidly isolate the effects of attacks. The use case is a causality analysis or causal learning in action where cause can be learned using a small number of effects because the human knowledge is applied.

Keywords Big data · Adversarial learning · Lexical link analysis · Clustering · Cyber security · Network attacks · Causality

Y. Zhao (✉) · L. Jones
Naval Postgraduate School, Monterey, CA, USA
e-mail: yzhao@nps.edu

© Springer Nature Switzerland AG 2021
P. Dasgupta et al. (eds.), *Adversary-Aware Learning Techniques and Trends in Cybersecurity*, https://doi.org/10.1007/978-3-030-55692-1_8

1   Introduction

The US Department of Defense (DoD) computer networks, like many other enterprise computer networks, require strong cyber security because adversaries deploy increasingly sophisticated malicious activities against the networks and therefore demand the capture and inspection of big data transmitted within the networks to assess the cyber security questions of who, what, where and when. The US DoD needs to develop Cyber Situational Awareness Analytic Capabilities (CSAAC) for enterprise networks to [9]:

- Prevent expensive and damaging distributed denial of service (DDOS) attacks
- Maintain a competitive advantage of the military or businesses by protecting expensive research and intellectual capital
- Prevent malware and viruses going through emails and other channels
- Better secure vital networked infrastructures

Most cyber events are benign, however the relatively small number of malicious activities can often hide within the large volume of data generated by network activities. Human cyber analysts have to manually sift through to look for suspicious activities.

New big data analytical tools and technologies bring fresh hope to help analysts automate the data analysis. Data analysis in cyber domain is a difficult problem for machine learning to solve since adversarial behavior data are small. Furthermore, the techniques and mechanism behind malicious attacks used by adversaries are constantly changing and evolving, making them ever more difficult to be detected and captured in real-life.

Should an attack occur, cause and effect analysis is important in order to quickly narrow the relevant search area and isolate the spread of the attacks among the enterprise computers and networks. Considering hacking or being hacked for a computer is the cause, effect can be measured from various computer's activities. The authors presented a use case on how to integrate human reasoning, data mining, and machine learning to improve CSAAC by effectively and efficiently prioritizing, aggregating, and modeling the big data from disparate sources to provide more accurate early detection and prediction of future network vulnerabilities, threats, and attacks.

2   Data Set Description

The cyber data in the study was taken from multiple routers in the Los Alamos National Laboratory's internal network [30]. The data set contains windows authentication events and processes, domain name lookups, network flow data, and hacking events. The data contains 58 days and total 12 gigabytes (compressed) of network information and 1.6 billion events. There are known malicious activities (identified as Red Team Actions) conducted within this network during this time period.

Some of the information contained within the dataset was anonymized or deidentified. While this removes significant amounts of information from the data set, there is still valuable information to be gleaned about the behavior of the network due to the unity of identification across the five different files (i.e., User 1 or U1 is the same user across all data sets and Computer 1 or C1 is the same computer across all data sets).

Some of the well-known ports (e.g., http port 80 and 443), protocols (e.g., 6 for Transmission Control Protocol), and system users (e.g., SYSTEM or Local Service) are left identified within the datasets. Time is captured in one-second intervals, starting with a time epoch of (1).

The LANL cyber data set was chosen over other popular open source data sets (e.g., DARPA [7] or KDD [14] data sources) because of its size, complexity, and recency (2015), which contains the activities of some newer malicious attack methodologies. This data also represents a generic and typical enterprise network cyber picture. The network includes about total 15,000 computers and 2% of the computers were hacked or hacking. The goal is to accurately classify the hacked or hacking computers from the rest of the normal ones.

3 Methods

3.1 Analysis Plan

In order to incrementally analyze the cyber data set using big data and deep models including machine learning methods, the LANL-DNS data file is initially pre-processed, analyzed, and interpreted in this paper before testing on other more complex data sets. The authors started with the "Domain Name Service" (DNS) data set because it is the smallest data in all the data sets. Figure 1 shows a snapshot of the LANL-DNS data. Time, source computer, and computer resolved are the attributes. A source computer is a computer which requested a name lookup and a resolved computer is the name server computer which resolved the request from the source computer.

The authors performed the following steps for understanding the data:

```
31,C161,C2109
35,C5642,C528
38,C3380,C22841
```

Fig. 1 The LANL-DNS log data

- Perform data visualization and exploration for the LANL-DNS data set: The goal was to display and visualize data initially, check data quality, and gain insights for further data analysis.
- Perform data mining and unsupervised machine learning to discover initial associations, correlations, and probability rules.
- Apply supervised machine learning to generate more precise classification and prediction models.

3.2   Data Visualization and Exploration

The Big Data Platform (BDP), which has been developed by the Defense Information Systems Agency (DISA) as a CSAAC tool [3], runs on on Amazon Web Services (AWS) including a mix of big data standard tools and customized tools for data ingestion, management, security, exploration, and analysis. These functions are supported by open source tools including Apache Spark [1], Apache Storm [2], Hadoop Map/Reduce, Kibana [15], NodeJS [20], and R-Shiny [24].

BDP can process large-scale real-time data feeds to provide useful visualizations of the data for initial data exploration and discovery of anomalous events. Ingestion of the LANL-DNS data into the BDP cluster included the following steps:

- Customize and format a rapid deployment archive (RDA) for parsing the csv file data.
- Connect a puppet server to upload data to the Apache Storm server which ingests and parses the data.

For the data visualization and exploration, the authors used Unity and Kibana. Unity is a visualization tool with the BDP software package. It uses queries to visualize time series, histograms, and pie charts for the initial examinations of the data. Kibana creates Data-driven documents (D3) visualizations including heat maps, graphs, and charts which could indicate threats. Figure 2 shows a Kibana heat map of a number of connections made for each computer (y-axis) over time (x-axis) for the data set LANL-DNS. These tools could show big data in a near real-time or replay of a real-time data to provide rapid updates for a focused segment.

For the data exploration, the authors also used an open source network display program Gephi [11] to visualize the connections among computer nodes for the LANL dataset. Gephi is not part of the BDP software package. Gephi uses Source and Target fields to draw network graphs. Gephi includes a timeline function to allow a user to view the connections between nodes at specific times or in a range of times. Each node is a computer. Figure 3 shows the hacking events during a 24-hour period.

The red team creates hacking events such as teal colored computer nodes are shown in Fig. 3. One teal node is hacking, the orange nodes are being hacked, purple nodes are neither hacking nor being hacked. The color of the edges between nodes

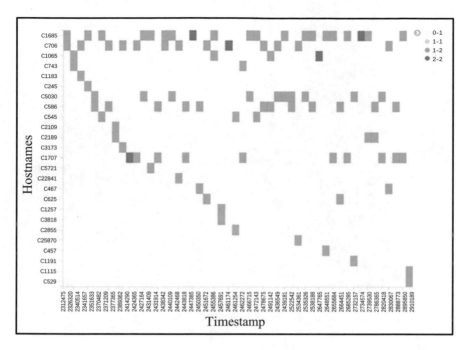

Fig. 2 BDP data exploration: A heat map showing the number of connections made for each computer (*y*-axis) over time (*x*-axis) from Kibana

represents the protocols used for the connections. Purple edges are most likely TCP. Green connections are "protocol-1" which relate to the hacked computers.

The shape of the graph provides clues as to the nature of the nodes. Nodes that are highly connected to other nodes may be name servers or popular web servers. The hacked nodes seem to be in the area of the nodes with higher numbers of connections (high centrality nodes in the middle).

3.3 Unsupervised Machine Learning Using Lexical Link Analysis (LLA)

An LLA [36] describes the characteristics of a complex system using a list of attributes or features with specific vocabularies or lexical terms. Because the number of lexical terms can be potentially very large from big data, the model can be viewed as a deep model for big data. For example, we can describe a system using word pairs or bi-grams as lexical terms extracted from text data. LLA automatically discovers word pairs, and displays them as word pair networks. The word pair model can further be extended to a context-concept-cluster model [29]. A context can represent a location, a time point or an object (e.g. file name) shared across

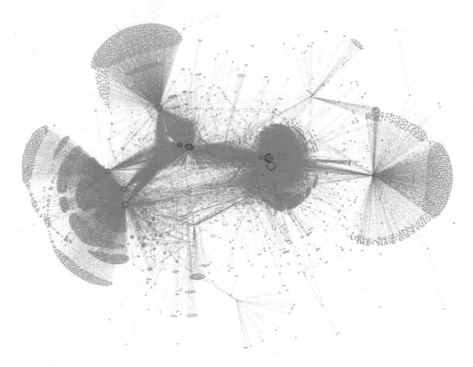

Fig. 3 Gephi network visualization of computers

data sources. For example, in "information assurance", "information" is the context, "assurance" is the concept. The timestamp, computer name are the contexts to link different data sources.

Figure 4 shows an example of such a word network discovered from text data. "Clean energy", "renewable energy" are two bi-gram word pairs. For a text document, words are represented as nodes and word pairs as the links between nodes. A word center (e.g., "energy" in Fig. 4) is formed around a word node connected with a list of other words to form a word network.

Bi-grams allow LLA to be extended to numerical or categorical data. For example, for structured data such as attributes from databases, we first discretize numeric variables and use categorical variables as word-like features. These word-like features are nodes in the word networks, the link among the features or nodes are the correlations. Figure 5 shows an example of a LLA network discovered from the LANL-DNS data. For the LANL-DNS data set, we compute associations and links as pairs of a source computer and a resolve computer. The strength of the associations or links are defined as how many time points or events that the two computers are linked via "source" or "resolve" in Fig. 5.

The detail LLA outputs for the LANL-DNS data set are listed as follows:

Output 1 The list of words representing the computers in the data set and nodes in the network with the following characteristics computed as follows:

Fig. 4 An example of word network from a text data by LLA

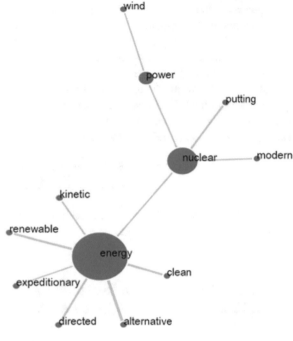

Fig. 5 The links of computer nodes

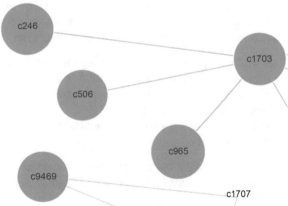

- Group: what group a node belongs. A node or a word is a computer.
- Type: group type from LLA.
- Degree: how many connections each node has.
- Betweenness: how many connections belong to the different groups.
- Degree in: how many connections for a computer as resolve.
- Degree out: how many connections for a computer as source.

Output 2 The list of association and correlation of computer nodes. The output from LLA for the LANL-DNS data processing identified 15,237 unique active devices (computers). There are no identifying features differentiating an end user device such as a personal computer versus a DNS server; all are identified as anonymous devices, such as C123. As in the example of a LLA network discovered from the LANL-DNS data in Fig. 5, each node or word is a computer. The links represent how likely two computers are linked as a "source" and "resolve" pair in the events (timestamps). An event is single timestamped record in the data referring to a source or resolve computer. The linked events for computer i and j are the events (data records) that two computers either source or resolve computers show together at the same time points. A correlation measure is computed using Eq. (1).

$$r_{ij} = \frac{(Linked\ Events\ Computer\ i\ and\ Computer\ j)}{\sqrt{(Events\ Computer\ i)(Events\ Computer\ j)}} \tag{1}$$

r_{ij} is used to indicate how often two computers appear together as a strength of association of the two computers.

4 Results Using Human Reasoning After the Exploratory and Unsupervised Machine Learning

After the initial data exploration, the research focused on how to classify the hacking and hacked computers from the data sets. There are several reasoning factors for a human analyst with domain knowledge to consider:

1. If a computer is hacked or hacking other computers, its activity, which can be measured in various ways, e.g., total activity from BDP, has to increase.
2. If a computer is a normal domain name server, it should not request any name lookups to other computers.
3. If a computer is a normal computer, it should not perform any name lookups from other computers.

The LLA outputs include measures of degree in and degree out for each node (computer), the authors computed additional metrics based on the outputs of LLA as follows:

- Multi: degree in*degree out;
- DIV: degree in/degree out if degree out not 0; else 0;
- SUM: degree in+degree out;
- DIFF: degree in-degree out

Figure 6 show a gains chart for predicting the hacked and hacking computers. The x-axis shows the computer sequence number ranked by the four metrics. The y-axis shows the percentage of hacked or hacking computer nodes. 1.75% out of 15,237 total computers are either hacked or hacking as the percentage of the ground truth. If there is a perfect prediction algorithm, the top 1.75% of the sorted nodes (based on the perfect scores) should predict 100% of the hacked or hacking computers as shown in the leftmost curve (two straight lines).

The two results are interesting from human analysts' perspective:

- The best performed prediction metric is Multi (degree in*degree out) where the top 2160 nodes (14%) include 62% of the total hacked or hacking nodes. This is the best gain over other scores: For example, if sorted by the "degree in" scores, the top 14% contains 56% of the total hacked or hacking nodes. If sorted by the random scores, 14% contains 14% of the total hacked or hacking nodes, which is the worst performing prediction.
- The bottom ranked 40% of the nodes (from 9112 to 15,237) are normal. This is also significant since one can eliminate the 40% nodes when examining hacked or hacking nodes, which is a big labor saving for cyber security analysts.

The metric "degree in*degree out" indicates highly active devices are more likely to be hacked. Highly active devices do not mean they are anomalous, however, a common behavior observed in malicious actions is increased activity of devices that may be participating involved in the unauthorized action. We later compute an activity metric by counting the number of event (i.e. timestamps) a computer is associated in the data set from BDP. This is a simpler metric to compute than the associations in LLA. The "total activity from BDP" metric shows a similar gain to the best LLA metric.

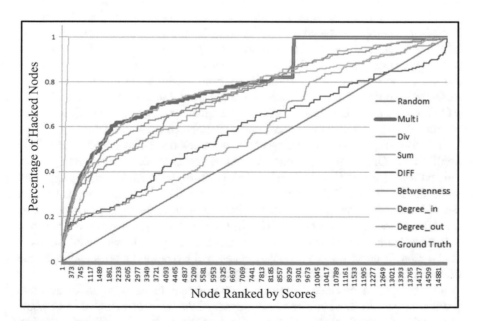

Fig. 6 Gains chart using centrality node scores computed from LLA and derived metrics

5 Results Using Supervised Machine Learning of the Combined Data

5.1 Relations of Deep Analytics, Machine Learning (ML), and Artificial Intelligence (AI) Algorithms

The supervised learning algorithms are among the natural choices for the classification and prediction tasks such as for the LANL data set. In this section, the authors review briefly the relations among deep analysis, ML/AI algorithms including traditional statistical analysis.

In recent years, the state-of-art ML/AI algorithms have been used to process big data for breakthrough applications to reach human level performance such as AlphaGo [25], AlphaZero [26] (convolutional neural networks or CNN [18] and reinforcement learning [28] based methods), and Libratus [5, 6] (a poker based on game theory AI algorithms). The techniques have been used to solve difficult problems, however, have been criticized for being black boxes and lacking understanding of causality [19].

Traditional statistical analysis heavily depends on hypothesis tests, where the likelihood of the data $P(X|H)$ given a hypothesis H is compared to the a null hypothesis H0. This also relates to the maximum likelihood estimation (MLE) where the likelihood of the data $P(X|M)$ given a model M is estimated from the data. The general assumption is that the model is generative of the data if the likelihood is maximized compared to all other models, therefore, the model is the cause of the data (effect). The generative models of the current ML/AI [22, 23], related to the hypothesis tests and MLE, also consider given classification labels, what are the likelihood of the data observed. The current machine learning techniques are different from the MLE approach, for example, neural networks or many other so-called machine learning classifiers directly estimate posterior probabilities (PP) of the models (e.g. classification labels) given the data, i.e., estimate $P(M|X)$.

The two MLE and PP approaches have been competing historically for ML/AI applications. One of the important ML/AI is the automatic speech recognition, where the MLE based Hidden Markov Model (HMM) has been the leading approach since the late 1980s [13], yet this framework has been gradually replaced with deep learning components and now the leading approaches to speech recognition are fully neural network systems [12]. In other words, although these black box ML/AI techniques are not often causal or explainable, they do work well for many applications because the cross-validation and regularization theories employed are effective for accurate prediction and classification [4, 33].

For supervised machine learning algorithms, the focus is to make accurate prediction or classification for out-of-sample data (new data that do not show in sample of train data). For example, for machine learning classifiers, a typical classification error graph or train (in-sample) and test (out-of-sample) errors, with respect to the complexity of the models, e.g., measured by so called Vapnik–Chervonenkis dimension or VC dimension [2] (e.g., number of parameters). From supervised machine learning perspective, out-of-sample error is always larger than the in sample error (i.e., so-call overfitting problem), there is an optimal model complexity d*vc which gives the lowest test error for a given train data. This is usually accomplished using cross-validation or regularization to avoid the overfitting [4, 33]. The methods keep the model as small and smooth as possible so the difference between in sample error and out of sample error is minimized. When the applications required causality analysis such as the cyber data set LANL in this paper, we need to integrate the reasonable causal elements with data-driven ML approaches together, and always keep human experts on-the-loop for interpreting the cause and effect relations. Causal learning relate to the subclass of generative models because, at an abstract level, that resembles how the data are actually generated [28].

5.2 Results

Supervised learning are usually better when there are the labeled data for training models as in the LANL data set. The algorithms, the authors used from using the open source data mining tool Orange [21], include logistic regression, neural networks (NN), naive Bayes (NB), decision trees, and support vector machines (SVM).

The authors appended other features from all the data sets combined and applied the algorithms. The features are listed as follows:

- computer ID
- hacked/hacking or not
- degree
- betweenness
- degree in
- degree out
- degree in*degree out
- number of unique processes
- number of total Processes
- total number of destinations
- total number of authorization
- total number of successful logon
- number of authorization types
- number of logon types
- number of orientations
- number of connections
- number of source ports
- number of destination ports
- total duration of connections
- total packets of connections

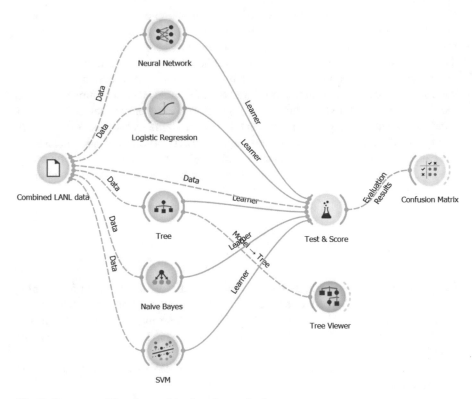

Fig. 7 Orange workflow for machine learning methods

- total bytes of connections

Figure 8 shows the the gains chart comparison of typical supervised machine learning methods including the NN, logistic regression, NB, decision trees, and SVM. The NN contains 100 neurons for one hidden layer, the learning rate is 0.0001 and the max iteration is 200. The decision trees include an induce binary tree, the minimum number of instances in leaves is 5 and the limit the maximal tree depth is set to 100. The SVM includes a radial basis function (RBF) kernel with the numerical tolerance 0.001 and iteration 100. The NB uses an automatic setting in Orange. The combined LANL data set is not split into training and test set in order to compare with the LLA method and a 10-fold cross-validation is used for validating for supervised machine learning algorithms.

Figure 7 shows a workflow to execute the supervised machine learning algorithms in the tool. The random strategy sorts the nodes randomly and calculates how many targets (hacked or hacking) computers are included on the top of the sorted computers (by random scores). Other supervised machine learning algorithms are used more intelligent scores to sort the same computers in descending orders, the nodes or computers on the top of the sorted lists are more likely to be the targets.

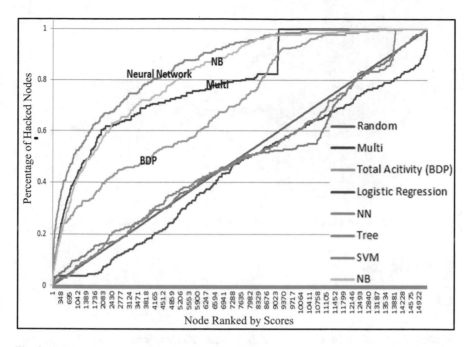

Fig. 8 Gains chart using machine learning algorithms

With a same cut off percentage of selected population (e.g., 14% of the sorted computers) for all the methods including the random strategy, machine learning algorithms should give higher percentages of targets (e.g., 62% for the Multi). Only the neural network shows a better gain than the "Multi" (i.e., "degree in*degree out") metric. The total activity from BDP performs well in the beginning of the curve. Surprisingly, these machine learning methods did not gain much edge over the metric "degree in*degree out" as the "Multi" in Fig. 8 from unsupervised LLA or the total activity measure from BDP.

The threshold for "degree in*degree out" is zero which came from the human analysts' intuition and the threshold enabled filtering out the "absolute" benign nodes. The machine learning algorithms usually generate sorted priority lists used for checking. The heuristics used are generalizable for other computer networks while possibly different in size and architecture will generally be comprised of the same protocols and structure. When filtering out normal activities in data sets, analysts can focus the resource on more difficult nodes.

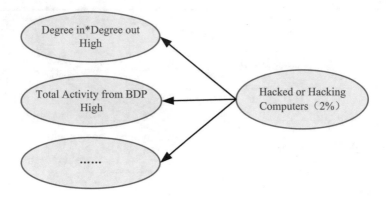

Fig. 9 Associations and correlations discovered from data as probabilistic rules

6   Discussion

6.1   Human Reasoning and Causal Learning

A unique aspect of human reasoning is that humans heavily rely on causality analysis. For any decision making activity, humans naturally analyze causes and effects. Causality analysis is closely related to anticipatory thinking of human cognition.

Human decision makers are always interested in discovering and understanding the reasons and causes from data for an effect. This calls for a systematic study of causal learning to be integrated into machine learning. The key factors for causal learning includes the three layers of a causal hierarchy [22]—association, intervention and counterfactuals.

6.1.1   Association

The common consensus is that data-driven analysis or data mining can discover initial statistical correlations and associations from big data. Figure 9 shows conceptually how the associations and correlations as probability rules were discovered from data via machine learning algorithms, i.e., both following probabilities are high: $P(Hacked\ or\ Hacking\ Computers | Degree\ in * Degree\ out\ High)$, and $P(Hacked\ or\ Hacking\ Computers | Total\ Activity\ from\ BDP\ High)$. These rules can be discovered using LLA with a threshold for the bi-gram strength. Meanwhile, human analysts need to validate if they make sense and what are causes and effects. In this case, "Degree in*Degree out" and "Total Activity from BDP High" are both effects caused by "Hacked or Hacking Computers."

6.1.2   Intervention

In machine learning practices, the associations, correlations or probabilistic rules are typically cross-validated using separate or new data sets. In causal learning, this relates to the intervention layer. A typical question at this level would be: What will happen if one takes an action? For example, instead of examining $P(X|M)$, one might further ensure M is actionable or $P(X|do(M))$ [19] can be examined. The answers to the question are more than just mining the existing data. The action needs to generate new observable data as an effect of the intervention to determine if the underlying action causes the effect. In Fig. 9, if the conditions for the probabilistic rules indeed relate to actions "hacked" or "hacking," then rules are causal rules.

6.1.3   Counterfactuals

A typical question asked is: "What if I had acted differently?" or counterfactual reasoning as shown in Fig. 9. If $P(E|C)$ is high-probability rule discovered from data and C is actionable, $P(E|Not\ C)$, $P(Not\ E|C)$, and $P(Not\ E|Not\ C)$ are the counterfactuals needed in the reasoning as shown in Fig. 10. Traditionally, the counterfactual is defined as the effect of an action for an entity and for the same entity without the action, i.e., $P(E|C)$ and $P(E|Not\ C)$. However, since the same effect is impossible to directly observe for the same entity, this is commonly referred to as the fundamental problem of causal inference [19]. The potential-outcome or counterfactual-based model of casual inference explores the idea of an entity-level treatment effect, although it is unobservable as well, it can be aggregated in various ways.

For example, the causal effect is typically measured using two randomized populations, one with the action (or with C) and another one without the action (Not C or control group). The two populations are randomized to ensure they are similar to each other (as if they were the same entity). This is the Randomized Control Treatment (RCT) theory [19], which is a standard practice found in social sciences, drug development, and clinic trials. With recent data-driven approaches such as data mining and machine learning, if people can robustly estimate a local average effect using machine learning algorithms [10] that are mostly nonparametric models such as nearest neighbors and random forests [32], i.e., use the effect of the nearest neighbor of an entity as the surrogate for the unobservable effect of the same entity for the counterfactual action.

6.2   Predicting Causes

In a real-life application, one often wants to predict causes based on the data of effects, i.e., computing and validating $P(C|E)$. Effects are often observable data, e.g., "total activity from BDP high" or "degree in*degree out high" in the

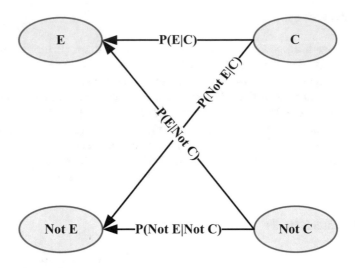

Fig. 10 Four probabilistic rules related to counterfactuals

example. Causes, e.g., "hacked or hacking computers," need to be predicted from the observable data. $P(C|E)$ is difficult to discover because causes are often hidden, anomalous, and capricious.

In recent research, modified algorithms gained rigorous research and attention related to an old economics method, i.e., generate an instrumental variable I [35] to discover the cause. An instrumental variable can be only correlated with the effect E through the cause C [27]. For example, a tobacco tax could be an instrumental variable for smoking which might be a cause for a poor health. Therefore, if one observes the correlation between tobacco tax and a better health, and given the known causal relation of tobacco tax and smoking, one can discover the hidden cause smoking for a poor health. Researchers also explore the emergence of causal reasoning and intervention strategies from simpler reinforcement learning algorithms using a meta-reinforcement learning framework [8]. This type of algorithms need to deploy agents to generate new data, resolve confounders, select informative interventions, and make counterfactual predictions. They are not suitable for data-driven causal learning where one can not change the big data that is already collected.

The innovation approach shown in this paper indicates that human intelligence sometimes can quickly discover the rules such as $P(Not\ C|Not\ E)$ with a high probability to reduce big data and allow resource such as ML/AI algorithms to focus on a much smaller population. In Fig. 11, high pair-wise predictive probability rules reveal necessary factors for causes, which are not enough for predicting causes. Human intelligence may capture sufficient non-effect factors to predict non-cause factors. For example, "degree in*degree out=0" indicates "not hacked and not hacking computers." The high values of these effect factors are also more

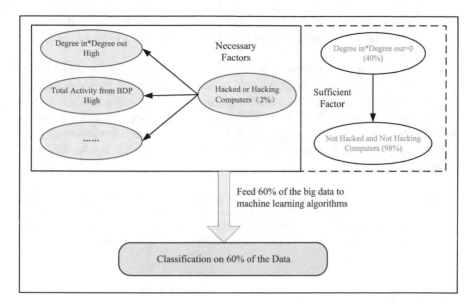

Fig. 11 Human causality reasoning process

likely linked to high values of cause factors. In other words, if $P(Not\ C|Not\ E)$ is high, $P(C|E)$ is probably high as well. This is why in our example, high "degree in*degree out" is a better predictor than any other factors or derived factors for "hacked or hacking computers." In real-life applications, this means that a supervised machine learning algorithm needs to choose to predict either the cause factor or the non-cause factor if one is more predictable than the other, then use the results to reduce big data and focus on the areas that are more confusing for predictive algorithms or classifiers.

7 Conclusion

The authors presented a use case that integrates human reasoning and domain knowledge to quickly narrow the search area down for the cyber attacks. It is a causality in action where cause can be measured using a small number of effects because the domain knowledge was applied. Data mining of exploratory visualization using BDP provides insights for human analysts. The unsupervised learning method of LLA computes the associations, statistics and centrality measures for nodes (computers) and derived metrics are significantly useful to predict hacked or hacking nodes in the gains chart evidently. The human reasoning and LLA allows us to identify a single best metric of the top 14% of the sorted nodes attributed to 62% hacked or hacking nodes and the bottom 40% of the nodes are 100% normal, and can be eliminated from examination. Supervised machine learning methods can further improve the model by incorporating more data. Human reasoning and machine learning need to be integrated to handle cyber security and isolate the effects of attacks rapidly.

In this paper, the authors used a static data set to demonstrate the methodology of integrating human reasoning and machine learning to classify cyber attacks, the established model, however, can potentially process real-time streaming data from online network sensors. The use of GPU, cloud technology, parallel processing, and standard big data processing such as BDP should handle the processing and monitoring of real-time network activities and provide updated status of network security.

Acknowledgments The authors would like to thank the Naval Research Program at the Naval Postgraduate School and Quantum Intelligence, Inc. for the research support and collaboration. The views and conclusions contained in this document are those of the authors and should not be interpreted as representing the official policies, either expressed or implied of the U.S. Government.

References

1. Apache Spark: https://spark.apache.org/
2. Apache Storm: http://storm.apache.org/
3. BDP: https://disa.mil/Cybersecurity/Analytics/Big-Data-Platform
4. Bishop, C.M.: Pattern Recognition and Machine Learning (Corr. printing. ed.). Springer, New York (2007). ISBN:978-0387310732
5. Brown, N., Sandholm, T.: Superhuman AI for heads-up no-limit poker: libratus beats top professionals. Science (2017). https://doi.org/10.1126/science.aao1733
6. Brown, N., Sandholm, T.: Safe and nested subgame solving for imperfect-information games. In: Neural Information Processing Systems (NIPS) (2017)
7. DARPA dataset: DARPA Intrusion Detection Scenario Specific Data Sets (2000). https://www.ll.mit.edu/r-d/datasets
8. Dasgupta, I., Kurth-Nelson, Z., Chiappa, S., Mitrovic, J., Ortega, P., Hughes, E., Botvinick, M., Wang, J.: Meta-reinforcement learning of causal strategies. In: The Meta-Learning Workshop at the Neural Information Processing Systems (NeurIPS) (2019)
9. Jones, L.M.: Big Data Analysis for Cyber Situational Awareness Analytic Capabilities. Master of Science, Naval Postgraduate School, September (2018)
10. Gelman, A.: Donald Rubin (2018) . Retrieved from http://www.stat.columbia.edu/~gelman/research/published/rubin.pdf
11. Gephi: The Open Graph Viz Platform (2018). https://gephi.org/
12. Hinton, G.E., et al.: Deep neural networks for acoustic modeling in speech recognition. IEEE Signal. Process. Mag. 29, 82–97 (2012)
13. Juang, B.H., Rabiner, L.R.: Hidden Markov models for speech recognition. Technometric 33(3), 251–272 (1990)
14. KDD dataset: The UCI KDD Archive, Information and Computer Science, University of California, Irvine (1999). http://kdd.ics.uci.edu/databases/kddcup99/kddcup99.html
15. Kibana: https://www.elastic.co/products/kibana
16. Lake, B.M., Ullman, T.D., Tenenbaum, J.B., Gershman, S.J.: Building Machines That Learn and Think Like People (2016). Retrieved from https://arxiv.org/abs/1604.00289
17. Lake, B.M., Ullman, T.D., Tenenbaum, J.B., Gershman, S.J.: Building Machines That Learn and Think Like People (2016). Retrieved from https://arxiv.org/abs/1604.00289

18. LeCun, Y., Bengio, Y., Hinton, G.: Deep learning. Nature **521**, 436–444 (2015)
19. Mackenzie, D., Pearl, J.: The Book of Why: The New Science of Cause and Effect. Basic Books, New York (2018)
20. NodJS: https://nodejs.org/en/
21. Orange data mining tool: https://orange.biolab.si/download/
22. Pearl, J. (2018). The Seven Pillars of Causal Reasoning with Reflections on Machine Learning. Retrieved from http://ftp.cs.ucla.edu/pub/stat_ser/r481.pdf
23. Rezende, D.J., Mohamed, S., Wierstra, D.: Stochastic backpropagation and approximate inference in deep generative models. In: International Conference on Machine Learning (ICML) (2014)
24. R-shiny:https://shiny.rstudio.com/
25. Silver, D., et al.: Mastering the game of Go with deep neural networks and tree search. Nature **529**(7587), 484–489 (2016)
26. Silver, D., et al.: Mastering the game of Go without human knowledge. Nature **550**, 354–359 (2017)
27. Singh, R.,Sahani, M., Gretton, A.: Kernel instrumental variable regression. In: The Proceeding of the Neural Information Processing Systems (NeurIPS) (2019)
28. Sutton, R.S., Barto, A.G.: Reinforcement Learning: An Introduction. MIT Press, Cambridge (1998, 2014)
29. System and method for knowledge pattern search from networked agents. US patent 8,903,756 (2014). https://www.google.com/patents/US8903756
30. The LANL cyber data (2017). https://csr.lanl.gov/data/cyber1/
31. Vapnik, V.: The Nature of Statistical Learning Theory. Springer, New York (2000)
32. Wager, S., Athey, S.: Estimation and inference of heterogeneous treatment effects using random forests. J. Am. Stat. Assoc. **113**(523), 1228–1242 (2018)
33. Wager, S., Athey, S.: Estimation and inference of heterogeneous treatment effects using random forests. J. Am. Stat. Assoc. (2018). https://doi.org/10.1080/01621459.2017.1319839
34. Watkins, C.: Learning from Delayed Rewards (PDF) (PhD thesis). King's College, Cambridge (1989)
35. Wright, P.G.: Tariff on Animal and Vegetable Oils. Macmillan Company, New York (1928)
36. Zhao, Y., MacKinnon, D.J., Gallup, S.P.: Big data and deep learning for understanding DoD data. J. Defense Softw. Eng. Spec. Issue Data Mining Metr. (2015)

Homology as an Adversarial Attack Indicator

Ira S. Moskowitz (ID), Nolan Bay, Brian Jalaian, and Arnold Tunick

Abstract In this paper we show how classical topological information can be automated with machine learning to lessen the threat of an adversarial attack. This paper is a proof of concept which lays the groundwork for future research in this area.

Keywords Homology · Topology · Handwritten digit recognition · Adverarial attack

1 Introduction

In this paper we show how classical topological information can be automated to lessen the threat of an adversarial attack. This paper is a proof of concept which lays the groundwork for future research in this area. We note that we take a step backwards from the current approach of Topological Data Analysis (TDA) [27] that uses persistent homology groups. Rather, we use the standard singular homology groups, and show how these groups relate to the modern work in persistent homology groups.

In [7] the authors showed how to apply the TDA technique of persistent homology to identifying the number 8 in the Modified National Institute of Standards and Technology (MNIST) data set of handwritten digits [19]. In [17] the authors discuss how to add persistent homological signatures into the training phase. Our approach is different. We show how topological information can be used after a machine learner classifies an image.

I. S. Moskowitz (✉) · N. Bay · B. Jalaian · A. Tunick
Information Management and Decision Architectures Branch, Naval Research Laboratory, Washington, DC, USA

U.S. Army Combat Capabilities Development Command, Army Research Laboratory, Adelphi, MD, USA
e-mail: ira.moskowitz@nrl.navy.mil

P. Dasgupta et al. (eds.), *Adversary-Aware Learning Techniques and Trends in Cybersecurity*, https://doi.org/10.1007/978-3-030-55692-1_9

We do not emphasize barcodes from persistent homology groups in this paper, rather we just use the first Betti number (rank of the first homology group with $\mathbb{Z}_2$ coefficients) to assist in identifying MNIST digits misclassified by a neural network (NN). It is our paradigm to start with the classical basics, and then build up to fancier, modern approaches.

Our approach is not meant to be the ultimate defense against adversarial attacks. Rather, the purpose of this paper is to examine a new technique in our arsenal of machine learning capabilities.

The contributions of this paper are:

- We show how to derive and use the first Betti number of an MNIST digit to detect certain adversarial attacks.
- We show how to relate the standard singular homology of an image to its persistent homology.
- Although our approach is not successful for all adversarial attacks, it gives a road map as to how to develop more advanced tools. In particular, we wish to use the more general approach of persistent homology in conjunction with the curvature of the image as a detection tool. We concentrate on three types of adversarial attacks using the Foolbox toolkit. The next section explains these attacks.

1.1 Why Topology?

Much of the data that neural networks attempt to classify is image data. Certainly the MNIST data that we are concerned with is image data. Mathematics has beaten neural networks to the punch in image classification by developing the field of Algebraic Topology, [24]. With the advent of high speed computers Algebraic Topology has been extended to the field of Topological Data Analysis, which includes Persistent Homology [14, 26, 27]. Therefore, it is natural to see if topology can assist with adversarial attacks.

2 Adversarial Attacks

In this section we review three of the gradient descent based methods of Adversarial Machine Learning (AML) used in our analysis (Table 1).

They are white-box because they have full access to the Deep Neural Network (DNN) that we trained on. Untargeted attacks attempt to fool, whereas targeted attacks fool in a specific manner. Gradient descent based methods utilize an optimization algorithm to minimize the loss function, i.e., $L = f(x - x')$, by iteratively stepping in the direction of steepest descent defined by the negative of the gradient. In AML, gradient descent is used to update the model weights. We do not discuss the forward derivatives approach, nor gradient-free optimization methods which involve black-box techniques, in this paper.

Table 1 Representative gradient descent based methods to generate adversarial attacks

Method	Black-box/white box	Targeted/untargeted
FGSM	White-box	Untargeted
PGD	White-box	Untargeted
BIM	White-box	Untargeted
DeepFool	White-box	Untargeted
Features Adversaries	White-box	Targeted
C-W	White-box	Targeted
EAD	White-box	Targeted, untargeted

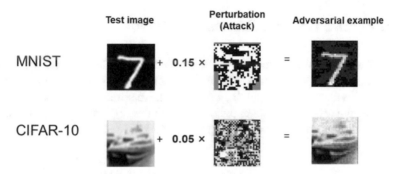

Fig. 1 A visualization of the FGSM attack for a selected MNIST and CIFAR10 image. The attack strengths are $\epsilon = 0.15$ and 0.05, respectively

2.1 Fast Gradient Sign Method (FGSM) [15]

This is a simple and popular method for generating adversarial examples. This approach modifies the image by using an algorithm based on the first-order gradient of the loss function using the L_∞ distortion metric, which uses the maximum difference between x and x' corresponding to the maximum changes in pixel values. The method is based on a simple equation involving the gradient ∇_x of the cost function $J(x)$:

$$x' = x + \epsilon \cdot sgn(\nabla_x J(f, \theta, x)), \tag{1}$$

where θ represents the parameters of the model f, and ϵ is a parameter controlling the magnitude of the perturbation introduced, and sgn is the sign of the value (or 0). Larger values of ϵ increase the likelihood that x' will be misclassified by f, but make the perturbation easier to detect visually. Figure 1 shows a visualization of the FGSM attack for selected MNIST [19] and CIFAR-10 [18] images. Note that the adversarial images appear distorted for FGSM.

Goodfellow et al. [15] discusses some defenses against this attack via a modified "adversarial" loss function.

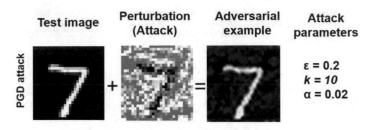

Fig. 2 A PGD attack for a selected MNIST image

2.2 Projected Gradient Descent (PGD) [20]

The PGD attack is similar to the FGSM attack but includes iterative steps when developing the adversarial attack. The PGD attack applies FGSM k times (number of iterations) with step-size $\alpha \leq \epsilon/k$, where ϵ is the maximum distortion (i.e., attack strength) of the adversarial example compared to the original input. The resulting adversarial example x^{t+1} corresponding to input x is:

$$x^{t+1} = \prod_{x+S}(x^t + \alpha sgn(\nabla_x J(f, \theta, x))), \tag{2}$$

where $\prod_{x+S}(\ldots)$ is the product operator that multiplies each successive adversarial example generated by adding the perturbation S to each data point x. A PGD attack is considered a first-order adversarial attack. These methods pick up on slight perturbations. Note that the modified inputs are visually indistinguishable from the originals. Figure 2 shows a visualization of the PGD attack for a selected MNIST [19].

2.3 Carlini-Wagner (C-W) [8]

The C-W targeted white-box attack generates an adversarial example such that given an input image x and any target classification T, it is possible to find a new input x' that is similar to x but is classified as T. The C-W attack generates low distortion adversarial examples that are almost always visually indistinguishable from the original input. Instead of generating adversarial examples based on the training loss, Carlini and Wagner [8] utilized an L_2-regularized loss function based on the logit layer of the DNN, i.e., the last neuron layer which produces the classification predictions. The distortion metric L_2 is defined as the root-mean-square distance between the input and the adversarial example. So far, the Carlini-Wagner attack is undefeated even though Papernot et al. [22] proposed a defensive distillation method to defend against most of the other adversarial attacks.

We also note that the C-W attack is capable of generating high-confidence adversarial examples, i.e., adversarial examples that are strongly misclassified by the DNN. To do this, Carlini and Wagner [8] define the loss function $g(x')$ for L_2 attacks as the maximum difference between the DNN softmax (confidence level) prediction for all of the classes other than the target, $Z(x')$ and the softmax prediction for the target class, $Z(x')_T$ scaled by the factor κ, i.e.,

$$g(x') = max(max Z(x')_i, i \neq T - Z(x')_T - \kappa), \tag{3}$$

where the parameter κ acts to modify the confidence score for the resulting adversarial output: the larger κ, the stronger the classification. In contrast, the results reported by Chen et al. [10] showed that target class probabilities could be less than 1%, albeit representing the top-1 prediction. Figure 3 illustrates a representative low distortion C-W adversarial example in comparison to representative FGSM and PGD adversarial examples.

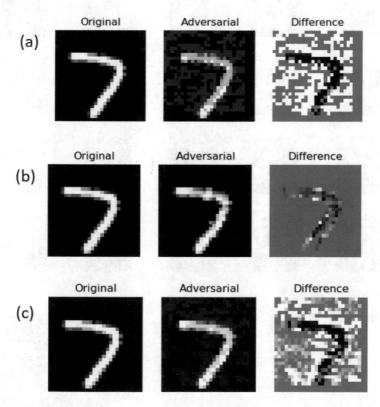

Fig. 3 Representative visual demonstrations of original input images and the adversarial examples/perturbations generated by (**a**) the FGSM attack, (**b**) the C-W attack, and (**c**) the PGD attack. C-W attacks have the least distortion

3   MNIST Dataset

This dataset [19] is a database of 60,000 28×28 grayscale images of the handwritten digits $\{0, 1, 2, 3, 4, 5, 6, 7, 8, 9\}$. Labels for the images are also part of the database. In Fig. 4 below are the first twenty images [11], displayed from left to right, top to bottom, and indexed 0–19 (i.e., starting with 0 in 4 rows $\times$ 5 columns for 20 images).

We concentrate on the 18th image (index 17), the only 8 number in Fig. 1, see Fig. 5.

This image only appears to have, as it should, two holes. However, this is a pixelated gray scale image of a hand written digit. Therefore, the pixel values are 0 only where there was no drawing. But we run into complications of hand movements

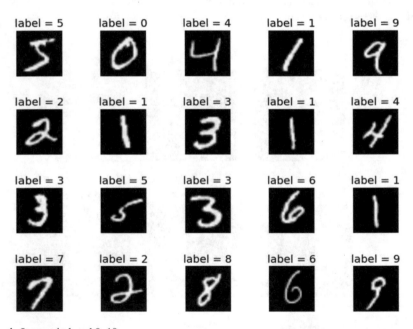

Fig. 4 Images indexed 0–19

Fig. 5 Image index 17, I_{17}

Fig. 6 $\mathscr{I}_{17}$: pixel value = 0 is white, pixel value > 0 is green

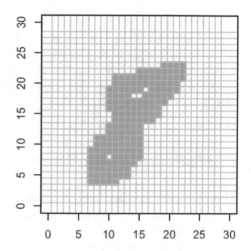

and quantization errors due to pixelations. For preliminary analysis, we say that a pixel is "empty", if its value is 0, elsewise it is said to be "colored" (pixel values between 1 and 255). (Please note that later in this paper we change this colored cutoff value to 64.) The image actually has three holes as we explain.

In Fig. 6 we consider the same image where we mapped every pixel value greater than 0 to 255, and 0 to 0. Thus, we separated the empty from colored pixels. In Fig. 6 one can easily see the three holes.

Due to the quantization error when we pixelate an image we make the following assumption: We associate a topological space (defined below) $\mathscr{I}_j$ to an MNIST image I_j as a subspace of $\mathbb{R}^2$ as follows (the process is modeled by the fact that the image is a quantized representation of an actual hand-drawn numeral):

For guidance, but not part of $\mathscr{I}_j$, we imagine a grid over the $[.5, 28.5] \times [.5, 28.5]$ subspace of $\mathbb{R}^2$ to aid in the visualization. If a pixel (i, j) is colored we assume that the entire grid square $SQ_{i,j} = [i - \frac{1}{2}, i + \frac{1}{2}] \times [j - \frac{1}{2}, j + \frac{1}{2}]$ is part of X. We define our topological space as

$$\mathscr{I}_j := \cup_{(i,j) \text{is colored}} SQ_{i,j}$$

which corresponds to what appears on the computer monitor, with respect to pixels.

(Note, we do not distinguish between connected components in this paper. It is a nonissue for us. However, for persistent homology it is important and gives rise to many barcodes for the dimension 0 homology.) Thus, we see that corners of colored pixel squares are part of $\mathscr{I}_j$ and can separate holes. This is illustrated in Fig. 6 where there are three holes—the top two are separate holes. We see that $\mathscr{I}_{17}$ has three holes–the lower hole which consists of one pixel, the uppermost hole of one pixel, and a middle hole of two horizontal holes. Under our assumption there is a corner point in green keeping the two holes from becoming one. Figure 6 is Fig. 5 with pixel value 0 equated to white, and pixel value greater than 0 to green, and a grid for visual use only. From singular homology theory (see the next section) in algebraic topology [24] we have that $H_1(\mathscr{I}_j; \mathbb{Z}_2) = \mathbb{Z}_2 \oplus \mathbb{Z}_2 \oplus \mathbb{Z}_2$. Thus, the first Betti number $\beta_1 = 3$, which of course, in lay terms is the number of holes. We introduce the concept of Betti numbers to lay the groundwork for our future research which will involve more complicated spaces, and to show how our work relates to that of persistent homology theory [27]. For simplicity, we will restrict ourselves to simply the number of holes β_1.

4 Algebraic Topology Review

There are many standard texts in this area (e.g., [16, 24]). In this paper we will not go into the details of (singular) homology theory. We will assume that the reader is either familiar with, or willing to accept, certain basic principles. This is a non-trivial subject that has taken many years to mature [12].

The precursor to homology theory is homotopy theory, which is a bit easier to visualize. Also, there are ways to interpret homotopic information as homological information.

Homotopy and homology theory are both parts of algebraic topology. We concentrate on homology in this paper. Algebraic topology assigns algebraic information to topological spaces as a means to distinguish the topological spaces. By this we mean that spaces with different algebraic information cannot be homeomorphic (topologically the same). Homotopy is concerned with being able to continuously deform loops (continuous map of the circle S^1 into the topological space). If the topological space is $\mathbb{R}^2$, and we fix a base point x, we see that any two loops at x are homotopic. However, if we let our topological space be $\mathbb{R}^2 - B(0, 1)$ (the plane with the open ball of radius 1 about the origin removed), we see that $\mathbb{R}^2 - B(0, 1)$ behaves very differently from $\mathbb{R}^2$. Any loop that goes around the open ball cannot be continuously deformed to the constant loop (the additive identity 0 loop) that continuously maps S^1 to x. In fact we see the loop that goes around once is not "homotopic" to the loop that goes around twice, or three times, or goes around in the other direction (the - loop), etc. This leads us to the calculation of the first homotopy group π_1 of a topological space. Note that a (hollow) torus $T^2 = S^1 \times S^1$ has inner and outer circles whose loops form subgroups isomorphic to $\mathbb{Z}$, see Fig. 7.

In the next subsection we give a quick review of homology theory, which is more complicated than homotopy theory. Before doing that we note though that there is a nice relationship between the first homotopy and homology groups. Given a group G, the notation $[G, G]$ denotes the commutator subgroup of G.

Theorem 1 (Hurewicz Isomorphism Theorem [24]) *If X is connected then the first homology group (with $\mathbb{Z}$ coefficients), $H_1(X) \cong \frac{\pi_1(X)}{[\pi_1(X),\pi_1(X)]}$.*

In other words $H_1(X)$ is the Abel-ization of $\pi_1(X)$.

Note we have:

$$\pi_1(\mathbb{R}^2) \cong 0$$

Fig. 7 T^2

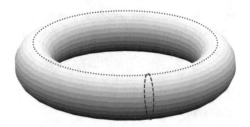

$$\pi_1(\mathbb{R}^2 - B(0, 1)) \cong \mathbb{Z}$$

$$\pi_1(T^2) \cong \mathbb{Z} \oplus \mathbb{Z}.$$

4.1 Homology

Homology involves continuous maps of simplices into the topological space X and the study of graded chain complexes. As mentioned above we just touch on the subject. An *n-simplex* Δ^n is the generalization of a triangle (2-simplex) and tetrahedron (3-simplex) to higher dimensions. We always give a simplex an orientation based on an orientation of the vertices, $[v_0, v_1, \ldots, v_n]$, and its lower dimensional faces (subsets of the vertices) inherit this orientation. A singular n-simplex σ_n is a continuous map

$$\sigma_n : \Delta^n \to X$$

We can add and subtract these maps to form a free Abelian group (with coefficients from a ring such as $\mathbb{R}$, $\mathbb{Z}$, or as we will use later, $\mathbb{Z}_2$, etc.) denoted as $C_n(X)$, with the elements of this group called n-chains. This is graded by n. There is a graded homomorphism map called the boundary map [24] (we ignore ∂_0)

$$\partial_n : C_n(X) \to C_{n-1}(X)$$

and is the linear operator derived by extending on the oriented simplex $[v_0, v_1, \ldots, v_n]$

$$\partial_n([v_0, v_1, \ldots, v_n] = \sum_{i=0}^{q}(-1)^i[v_0, v_1, \ldots, \hat{v}_i, \ldots, v_n], \text{ the } i\text{th vertex is removed}$$

The boundary map is the restricting of the singular simplex to the faces of Δ^n with the proper orientation. The elements of C_n that map to 0 under ∂_n are called the cycles and denoted as $Z_n(X)$. The images in C_n from ∂_{n+1} are called boundaries. Note that the composition map $\partial_n \circ \partial_{n+1}$ is the zero homomorphism, because of the simplex orientations. Thus, every boundary is a cycle. We then form the factor group (or ring module) with the coefficients from the given ring,

$$H_n(X; R) := Z_n(X)/B_n(X)$$

If the coefficients are $\mathbb{Z}$, one can view $H_1(X)$ as the commutative part of $\pi_1(X)$. This gives us

$$H_1(\mathbb{R}^2; \mathbb{Z}) \cong 0$$

$$H_1(\mathbb{R}^2 - B(0, 1); \mathbb{Z}) \cong \mathbb{Z}$$

$$H_1(T^2; \mathbb{Z}) \cong \mathbb{Z} \oplus \mathbb{Z}$$

Note For the rest of this paper we set the ring of coefficients to be $\mathbb{Z}_2$ and no longer denote it. The above easily tells us that

$$H_1(\mathbb{R}^2) \cong 0$$

$$H_1(\mathbb{R}^2 - B(0, 1)) \cong \mathbb{Z}_2$$

$$H_1(T^2) \cong \mathbb{Z}_2 \oplus \mathbb{Z}_2$$

What is especially important to us is the rank of $H_n(X)$, we define this to be the n-th Betti number β_n. Thus, we have:

$$\beta_1(\mathbb{R}^2) = 0$$

$$\beta_1(\mathbb{R}^2 - B(0, 1)) = 1$$

$$\beta_1(T^2) = 2$$

The lowest Betti number β_0 counts the number of connected components of X. Therefore for the three spaces above $\beta_0 = 1$. For the three spaces above one can show that $\beta_n, n > 2 = 0$ and that

$$\beta_2(\mathbb{R}^2) = 0$$

$$\beta_2(\mathbb{R}^2 - B(0, 1)) = 0$$

$$\beta_2(T^2) = 1 \ .$$

Definition 1 (Working, But Not Technical Definition, See [24] for Details) We say that topological spaces X and Y are **homotopy equivalent** if one space can be continuously pulled, stretched, squashed, etc. (but not ripped!) into the other space and vice versa.

Theorem 2 *Homotopy equivalent spaces have isomorphic homology and homology groups [24].*

Proof This follows from the functorial view of the category of topological spaces and continuous maps being mapped into the category of groups and homomorphisms.

Note $\mathbb{R}^2$ is homotopy equivalent to a 0-dimensional point, $\mathbb{R}^2 - B(0,1)$ is homotopy equivalent to a 1-dimensional circle, but the torus is a nice compact (closed and bounded) 2-dimensional manifold.

We see that the Betti numbers are a very good way to distinguish topological spaces (up to homotopy type).

One can see that X_{17}, which is the topological space associated to $\mathscr{I}_{17}$, is homotopy equivalent to K^3 illustrated Fig. 8 below (which is homotopy equivalent to $S^1 \vee S^1 \vee S^1$). The fundamental group $\pi_1(S^1 \vee S^1 \vee S^1) \cong \mathbb{Z} * \mathbb{Z} * \mathbb{Z}$, which is the triple free product of $\mathbb{Z}$. Thus, $\pi_1(X_{17}) \cong \mathbb{Z} * \mathbb{Z} * \mathbb{Z}$.

By the Hurewicz theorem we can easily show that

$$H_1(X_{17}) \equiv \mathbb{Z}_2 \oplus \mathbb{Z}_2 \oplus \mathbb{Z}_2 \, .$$

Now that we have a background in homology theory let us proceed to persistent homology theory. We must use a different homology theory though called "simplicial homology". Simplicial homology can be calculated by a machine [26, Ch. 7], and interestingly it is an historical predecessor to (singular) homology theory.

After Sect. 5 we return to our discussion of algebraic topology. In that section we show how the concept of holes is a special case of persistent homology characteristics, and discuss how to use persistent homology as a better discriminator of adversarial attacks.

4.1.1 (Abstract) Simplicial Complex

Originally, algebraic topology broke a space up into a combination of generalizations of the n-simplex. What mattered were the vertices and edges, or faces of the

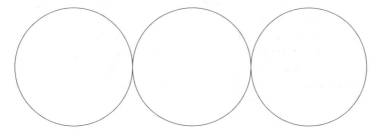

Fig. 8 K^3: three kissing circles

simplex, not the lengths. This leads to an abstraction called the simplicial complex (what follows is from [24]).

Definition 2 A **simplicial complex** K consists of a set $\{v\}$ of vertices and a set $\{s\}$ of finite nonempty subsets of $\{v\}$ called simplices such that

- Any set consisting of exactly one vertex is a simplex.
- Any nonempty subset of a simplex is a simplex.

A simplex s containing exactly $q + 1$ vertices is called a q-simplex (or dimension q). If $s' \subset s$, then s' is a face of s.

Note, we are concerned with simplicial complexes in the plane $\mathbb{R}^2$, thus our simplices of dimension higher than 2 are squashed down to the plane, but it is their abstract qualities that we are interested in. Also note that we supply an orientation to each simplex by ordering the vertices.

4.2 Holes

We are interested in the number of holes in $\mathscr{I}_j$. Since we are dealing with homology with $\mathbb{Z}_2$ coefficients and all the topological spaces $\mathscr{I}_j$ are simple combinations of filled in, or blank, pixel blocks, it suffices just to be concerned with the rank, that is the Betti number, of $H_1(\mathscr{I}_j)$ for now.

It turns out that determining the number of holes is not a complex task, there is existing code [1, 2, 4] which we modify for our means. Basically, we move the filter $\begin{pmatrix} 0\ 1\ 0 \\ 1\ 1\ 1 \\ 0\ 1\ 0 \end{pmatrix}$ over the image which picks out the left, right, up, down, but not diagonal paths, that connects the holes. Note (that our code swaps 0 with 1, and) we do not use images that touch the boundary. We can easily get around the boundary condition by enlarging our images to 29×29, but we choose not to for the proof of concept in this paper.

Note we could have directly gone to holes, without discussing homology theory. However, this would not tie in with the general approach of using TDA to assist in neural net analysis of images. Later in the paper we will show how the hole counting that we perform is in fact a special case of persistent homology.

We assign any pixel value less than 64 to zero and the others to a non-zero value. Our algorithm counts the number of connected components of zero, via the left, right, up, down paradigm. Since there is one component exterior to the image, we subtract one from the total count (this is why we do not allow the image to touch the boundary of the 28×28 space).

5   Adversarial Attack Using Foolbox

We describe our method on adversarial learning using the Foolbox toolkit with the Fast Gradient Sign Method (FGSM). The Foolbox C-W and Foolbox PGD attacks follow by adjusting the code (see the comments in our included code—note we use the default parameters of Foolbox). Our approach worked well on FGSM as we will show. However, when we used a more sophisticated adversarial attack such as the C-W or the PGD method our results were no better than a random guess. This is not to say that our method only works on simple adversarial attacks. Rather, simply counting holes is not complex enough, and a richer topological structure is called for and/or adjustments to the gradient descent/back propagation algorithms. This is not totally surprising to us and we are researching more sophisticated topological methods using persistent homology theory. The final section of this paper shows how our holes method is actually a persistent homology approach, but only within certain parameters.

We start by training an 8-layer (including the input layer, see the code Finalconvolutionalnetdefault.py in the Appendix) convolutional neural net (CNN) [6] with the standard training set of 60,000 MNIST images, with another 10,000 set aside for testing.

This discussion centers around Foolbox, with the other attacks summarized later. First we modify Foolbox code, ver. 1.8.0 [23]. Note, we use [3] in conjunction with [5] via

```
foolbox.attacks.GradientSignAttack(model=None,
 ↪   criterion=<foolbox.criteria.
Misclassification object>,distance=<class
 ↪   'foolbox.distances.MeanSquaredDistance'>,

 threshold=None).
```

- We run `Finalconvolutionalnet.default.py` saving the model to `model1.json` and its weights to `model1_weights.h5`. We ran this for 5 epochs which suffices for a very high accuracy on both the training and test data. This code has options for the different adversarial attacks, along with other items not discussed in this paper.
- We then run `FinalAttack.py`. This uses, from above, the model and weights of the training data and attempts to create adversarial images from the test data (10,000 images). But first, our code goes through all of the MNIST training data (60,000 images) and removes the few MNIST images that touch the boundary, this is our *filtered training data*. This is done to facilitate our hole counting algorithm, which is also in this code. Our cut-off for hole counting is now shifted from what we originally discussed as being 1 to pixel value 64. This is done to remove most of the noise from the adversarial attacks later in the code. For each digit d, we find the sample conditional probability $P(i|d)$, where i is the number of holes ranging from 0 to 7 by simply counting. Therefore,

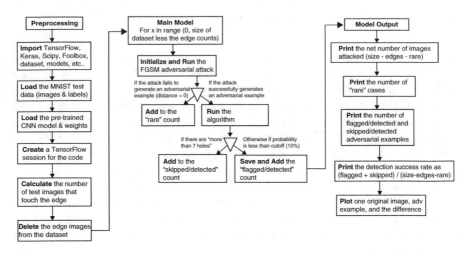

Fig. 9 Flowchart

Fig. 10 Training Data for a representative run

we have the sample conditional distributions from the filtered training data $P(H|d); i = 0, \ldots, 7; d = 0, \ldots, 9$ (note we never have more than 7 holes).

- We first ignore the images in test data that touch the edges (101 images), leaving us with a *filtered test set* of 9899 images. We now go image by image in the filtered test set and generate adversarial images. For each adversarial image that exists we calculate the number of holes (if the adversarial image has more than 7 holes, we mark it as suspect and stop analysis on it, and move onto the next adversarial image). If this adversarial digit is classified as d', and has i' holes, we now use Bayes' formula on the filtered training data to generate the conditional probability $P(d'|i')$. The reason we swap the conditional probabilities is that this gives us a base to compare probabilities from.

- If $P(d'|i') < .10$, (experimentation showed this to be a good value) we flag this image as suspect. By dividing the sum of the adversarial images with more than 7 holes and those with probability less than .10, we arrive at a probability of suspect adversarial image of approximately 2/3. Note, that there are no images with more than 7 holes, so we do not run that test. See Figs. 9, 10, and 11.

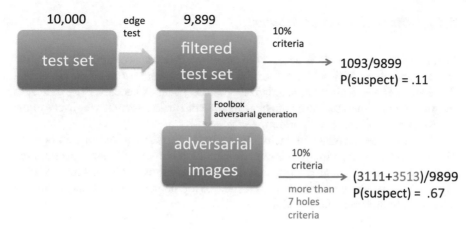

Fig. 11 Test Data for a representative run

	# of adversarial examples had prob's of <10%	skipped	sum/9899
1	3111	3513	66.9%
2	3582	2869	65.2%
3	4032	2289	63.9%
4	3219	3993	72.9%
5	3621	3194	68.8%
6	3239	4290	76.1%
7	3351	3059	64.8%
8	3652	2752	64.7%
9	3603	2633	63.0%
10	3340	4064	74.8%
Sample Mean :	3475	3265.6	68.11
Sample Variance:	75339.6	455552.5	23.2
Sample standard deviation	274.5	674.9	4.8

Fig. 12 Results for representative runs of our code using the Foolbox FGSM adversarial attack

Figure 12 shows the results of ten runs. On average, we pick up 68% of the Foolbox FGSM adversarial attacks. Granted this is not that high a percentage, but it is an improvement over a random guess.

5.1 Other Adversarial Attacks

When we run a Foolbox C-W adversarial attack we detect approximately 50% of the attacks, and about 51% with Foolbox PGD. (Attacks were run multiple times and these are averages with small standard deviations.) This is because FGSM distorts the image more than the other attacks. In the conclusion section we discuss how Gaussian noise affects the algorithm.

Note, we experimented with including the hole values as part of the training data. However with a 28×28 image this extra information is not important to the training. Our next step is to change the gradient descent algorithms in the back propagation algorithm to weight them heavily with respect to topological information, and to use additional homological information.

6 Persistent Homology

We will develop some of the machinery of persistent homology, and then show that the hole counting that we do corresponds to a certain range of the ranks of the first persistent homology groups. This lays the groundwork for vastly extending our topological approach to deep neural net machine learning.

6.1 What Is Persistent Homology

Persistent homology [25–27] is concerned with algebraic topology features that are born and die, it sees how certain features may, or may not persist—this is given by barcodes [14]. That is if something is born at 1 and dies at 3, it contributes the interval [1, 3] to the barcode plot.

One must keep in mind when dealing with algebraic topology that there is the modern singular viewpoint as discussed in Sect. 4 above. However, this is not the way algebraic topology developed. It developed by cutting a space up into fundamental geometric pieces, such as simplicial (or CW) complexes. What is amazing is that the different theories all give the same results. This is because the singular approach we used above is the modern refinement of many years of research in the area [12, 16]. Now however, we will take a step backwards and look at simplicial complexes via the work of Ghrist [14] on Vietoris-Rips complexes and barcodes. Note that in general, persistent and simplicial homology give very different answers. An exception is our theorem below.

Figure 13 illustrates a Vietoris-Rips complex where the distances between D, C, and E are less than ϵ, the distance between C and A is less than ϵ, and all other distances are greater than ϵ. We form four 1-simplices, and one 2-simplex. This information can be lossy compressed into a birth death diagram as given in Fig. 14.

Fig. 13 Illustration of
Vietoris-Rips Complex with
parameter ϵ

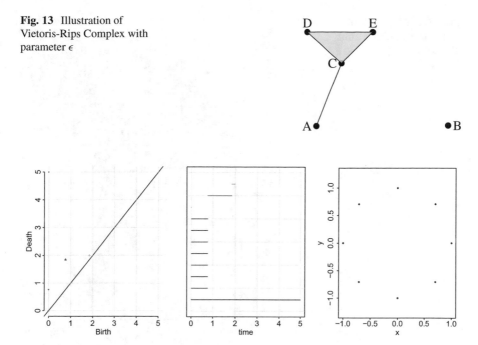

Fig. 14 Birth death diagram, barcode, point cloud

As discussed by [13] "Each horizontal bar shows the lifetime of a topological feature as a function of ϵ for the homology groups ... Significant features have long horizontal bars. ... The birth and death times of the barcode become the x- and y-coordinate of the persistence diagram. ... "

For us a *point cloud* P is a finite set of points in $\mathbb{R}^2$. Now, following [9], and using the fact that P inherits the natural metric from $\mathbb{R}^2$:

Definition 3 The **Vietoris-Rips complex** for P, with parameter $t \geq 0$, denoted $VR(P, t)$, is the simplicial complex whose vertex set is P. A collection of $q + 1$ distinct points X spans a q-simplex iff $d(x_\alpha, x_\beta) \leq t$, for any $x_\alpha, x_\beta \in X$.

The parameter t above is our *persistence parameter* (some authors use ϵ). We see that as t grows the simplicial complex changes, it is stable for awhile and then changes. We assume that the simplicial complex is oriented and use the boundary map ∂_q to calculate the homology groups of $VR(P, t)$, and denote them as $H(P, t)$. Thus we have $H_0(P, t), H_1(P, t), \ldots$. The rank of $H_i(P, t)$ is the ith Betti number $\beta_i(t)$ at parameter t and tells us how many generators we have of $H_i(P, t)$. We now form the persistence diagram by plotting the life span of the generators with a horizontal axis of t and a vertical axis going from the 0th to the last homology group of interest.

By looking at a pixelated black and white image we see that (note we ignore H_0 which just counts connected components) generators of H_1 can only be born for

Fig. 15 A Blue and White scaled 64 cut-off of the fifth MNIST digit

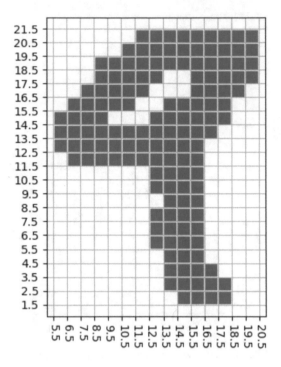

values $\sqrt{2}, 2, \ldots$, which is based on the distance between the pixel coordinates. If a generator for our black and white MNIST (scaled at < 64) digit is born before 1.5 and dies after 1.5 it corresponds to an actual generator of the simplicial H_1. This also holds for barcodes containing the interval $(\sqrt{2}, 2)$. Thus we have a theorem equating persistent and singular homology in certain cases.

Theorem 3 *For the black and white pixelated image the rank of the first homology group is the same as the number of dimension-1 barcodes born before 1.5 and dying after 1.5*

This discussion is only outlined. Its purpose is to show how we can go from using holes to detect adversarial attacks to using more sophisticated techniques such as barcodes from persistent homology.

In Fig. 15 we see how 1-cycles start at distance 1, and become boundaries by distance 3 (center of pixels is where distance is measured from). Thus, as homological information they are born at 1 and die at 3, thus this contributes the interval [1, 3] to the barcode plot and corresponds to the point (1, 3) in the birth death diagram (Fig. 16).

The first Betti number is 1, which corresponds (point at (1,3)) to the only H_1 born before 1.5 with death after 1.5.

Fig. 16 Birth death diagram
of the fifth MNIST digit in
question

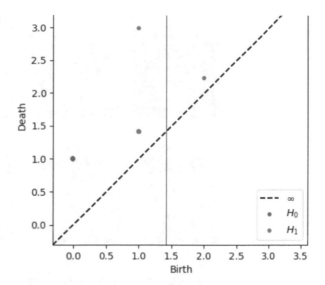

7   Conclusion and Future Work

In terms of Topology: we showed how calculating a topological invariant, derived
from singular homology theory, can be easily calculated via a simple hole counting
algorithm. We show how this can also be calculated from persistent homology, and
thus instead of using just this one invariant we have a wide range of indicators from
barcodes and birth death diagrams. We did not go into the details in this paper of how
the computer finds persistent homology groups. Due to their simplicial structure
they are actually calculated via matrix manipulation algorithms [26, Ch. 7] which a
machine can quickly and easily deal with.

In terms of Deep Neural Networks: our method did well against an FGSM attack,
but not against C-W or PGD. We note that C-W and PGD attacks do not distort
the image as much as FGSM attacks. Furthermore, by just adding Gaussian noise
as a Foolbox option we were able to get a very high (80%) false alarm rate. Of
course the Gaussian noise greatly distorts the image (see Fig. 17). Our topological
approach has to be extended to detect more subtle image changes. This is why we
feel that extending simplicial homology calculations (holes) to persistent homology
will detect these more subtle changes. We will perform experiments in future work
to see if this hypothesis is correct.

We conclude with Fig. 17 showing the impact of FGSM, C-W, PGD and added
Gaussian noise on an MNIST image via the Foolbox toolkit.

A future consideration is to incorporate holes as part of the gradient descent/back
propagation algorithms by changing that algorithm so it emphasized information
from holes. The other approach is, as we discussed, to widen the field of topological
information that we are using. Our approach can be modified to use the full power of
persistent homology. We only used the range where the persistent homology agreed

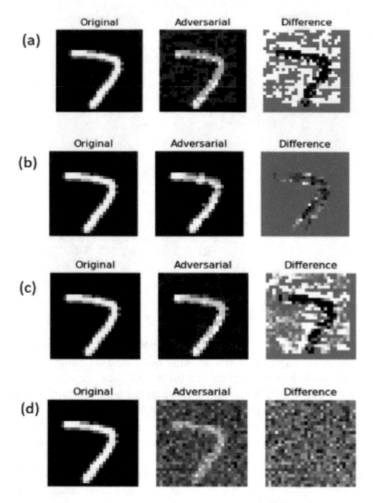

Fig. 17 Representative visual demonstrations of original input images and the adversarial examples/perturbations generated by (**a**) the FGSM attack, (**b**) the C-W attack, (**c**) the PGD attack, and (**d**) adding Gaussian noise

with the actual homology. Hopefully using the full spectrum of the Betti numbers will enable us to improve upon defenses against adversarial C-W attacks.

Aside from improving the algorithm by not just using one cut-off value for hole detection we need to test it on other related databases. One such database is the Street View House Numbers dataset [21], which will be the subject of a future study.

Acknowledgments We thank Zhuming Ai, Paulita Ball, Sophie Cissé, Prithviraj Dasgupta and Rish Heilizer for their assistance and helpful discussions. We very much appreciate the thorough and helpful reviews given to this paper.

Appendix

Listing 1: Finalconvolutionalnetdefault.py

```python
#tensorflow library/package that makes it easy to get a neural net running
import tensorflow as tf
#keras implementation on top of tensorflow to create the model and add layers
from tensorflow.keras import datasets, layers, models

#package for plotting the mnist images
import matplotlib.pyplot as plt
#import numpy to be able to access the mnist arrays
import numpy as np
#import the mnist dataset
from keras.datasets import mnist
#import the type of keras model that will be used
from keras.models import Sequential
#import the type of keras layers that will be used
from keras.layers.core import Dense, Activation
#import keras Gradient descent function
from keras.optimizers import SGD
from keras.utils import np_utils


#for saving the model after use
import json

#importing the MNIST dataset
(X_train, y_train),(X_test,y_test)=mnist.load_data()

#plotting MNIST image example
plt.imshow(X_train[0].reshape(28,28))

#code if you wanted to save a numpy array as a .csv file
#np.savetxt('newArr2.csv',X_train[0].reshape(28,28),fmt='%1.0f',delimiter = ',')

#reshape or flatten the mnist dataset to prep it for model input
X_train=X_train.reshape((60000,28,28,1))
X_test=X_test.reshape((10000,28,28,1))

#normalize all values to between 0 and 1
X_train, X_test = X_train/ 255.0, X_test/255.0

#Model starts here
#First, create a sequential keras model using the tensorflow framework
model = models.Sequential()
#first convolutional layer, which applies 32 3x3 filters that iterate over
#each image looking for features
model.add(layers.Conv2D(32, (3,3), activation='relu', input_shape=(28,28,1)))
#max pooling layer shrinks the image by pooling regions and taking the regions largest value
model.add(layers.MaxPooling2D((2,2)))
#applying the second convolutional layer, which applies even more filters for more
#detailed feature detection
model.add(layers.Conv2D(64,(3,3),activation='relu'))
#final pooling and convolutional layers are applied
model.add(layers.MaxPooling2D((2,2)))
model.add(layers.Conv2D(64,(3,3), activation='relu'))
#you are left with 64 3x3images, that are then flattened into a vector of shape 1x576 before
#going through densely connected hidden layer
model.add(layers.Flatten())
#first dense hidden layer
model.add(layers.Dense(64, activation='relu'))
#output layer. softmax activation is a probability distribution;all 10 neurons must sum to 1.
#highest value neuron is chosen as the models prediction
model.add(layers.Dense(10, activation='softmax'))

#to visualize all the layers in the model
model.summary()

#compiling the model for training and testing
model.compile(optimizer='adam',
              loss='sparse_categorical_crossentropy',
              metrics=['accuracy'])
#plot the model training as it goes
history = model.fit(X_train, y_train, epochs=5, validation_data=(X_test, y_test), shuffle=True)

#testing the model on the test data after the training is completed
test_loss, test_acc = model.evaluate(X_test, y_test)

#list of model predictions that were wrong, just to see which images it messes up on
predictions=model.predict(X_test)
wrongindex=[]
for i in range(0,len(X_test)):
    compare = np.argmax(predictions[i])
    if(compare!=y_test[i]):
        wrongindex.append(i)
```

```
# code to visualize the training history and test history of the model, seeing
#how fast it "learned" the data
'''
print(history.history.keys())
# summarize history for accuracy
plt.plot(history.history['acc'])
plt.plot(history.history['val_acc'])
plt.title('model accuracy')
plt.ylabel('accuracy')
plt.xlabel('epoch')
plt.legend(['train', 'test'], loc='upper left')
plt.show()
# summarize history for loss
plt.plot(history.history['loss'])
plt.plot(history.history['val_loss'])

plt.title('model loss')
plt.ylabel('loss')
plt.xlabel('epoch')
plt.legend(['train', 'test'], loc='upper left')
plt.show() '''

#for saving the model for future use
model.save('convdefault.h5')
json.dump({'model1': model.to_json()}, open("model1.json", "w"))
model.save weights("model1 weights.h5")
```

Listing 2: FinalAttack.py

```python
from __future__ import absolute_import, division, print_function, unicode_literals
import tensorflow as tf
from tensorflow.keras import datasets, layers, models
import matplotlib.pyplot as plt
# from __future__ import print_function
import numpy as np
from keras.datasets import mnist
from keras.models import Sequential
from keras.layers.core import Dense, Activation
from keras.optimizers import SGD
from keras.utils import np_utils
import numpy as np
import pandas as pd
import array as arr
from scipy.ndimage.measurements import label
from keras.models import load_model
from PIL import Image
import matplotlib.pyplot as plt
from sklearn import datasets
import os
import cv2
import random
import keras
from foolbox.attacks import FGSM
from foolbox.attacks.iterative_projected_gradient import ProjectedGradientDescentAttack
from foolbox.attacks.carlini_wagner import CarliniWagnerL2Attack
from foolbox.criteria import Misclassification
from keras import backend
import foolbox
import json
from foolbox.criteria import TargetClassProbability
from foolbox.criteria import TargetClass
from foolbox.distances import MeanSquaredDistance
from foolbox.distances import Linfinity


#p(numholes|zero)
zerozero=.072
onezero=.865
twozero=.051
threezero=.009
fourzero=.002
fivezero=.001
sixzero=.001
sevenzero=0

#p(numholes|ones)
zeroone=.995
oneone=.005
twoone=0
threeone=0
fourone=0
fiveone=0
sixone=0
sevenone=0

#p(numholes|two)
zerotwo=.563
onetwo=.364
twotwo=.061
threetwo=.01
fourtwo=.001
fivetwo=.001
sixtwo=0
seventwo=0

#p(numholes|three)
zerothree=.904
onethree=.082
twothree=.012
threethree=.002
fourthree=0
fivethree=0
sixthree=0
seventhree=0

#p(numholes|four)
zerofour=.867
onefour=.111
twofour=.019
threefour=.002
fourfour=0
fivefour=0
sixfour=0
sevenfour=0
```

```
#p(numholes|five)
zerofive=.916
onefive=.076
twofive=.007
threefive=.001
fourfive=0
fivefive=0
sixfive=0
sevenfive=0

#p(numholes|six)
zerosix=.162
onesix=.645
twosix=.145
threesix=.034
foursix=.01
fivesix=.004
sixsix=0
sevensix=0

#p(numholes|seven)
zeroseven=.964
oneseven=.033
twoseven=.002
threeseven=0
fourseven=0
fiveseven=0
sixseven=0
sevenseven=0

#p(numholes|eight)
zeroeight=.026
oneeight=.231
twoeight=.609
threeeight=.107
foureight=.022
fiveeight=.004
sixeight=.001
seveneight=0

#p(numholes|nine)
zeronine=.136
onenine=.728
twonine=.112
threenine=.020
fournine=.004
fivenine=.001
sixnine=0
sevennine=0

#p(num)
probzero=.1
probone=.11
probtwo=.1
probthree=.1
probfour=.1
probfive=.09
probsix=.1
probseven=.1
probeight=.1
probnine=.1

#p(numholes)
zeroholes=.561
oneholes=.313
twoholes=.102
threeholes=.018
fourholes=.004
fiveholes=.001
sixholes=0
sevenholes=0
'''
checkedges: Code that marks images that have pixels that touch the edge of the image,
which would split up the
image into two sides and over-count the correct number of holes.

Checks edge rows and columns to see if any item has the value '0',
which is the value assigned to pixels
that make up the drawing of the number. 1's represent holes.
'''
```

```
touching=0
def checkedges(a):
    rows=a.shape[0]
    cols=a.shape[1]
    #print("checking top row")
    for i in range(0,cols):
        if a[0,i]==0:
            global touching
            touching+=1
            break
    else:
        #print("checking leftmost column")
        for i in range(0,rows):
            if a[i,0]==0:
                touching+=1
                break
        else:
            #print("checking rightmost column")
            for i in range(0,cols):
                if a[i,cols-1]==0:
                    touching+=1
                    break
            else:
                #print("checking bottom row")
                for i in range(0,rows):
                    if a[rows-1,i]==0:
                        touching+=1
                        break
    return

'''runvalidation: function that calculates the number of holes in an adversarial image and
determines how likely an adversarial image is what the predicted label is given
the number of holes the image has.
if this probability is low, it means that the classification by the network
is most likely wrong.
in this example, every classification is wrong, we are just testing to see how
many examples we can flag '''
def runvalidation(adversarial, predict):
    #label that the network gave the adversarial image(which is the wrong label)
    fakelabel=predict
    #adversarial image resizing and rescaling back to a normal MNIST image
    a = adversarial.reshape(28,28)
    a=a*255

    #If the value of a given pixel is less than 64 (on a scale of 0-255),
    #it sets the value to 0, otherwise its a 1
    #normalizes all values of the matrix to either a 0 or a 1.
    b=np.where(a<64,0,1)
    #see noom.csv for how the matrix looks after it has been updated
    np.savetxt('noom.csv',b,fmt='%1.0f',delimiter = ',')

    f=pd.read_csv("noom.csv", sep=",",header=None)
    x=f.values

    #swapping the 0s and ones now.
    xs=np.where(x==1,-3,0)
    xn=np.where(xs==0,1,-3)
    xb=np.where(xn==-3,0,1)

    #P=np.ones((3, 3), dtype=np.int)
    #ncomponents is the same thing as the number of holes
    labeled, ncomponents = label(xb)#, P)
    holes=ncomponents-1
    #returning string with word representation of how many holes there
    #were (ie. 0 holes returns 'zero')
    numholes= findprob(holes)
    #returns a string with word representation of what the image's label
    #is (ie. label 7 returns 'seven')
    numlabels=findlabel(fakelabel)

    #in cases where the adversarial image generates too much noise, and thus too
    #many holes, we have to skip these
    #because our probability equation will not work with more than 7 holes
    if numholes=="more_than_seven":
        global skipped
        skipped+=1
        return 1
        #print("image had too much noise, and more than seven holes, cannot calculate
        #a probability")
    else:
        if eval(numholes+"holes")==0:
            return 0
        else:
            #equation p(label|numholes) is calculated, using the variables we assigned
            #at the very top of the code
            return ((eval(numholes+numlabels))*(eval("prob"+numlabels)))/(eval(numholes+"holes"))
```

```python
def findprob(holes):
    if holes==0:
        return "zero"
    elif holes==1:
        return "one"
    elif holes==2:
        return "two"
    elif holes==3:
        return "three"
    elif holes ==4:
        return "four"
    elif holes==5:
        return "five"
    elif holes==6:
        return "six"
    elif holes==7:
        return "seven"
    else:
        return "more_than_seven"


def findlabel(fakelabel):
    if fakelabel==0:
        return "zero"
    elif fakelabel==1:
        return "one"
    elif fakelabel==2:
        return "two"
    elif fakelabel==3:
        return "three"
    elif fakelabel==4:
        return "four"
    elif fakelabel==5:
        return "five"
    elif fakelabel==6:
        return "six"
    elif fakelabel==7:
        return "seven"
    elif fakelabel==8:
        return "eight"
    elif fakelabel==9:
        return "nine"
'''Noise Parameters
-----------
image : ndarray
    Input image data. Will be converted to float.
mode : str
    One of the following strings, selecting the type of noise to add:

    'gauss'      Gaussian-distributed additive noise.
    'poisson'    Poisson-distributed noise generated from the data.
    's&p'        Replaces random pixels with 0 or 1.
    'speckle'    Multiplicative noise using out = image + n*image, where
                 n is uniform noise with specified mean & variance.'''


def noisy(noise_typ, image):
    if noise_typ == "gauss":
        #print(image.shape)
        row, col, ch= image.shape
        mean = 0
        var = 0.1
        sigma = var**0.5
        gauss = np.random.normal(
                mean, sigma, (row, col, ch))
        gauss = gauss.reshape(row, col, ch)
        noisy = image + gauss
        return noisy
    elif noise_typ == "s&p":
        row, col, ch = image.shape
        s_vs_p = 0.5
        amount = 0.004
        out = np.copy(image)
        # Salt mode
        num_salt = np.ceil(amount * image.size * s_vs_p)
        coords = [np.random.randint(0, i - 1, int(num_salt))
                  for i in image.shape]
        out[coords] = 1

        # Pepper mode
        num_pepper = np.ceil(amount* image.size * (1. - s_vs_p))
        coords = [np.random.randint(0, i - 1, int(num_pepper))
                  for i in image.shape]
        out[coords] = 0
        return out
    elif noise_typ == "poisson":
        vals = len(np.unique(image))
        vals = 2 ** np.ceil(np.log2(vals))
        noisy = np.random.poisson(image * vals) / float(vals)
        return noisy
```

```
    elif noise_typ =="speckle":
        row,col,ch = image.shape
        gauss = np.random.randn(row,col,ch)
        gauss = gauss.reshape(row,col,ch)
        noisy = image + image * gauss
        return noisy

#loads the Xtest and Ytest MNIST data. It does not load the training set.
-, (images, labels) = tf.keras.datasets.mnist.load_data()

#The learning phase flag is a bool tensor (0 = test, 1 = train) to be passed as
#input to any Keras function that uses a different behavior at train time and test time.
tf.keras.backend.set_learning_phase(False)

#loading the default CNN
model = tf.keras.models.model_from_json(json.load(open("model1.json"))["model1"], custom_objects={})
#initializing the loaded model weights
model.load_weights("model1_weights.h5")
model.compile(optimizer='adam', loss='categorical_crossentropy',
              metrics=['accuracy'])
#creates a tensorflow session for the foolbox model to run on
with tf.keras.backend.get_session().as_default():
    fmodel = foolbox.models.TensorFlowModel.from_keras(model=model, bounds=(0.0, 1.0))

'''The following is the code to calculate the number of depicted digits that touch the edge
   of the image.
   It uses the function checkedges that was defined above '''
edgeitems = []
l=len(images)
#Performs check on the entire set of images
for i in range(0,l):
    a = images[i]
    b = np.where(a<64,0,1)
    np.savetxt('noom.csv',b,fmt='%1.0f',delimiter = ',')

    #reading the image from the saved .csv
    f=pd.read_csv("noom.csv", sep=",",header=None)
    x=f.values

    #Switches the 1's with 0's and vice versa. See 'XB.csv' to see what this looks like
    xs=np.where(x==1,-3,0)
    xn=np.where(xs==0,1,-3)
    xb=np.where(xn==-3,0,1)
    np.savetxt('XB.csv',xb,fmt='%1.0f',delimiter = ',')
    current = touching
    checkedges(xb)
    if (current+1==touching):
        edgeitems.append(i)

print("Number_of_test_images_touching_the_edge_is:_" + str(touching))
#deleting all MNIST edge items in the test set
images=np.delete(images,edgeitems,0)
labels=np.delete(labels,edgeitems,0)
print("New_test_set_has_" + str(len(images)) + "_images")

#reshaping test set in preparation for the adversarial image generator
images = images.reshape(images.shape[0], 28, 28, 1)
print(images.shape[0])
images = images/255
images = images.astype(np.float32)
print(images.shape)
skipped=0
skipped2=0
#if you want to run individual examples assign chosen image index to x and get rid of the loop x=100
size= len(images)
#list of how many adversarial examples we are able to flag
adversarialcatches =[]
#dictionary of indices of adversarial examples that were flagged and their labels
flagkeys={}
adversarial_images = np.empty([size ,784])
#whatever you want your probability cutoff to be
cutoff=.10
for x in range(0,size):
#for x in range(0,300):
    #initializes the FGSM adversarial the attack
    attack = foolbox.attacks.FGSM(fmodel, criterion=Misclassification())

    #initializes the C-W adversarial the attack
    #attack = foolbox.attacks.carlini_wagner.CarliniWagnerL2Attack
    #(fmodel, criterion=Misclassification(),distance=foolbox.distances.MeanSquaredDistance)

    #initializes the PGD adversarial the attack
    #attack = foolbox.attacks.iterative_projected_gradient.ProjectedGradientDescentAttack
    #(fmodel, criterion=Misclassification(),distance=foolbox.distances.Linfinity)

    #generates an adversarial image using the Fast Gradient Sign Method
    #(increasing loss until image is misclassified)
    adversarial = np.array([attack(images[x], label=labels[x])])
```

```
#generates images with gaussian noise
#adversarial = np.array(noisy("gauss",images[x]))
#adversarial = adversarial.reshape(1,28,28,1)
#print(adversarial.shape, ' =adv shape')

#in rare cases, an adversarial example cannot be found, we skip over these with this conditional
if adversarial.size==1:
    skipped2+=1
    print(x,"=x_{an_adversarial_examples_has_not_been_found}")
    continue
else:
    #model predicts wrong number on adversarial image
    add=adversarial.reshape(1,784)
    adversarial_images[x]=add
    model_predictions = model.predict(adversarial)
    predict=np.argmax(model_predictions)
    #calls method to calculate our probability that this image is misclassified
    finalprob = round(runvalidation(adversarial,predict),3)
    if finalprob <cutoff:
        adversarialcatches.append(finalprob)
        flagkeys[x]=predict

    if x % 100 == 0:
        print(str(x) + "_adversarial_examples_have_been_made")

#MODEL OUTPUT
print("MODEL_OUTPUT")
#print("the following is the list of the adversarial catch probabilities")
#print("Images with <"+str(cutoff*100)+"% probability: " + str(adversarialcatches))
#print("Indices of the flagged adversarial example images with their misclassified labels
#(index: label): " + str(flagkeys))
#print()
#print(str(len(adversarialcatches))+ " adversarial examples had prob's of
#<"+str(cutoff*100)+" percent.")
#print(str(len(adversarialcatches))+ " is the number of adversarial catches, i.e.,
#the number of adversarial examples that had prob's of <"+str(cutoff*100)+" percent.")
#print(str(len(flagkeys))+" is the number of flagged adversarial examples")
#for plotting individual adversarial examples
print(size-skipped2, "_=_NET_number_of_images_attacked")
print(str(skipped2), "_=_number_of_rare_cases_when_an_adversarial_example_cannot_be_found")
print(str(skipped), "_=_adversarial_examples_detected/skipped_due_to_having_too_much_noise_"
"(more_than_7_holes).")
print("Entire_analyzed_set_contains_{size-edge_counts}_"+ str(size)+ "_test_images.")
print(str(len(adversarialcatches)), "_=_number_of_adversarial_examples_detected_{Prob_<_10%}")
print("detection_success_rate_(%)_=_", 100.*(len(adversarialcatches)+skipped)/(size-skipped2))

#EXAMPLE ADVERSARIAL IMAGE PLOT
#resizing set of adversarial images
adversarial_images = adversarial_images.reshape(size,28,28)
#displaying an adversarial example
plt.imshow(adversarial_images[17], cmap='gray')

#PLOT OF ORIGINAL IMAGE, ADV EXAMPLE, AND THE DIFFERENCE
#adversarial and images[x] must be the same for this to see noise
#adversarial=adversarial.reshape(28,28)
adversarial=adversarial_images[17].reshape(28,28)
#a=images[x].reshape(28,28)
a=images[17].reshape(28,28)
#print(str(x), "=x")
plt.figure()
plt.subplot(1,3,1)
plt.title('Original')
plt.imshow(a, cmap='gray')
plt.axis('off')

plt.subplot(1, 3, 2)
plt.title('Adversarial')
plt.imshow(adversarial, cmap='gray')
plt.axis('off')

plt.subplot(1, 3, 3)
plt.title('Difference')
difference = adversarial - a
plt.imshow(difference / abs(difference).max() * 0.2 + 0.5, cmap='gray')
plt.axis('off')
plt.show()

model_predictions = model.predict(adversarial.reshape(1,28,28,1))
predict=np.argmax(model_predictions)
print("***The_model_predicted_label_for_the_plotted_adversarial_example_=_",predict)
```

References

1. https://docs.scipy.org/doc/scipy-0.16.0/reference/generated/scipy.ndimage.measurements. label.html
2. https://en.wikipedia.org/wiki/Blob_detection
3. https://github.com/bethgelab/foolbox/issues/175
4. https://stackoverflow.com/questions/46737409/finding-connected-components-in-a-pixel-array
5. https://stackoverflow.com/questions/55953083/ www.code-to-perform-an-attack-to-a-cnn-with-foolbox-whats-wrong
6. https://www.tensorflow.org/beta/tutorials/images/intro_to_cnns
7. Bell, G., Lawson, A., Martin, J., Rudzinski, J., Smyth, C.: Weighted persistent homology. Involve: J. Math. (2018, to appear) ePrint. arXiv:1709.00097v2
8. Carlini, N., Wagner, D.A.: Towards evaluating the robustness of neural networks (2016). CoRR abs/1608.04644. http://arxiv.org/abs/1608.04644
9. Carlsson, G.: Topology and data. Bull. Am. Math. Soc. **46**(2), 255–308 (2009)
10. Chen, P.Y., Zhang, H., Sharma, Y., Yi, J., Hsieh, C.J.: Zoo: zeroth order optimization based black-box attacks to deep neural networks without training substitute models. In: Proceedings of the 10th ACM Workshop on Artificial Intelligence and Security, pp. 15–26. ACM, New York (2017)
11. corochannNote MNIST dataset introduction: https://corochann.com/mnist-dataset-introduction-1138.html
12. Dieudonné, J.: A History of Algebraic and Differential topololgy, 1900–1960. Birkhäuser, Basel (1989)
13. Fasy, B., Lecci, F., Rinaldo, A., Wasserman, L., Balakrishnan, S., Singh, A.: Confidence sets for persistence diagrams. Ann. Stat. **42**(6), 2301–2339 (2014)
14. Ghrist, R., Muhammad, A.: Coverage and hole-detection in sensor networks via homology. In: Proceedings of the 4th International Symposium on Information Processing in Sensor Networks, ISPN'05, Los Angeles, CA, pp. 254–260 (2005)
15. Goodfellow, I.J., Shlens, J., Szegedy, C.: Explaining and harnessing adversarial examples. In: ICLR'15 (2015). Preprint. arXiv:1412.6572
16. Greenberg, M.J.: Lectures on Algebraic Topology. Mathematical Lecture Notes Series. W.A. Benjamin, New York (1967)
17. Hofer, C., Kwitt, R., Niethammer, M., UHl, A.: Deep learning with topological signatures. In: Proceedings of the 31st Conference on Neural Information Processing Systems (NIPS 2017) (2017)
18. Krizhevsky, A., Hinton, G., et al.: Learning multiple layers of features from tiny images. Tech. rep., Citeseer (2009)
19. LeCun, Y.: The mnist database of handwritten digits. http://yann.lecun.com/exdb/mnist/
20. Madry, A., Makelov, A., Schmidt, L., Tsipras, D., Vladu, A.: Towards deep learning models resistant to adversarial attacks (2017). Preprint. arXiv:1706.06083
21. Netzer, Y., Wang, T., Coates, A., Bissacco, A., Wu, B., Ng, A.Y.: Reading digits in natural images with unsupervised feature learning. In: NIPS Workshop on Deep Learning and Unsupervised Feature Learning, vol. 1 (2011)
22. Papernot, N., McDaniel, P., Wu, X., Jha, S., Swami, A.: Distillation as a defense to adversarial perturbations against deep neural networks. In: 2016 IEEE Symposium on Security and Privacy (SP), pp. 582–597. IEEE, New York (2016)
23. Rauber, J., Brendel, W., Bethege, M.: Foolbox: a python toolbox to benchmark the robustness of machine learning models (2018). arXiv:1707.04131v3
24. Spanier, E.H.: Algebraic Topology. McGraw-Hill, New York (1966)

25. Topology, C.: Computational Topology. AMS, Providence (2010)
26. Zomorodian, A.J.: Topology for Computing. Cambridge Monographs on Applied and Computational Mathematics, vol. 16. Cambridge University Press, Cambridge (2005)
27. Zomorodian, A., Carlsson, G.: Computing persistent homology. Discrete Comput. Geom. **33**, 249–274 (2005)

Cyber-(in)Security, Revisited: Proactive Cyber-Defenses, Interdependence and Autonomous Human-Machine Teams (A-HMTs)

William F. Lawless (ID)**, Ranjeev Mittu, Ira S. Moskowitz** (ID)**, Donald A. Sofge** (ID)**, and Stephen Russell**

Abstract The risks from cyber threats are increasing. Cyber threats propagate primarily with deception. Threats from deception derive from insider and outsider attacks. These threats are countered by reactive and proactive cyber-defenses. Alarmingly, increasing proactive cyber defenses simulate conflicts from the Wild West of yesteryear. However, deception is inadequately addressed with traditional theories based on methodological individualism (MI). Worse, MI's rational choice theory breaks down in the presence of social conflict. In contrast, interdependence theory addresses barriers, deception to penetrate the vulnerabilities of barriers and the conflict which ensues, topics where interdependence theory thrives. Interdependence includes the effects of the constructive or destructive interference that constitute every social interaction. Our research primarily addresses the application of interdependence theory to autonomous human-machine teams (A-HMTs), which entails artificial intelligence (AI) and AI's sub-field of machine learning (ML). A-HMTs require defenses that protect a team from cyberthreats, adverse interference and other vulnerabilities while affording the opportunity for a team to become autonomous. In this chapter, we focus on an introduction that includes a review of traditional methodological individualism and rational choice theory. Our intro-

W. F. Lawless (✉) · I. S. Moskowitz
Paine College, Augusta, GA, USA

Naval Research Laboratory, Washington, DC, USA
e-mail: w.lawless@icloud.com; ira.moskowitz@nrl.navy.mil

R. Mittu
Information Management and Decision Architectures Branch, Information Technology Division, U. S. Naval Research Laboratory, Washington, DC, USA
e-mail: ranjeev.mittu@nrl.navy.mil

D. A. Sofge · S. Russell ·
Army Research Laboratory, Adelphi, MD, USA
e-mail: donald.sofge@nrl.navy.mil; stephen.russell15.civ@mail.mil

© This is a U.S. government work and not under copyright protection in the U.S.; foreign copyright protection may apply 2021
P. Dasgupta et al. (eds.), *Adversary-Aware Learning Techniques and Trends in Cybersecurity*, https://doi.org/10.1007/978-3-030-55692-1_10

duction is followed by a discussion of deception and its implications for reactive cyber defenses. We next cover proactive cyber defenses in a separate section. Then we review our research on interdependence theory and its application to A-HMTs. We conclude that while cyber-risks are increasing, so too is the teamwork that strengthens cyber-defenses. The future belongs to a theory of interdependence that improves cyber-defenses, teams and the science that generalizes to A-HMTs.

Keywords Deception · Reactive and proactive cyber-defenses · Interdependence · Orthogonality · Human-Machine Teams (A-HMTs) · Autonomy

1 Introduction

Revolutionary changes in cyber-systems are occurring rapidly across the fields, for example, of medicine, transportation, and the military. In this chapter, we discuss four topics: First, in the introduction, we review the traditional model of methodological individualism (MI) and its rational choice theory which follows. Second, MI fails to come to terms with deception, which we review next. Third, we cover reactive and proactive defenses to cyber threats. With its focus on teams, while proactive defenses have evolved into the conflict common to the Wild West, unaccounted for by MI and rational choice theory, conflict and teams are central to interdependence theory, which we review last.

To reduce cyber threats in the US, information sharing is supported by the Department of Homeland Security. It is based on the 2020 counterintelligence strategy for America released to the public on January 8, 2020, for which it has been conceived as a "paradigm shift" [1]. It was established by the Office of the Direction of National Intelligence's (ODNI) National Counterintelligence and Security Center's Director. For its new policy, ODNI is planning to share more contextual information about cyber threats from the Cybersecurity and Infrastructure Security Agency and the National Security Agency with industry [2].

Information sharing, however, has raised significant theoretical questions by the Rand Corporation about the state of AI and its implications for DoD [3]. We paraphrase and review the key findings and recommendations from the Rand study that are relevant to this chapter.

- First, AI is underpinned by several technologies. Recent significant technological advances have primarily occurred in supervised machine learning, more specifically, in deep learning. But success in deep learning is predicated on the availability of large, labeled data sets coupled with computing power sufficient for users to train the models. Overall, however, the current result is fragile and with optimizations for commercial rather than DoD uses.
- Second, the current state of AI verification, validation, test, and evaluation (VVT&E) is unsatisfactory for ensuring the performance and safety of AI applications, particularly safety-critical systems. While this problem is not unique to DoD, it affects DoD significantly.

- Third, generalizing, AI investments made in DoD and industry today should become deployed in the near-term for enterprises, in the mid-term for the support of most missions, and in the longer-term for most operational AI systems, ranking team autonomy last (i.e., A-HMTs).

RAND further concluded that with AI today, DoD was significantly challenged across all of the dimensions that RAND assessed; i.e., again from our perspective,

- First, DoD lacks baselines and metrics for its AI vision (we take exception by claiming that autonomous teams may be easier to establish performance metrics than for independent autonomous robots; e.g., in [4, 5]).
- Second, current practices, processes and implementations in DoD may be hampering innovation (we later link innovation with education and competition; in [6]).
- Third, DoD's data are not always collected and stored when possible; access to existing data is limited; existing data sets are not always understandable or traceable; and when vendors are involved, ambiguity in data ownership is common. Lack of interoperability in systems across DoD adds additional challenges.

RAND also made various Recommendations (the relevant ones follow):

- First, DoD should adopt structures for the governance of AI that align DoD authorities, resources and missions to better scale AI (we agree; in [7]).
- Second, working in close partnership with industry and academia, DoD should advance the science and practice of VVT&E for AI systems.
- Third, DoD must recognize its data as a critical resource, it must institute practices for data collection and curation, and it must increase sharing while protecting its data after sharing and during its use and analyses.

In addition to RAND's questions, to advance autonomy, we add that before and after sharing cyber threats, we must know when autonomous teams, organizations and systems have performed poorly, satisfactorily, or at the highest level, viz., maximum entropy production (MEP). We must generalize the performance metrics used for human teams and systems to autonomous human-machine teams (A-HMTs). When changes are made to a team or system in proactive cyber-defense environments, we must know what identifies as a successful change, a poorly adopted change, or no change at all. And, most importantly, we must know how the deception used by an adversary is managed or discovered and how deception is implemented by friendly forces.

Autonomy is entering society first with automobiles. A draft of bipartisan legislation is already in Congress for a driverless bill, starting in the U.S. House of Representatives [8]. This bill sets extensive requirements to prevent vehicles from being hacked. The House has not yet decided whether to bar manufacturers from selling vehicles without cybersecurity protections or to allow only those with automated features.

Non-autonomous weapons systems not only are becoming more sophisticated, but they are integral to military defense systems (e.g., [9]). An example is the remotely controlled MQ-9,[1] which has several advantages over aircraft piloted by humans. These advantages include not needing to send rescue crews when an MQ-9 crashes; flying without the need of a restroom; staying aloft for extended periods (i.e., 32 h); and performing close air support (CAS), precision strikes, and intelligence, surveillance, and reconnaissance (ISR) missions. Although remotely controlled, the MQ-9 can also serve as armed reconnaissance, a coordinator for airstrikes, and an airborne forward air controller.

Preparations are underway for the future arrival of autonomous weapon systems [10], specifically lethal autonomous weapon systems (LAWS; in [11]). Autonomy to the military is also known as "human out of the loop" or full autonomy. While autonomous weapon systems are not yet ready for battle, nor do these systems yet exist, they are likely to operate where and when traditional weapon systems would be degraded, denied, or otherwise unable to operate. LAWS are a special class of weapon systems with sensor suites and algorithms that allow them to autonomously identify, target and destruct a target with a weapon unaided by human control.

The United Nation is considering a ban on LAWS due to the ethical concerns involved; supported by its Editors [12] the *New York Times* agreed. However, contrary to news reports (reviewed in [11]), U.S. policy neither forbids the development nor the deployment of LAWS. The United States military does not have an inventory of LAWS. But senior military and defense leaders believe that the United States must develop LAWS if U.S. adversaries develop them. Department of Defense Directive (DODD) 3000.09 defines LAWS weapons as those system[s] that, once activated, can select and engage targets without further intervention by a human operator.

However, DODD 3000.09 requires all systems, including LAWS, be designed to allow commanders and operators to exercise appropriate levels of human judgment over the use of force.

To address RAND's and our questions and other theoretical issues, we review the relevant issues in cyber: Deception; reactive and proactive cyber defenses; and our new theory of interdependence as applied to A-HMTs from a team's perspective for purposes of design and operation.

Autonomous submarines. Drone wingmen. Hypersonic missiles (e.g., [13]). The evolution of autonomous human-machine teams (A-HMT) is occurring when the need for the rapidity of making decisions exceeds the capabilities of humans, an issue central to military defense, operating complex systems, transportation, etc. This evolution includes retrofitting old systems; e.g., the U.S. Navy has converted a manned combat jet into an unmanned machine rebuilt to fly in a pair as drones under the command of a single fighter pilot [14].

Social science, however, with its basis in rational methodological individualism (MI), offers little in the way of theoretical guidance for the science of A-HMTs.

---

[1] The "M" is the DOD designation for multi-role, and "Q" means remotely piloted aircraft system. The "9" indicates it is the ninth in the series of remotely piloted aircraft systems (from the USAF; see https://www.af.mil/About-Us/Fact-Sheets/Display/Article/104470/mq-9-reaper/).

This basis for social science, often unaccompanied by theory, is likely at the root of the replication crisis in social science and its inability to make satisfactory predictions. MI has impeded the generalization of every social-psychological theory that has used it; e.g., game theory, the aggregation of data in economics, assembling automata, political science and philosophy.

In the laboratory and field, MI's rational collective theory tellingly fails in the presence of conflict, where interdependence theory thrives. Recently, however, social science has experimentally reestablished the value of interdependence to human team science [15], especially for the best of science teams [16], but not theoretically, making the results important but ad hoc.

Methodological Individualism's rational choice theory, the traditional model of decision-making, attempts to improve individual decisions by making them more consistent, mathematical, and in line with their preferences [17]. Israel [18] added that mathematics provides the rational criterion for truth, contradicted by other economists (e.g., [19]. This model is popular in military circles, where it is known as the perception-action cycle. Undercutting the value of consistency, however, consistency is not only prized by consensus-seeking rational choice theorists, but it is also prized by authoritarians and gang leaders [7].

Rational choice theory is based on three assumptions. First, it assumes that an individual's behaviors converge to what its brain sees and choses, where reality is sufficiently determinable to make individual decisions consistent. Second, by observing consistent behavior, trained observers (e.g., scientists) can impute the choices an individual makes, overcoming Kelley's [20] inability with subjective self-reports to determine individual preferences. Third, if the information collected converges, it forms the basis for a consensus by a collective.

But, in addition, the fatal flaw of rational choice theory is its inability to handle conflict, where interdependence theory thrives.

Arrow [21], a Nobel laureate in economics, was one of the first to contradict MI when he attributed the production, possession, and nature of knowledge exclusively to social effects:

> . . . technical information in the economy is an especially significant case of an irreducibly social category in the explanatory apparatus of economics . . .

Arrow had concluded that methodological individualism (MI), exemplified by game theory (1994, p. 4), could not explain knowledge acquisition; e.g., in game theory, scientists establish the context for every game by setting its rules and payoffs before they start an experiment with humans. For example, in Prisoners Dilemma Games, by cooperating, cooperators "win" more points than competitors, providing weak support for socialism, but with no support to reject capitalism [7].

Nonetheless, with these self-fulfilling rules, Axelrod [22] produced two claims based on repeated games run in laboratories: first, "the pursuit of self-interest by each [participant] leads to a poor outcome for all." And, second, this situation can be avoided when sufficient punishment exists to discourage competition. The first claim has not been established outside of the laboratory ([23], p. 422). As for the second claim, collective punishment can produce pernicious social effects; e.g., impeding the ability to innovate (e.g., promoted by the leaders in China, the theft of IP property is a common practice, but it is counterproductive; see [24]). An example of the perverse effects of collective punishment in China was reported by Friedman [25]:

> ... with the leak over the weekend of government documents describing ... a broad Chinese assault ... underway for several years on the ethnic minority Uighur community in ... Xinjiang ... [its] massive detention camps for "retraining" purposes and the separation of families on a scale that is startling even for China. Beijing clearly wants to break the back of Islam in the province.

A key problem with the use of collective punishment is the loss of trust, corruption and the lack of competence that follow [7]. For example, with the discovery, mismanagement and coverup of the use of deception by leaders to censor information about the spread of coronavirus in China, trust has been lost [26].[2]Those who discovered the virus were afraid to tell their superiors, their superiors were afraid to alert medical authorities to ask for help, and insiders were unable to trust the information received. This chain of failure indicates that the benefits of administering collective punishment to maintain central control are elusive.

Dictatorships, like those in Russia and China, prize rational consistency. To maintain it, whenever social chaos appears, their first weapon is censorship to gain control and to maintain it. For example, from ([28]; see also [29], *Los Angeles Times*; and [30], *The Guardian*), like China at the start of the coronavirus outbreak, in Soviet Ukraine the state's default mode was secrecy and denial. On April 26, 1986 when a reactor meltdown sent a radioactive cloud spewing from Chernobyl, Spring was occurring, school was following its routine, and the May Day parade was planned for International Workers' Solidarity Day. Initially, there was no warning and no panic. But the radioactive fallout from Chernobyl overcame the fear of the Russian state, creating an independence movement that rejected Communism and Moscow's rule. Similarly, in Wuhan, a handful of local doctors alerted their colleagues online about unusual cases of pneumonia. These doctors were visited by the police and warned to stay silent, preventing the residents of Wuhan from protecting themselves, allowing the virus to spread unchecked across and beyond China. Unlike Soviet Russia, China has a robust economy. But China's President Xi Jinping intensified the Chinese Communist Party's authority and repression of dissent after achieving power in 2012, replacing top party officials in Wuhan with loyalists to face the coronavirus. Unlike the information generated from the restraints afforded by checks and balances, dictatorships, like the Chinese party-state system, have severe economic, social and political costs from their secretive, central commands (e.g., news about the 1957 disaster near Kyshtym in the Urals, when a Soviet nuclear-weapons facility caught fire, scattering nearly half as much radiation as the Chernobyl reactor, was censored; after the 2008 earthquake in Sichuan that killed children in the thousands, Chinese authorities silenced parents

---

[2]Jimmy Lai, the cited author of this opinion piece in the Wall Street Journal, has since been arrested by the Chinese authorities [27].

complaining about shoddily constructed school buildings; and after the high-speed train crash near Wenzhou in 2011, the government bulldozed the wreckage, rumored with survivors trapped inside, while censoring the media).

The failure of rational competence as a means to achieve consistency in the governed was captured in a new report by Friedman [25]:

> The Communist revolution ... [in China] created a state based on ideology, the belief that what would emerge from the long revolution would be a nation based on communism, and that with that China would experience both a prosperity and community it had never had. But the price that had to be paid to reach that goal would be ruthless oppression and suffering. This was designed both to build communism and expunge the anti-communist habits that were ingrained in the Chinese people.

"China is ruled by thieves" [31]. But so is Russia. From Foxall [32],

> Russian ... kleptocracy is based on the "rule of law" ... [for] a State where corruption lies at the very epicentre of power, [where] the law serves to control and coerce the majority of the population while allowing Putin, his cronies, and other regime insiders to act with impunity ... [where] state agencies collude with business and organised crime in criminal activities ... supported by the Kremlin ... [and] Russian courts ... [combining] to undermine the rule of law in European states and multilateral treaty organisations

Command decision makers believe their better grasp of reality allows them to make the best decisions. However, Einstein's theory of relativity, Heisenberg's uncertainty principle, and Schrodinger's quantum mechanics are structured to recognize that physical "reality is not as it appears to us" [33]; and yet, like dictators, both social scientists and rational economists persist in believing that social reality can be determined based on individual perceptions that are unreliable, commonly leading to invalid concepts even about individuals' beliefs about their own actions [34]; e.g., social psychologists have spent decades trying but failing to make games work (viz., see the review by [35]).

Economic decisions are supposedly based on the rational choices that consistently maximize an individual's self-interest. But it has long been known that individual preferences in game theory do not predict the choices actually made in games [20]. Rational choice theorists correct for this problem by replacing stated individual preferences with *imputed* preferences based on the observed behavior of individuals [17], regardless of the preferences claimed by individuals.

Other limits to rational choice theory have been determined, including biases, but since biases often produce consistent behavior, they have been incorporated (e.g., [36]). Similarly, Robb [37] prefers purposeful choice to account for emotion in group impulses, such as the Good Samaritan, not as reason or profit dictate; but Robb, too, feels that his theory is rational.

The primary requirement to operate in social and physical reality requires a consensus about the assessment of a situation. Absent a consensus about a context, social reality cannot be predetermined by individuals de novo. Rational choice theorists need consistency to determine behavior; and they need a consensus among themselves to determine a collective's interpretation of a context. However, Mann [38] found that conflict disables rational choice, again, where interdependence theory thrives [7], discussed in the last section of our chapter.

At the very moment when social science is being asked to contribute to the advancement of a physical science, the science of human-machine teams, the discipline has faltered with little of substance to offer (e.g., [39]). We attribute the cause of failure of social science to methodological individualism's (MI) rejection of social effects (interdependence) in favor of a rational theory of behavior.

Failures occurred in social science not only with questionnaires that not only failed to measure implicit racial bias [40] and self-esteem [41], but also the social and political predictions that failed to occur; e.g., Tetlock and Gardner [42] technique to seek consensus among the best forecasters, finding and using what they described as superforecasters, but these superforecasters predicted incorrectly that Brexit would not occur and that Trump would not become President.

In the remainder of the chapter, we have divided the narrative into sections on deception, proactive cyber defense, and interdependence theory.

2 Deception

According to Gartner (from a Cryptologic Program budget analysis, in [43]), exclusive of the Internet of Things (IoT), despite the usual passive defense measures, industrial control systems (ICS), and the security of public and private transportation, the increase in cybercrime led to spending for cyber security of more than $86.4 billion in 2017. Moreover, the intelligence community invested roughly one-third of this budget for cyber-operations.

Deception can be expensive. From Kaste [44], a new scam, the "business email compromise," or BEC, uses phony emails to trick employees at companies to wire money to the wrong accounts. According to the FBI's Internet Crime Complaint Center, BEC losses of more than $1.2 billion in 2018, tripling what happened with this scam in 2016. The CEO of Agari, a firm specializing in protecting corporate email systems, Patrick Peterson, calls this "social engineering." He is using a hacker's-term for scams that rely less on technical tricks and more on exploiting human vulnerabilities:

> "It's using our own trust and desire to communicate with others against us," Peterson says. In the past, scammers have pretended to be business partners and CEOs, urging employees to send money for an urgent matter. But lately there has been a trend toward what Agari calls "vendor email compromise" — scammers pretending to be part of a company's supply chain.

Cyber-crime with crypto-currency is expanding rapidly [45]. For example, Ponzi schemes and other frauds involving bitcoin and cryptocurrencies lured at least $4.3 billion from investors in 2019, more than the combined $3 billion in 2017 and 2018 for cyber crypto-crime.

Cybercrime, however, is not unusual human behavior involving the use of deception. As a first example of ordinary human behavior, in baseball, the Houston Astros used an algorithm called "Codebreaker" to decode the signs of opposing catchers, the beginning of what has turned into one of the biggest scandals in Major League Baseball history (from [46]):

> Throughout the 2017 season and for part of 2018, Astros baseball operations employees and video room staffers used Codebreaker to illegally steal signs, which were then relayed to batters in real time. Another Astros employee referred to the system as the "dark arts."

As a second example from banking [47], an ordinary spying scandal that began last Fall when the head of Credit Suisse bank's former international wealth management group spotted and confronted an investigator employed by the bank to follow him in Zurich. For the bank's board, the multiple spying allegations since have formed a pattern that characterized the bank's culture under its Chief Executive Officer's (CEO) inner circle. Doubts existed about whether the CEO knew about the surveillance, but the bank's board concluded that they had lost confidence in their CEO, and replaced him.

Third, from the financial industry, where a crackdown of many years has taken place recently to stop what the Department of Justice (DOJ) regards as cheating in the futures markets, with the government's focus on a tactic known as "spoofing." Several critics of DOJ's campaign say prosecutors are trying to make ordinary, maybe cunning, behavior into a crime equal to insider trading. Instead, traders say spoofing, a form of bluffing where users enter bogus orders and then cancel them, is hard to distinguish when traders use algorithms to post, cancel and update prices. Jerry Markham, a professor at Florida International University and former regulator who has testified for traders accused of spoofing, said [48]:

> It sounds like a moral issue because deception is involved, but that is what trading is all about . . .

Deception has occurred in the computer industry almost from the very beginning (e.g., [49]). The dot-com bust and accounting scandals at WorldCom and Enron encouraged Congress to enact the Sarbanes-Oxley Act of 2002 to require the chief executive officer (CEO) and chief financial officer (CFO) of a company to certify that all of its financial statements were complete and accurate. The scandals also hastened a trend toward more independent corporate directors who were willing to challenge CEOs.

In recent news about hackers committing cyber-crimes ([50]; see also [51]; and [52]), the Department of Justice (DOJ) charged two alleged hackers of being controlled by the Chinese government, a cyber-threat known as an Advanced Persistent Threat, in what has been alleged to be a long-running scheme to steal American intellectual property and personal identification information. The charges were part of a broader move by President Trump's administration to push back against what U.S. officials describe as China's relentless drive to steal American business secrets (i.e., IP property).

Focusing on the cyber-theft news released by DOJ [50], a federal grand jury recently indicted four members of the Chinese People's Liberation Army (PLA) with hacking into the computers of Equifax, a credit reporting agency, to steal personal data from millions of American citizens and trade secrets from Equifax. From Attorney General William P. Barr, who made the announcement,

> This was a deliberate and sweeping intrusion into the private information of the American people. ... Today, we hold PLA hackers accountable for their criminal actions, and we remind the Chinese government that we have the capability to remove the Internet's cloak of anonymity and find the hackers that nation repeatedly deploys against us. Unfortunately, the Equifax hack fits a disturbing and unacceptable pattern of state-sponsored computer intrusions and thefts by China and its citizens that have targeted personally identifiable information, trade secrets, and other confidential information.

According to the indictment [50], the Chinese defendants exploited a vulnerability in Equifax's Apache Struts Web Framework software for its online dispute portal. With this access, the defendants reconnoitered in Equifax's portal until they obtained login credentials to navigate across Equifax's network. The defendants spent several weeks performing data queries to identify Equifax's database structure in their search for sensitive, personally identifiable information (PID) within Equifax's system.

After the Chinese hackers had accessed the files that they wanted, they stored the stolen information temporarily, compressed and downloaded it to computers outside the United States. The PID information that they had obtained from Equifax included names, birth dates and social security numbers. The defendants were also charged with stealing trade secrets from Equifax; i.e., its data compilations and database designs. Again from Attorney General Barr [50]:

> In short, this was an organized and remarkably brazen criminal heist of sensitive information of nearly half of all Americans, as well as the hard work and intellectual property of an American company, by a unit of the Chinese military ...

The Chinese defendants used deception to evade detection throughout the intrusion, as alleged in the indictment [50]. Traffic was re-routed through multiple servers located in nearly 20 countries to hide the hackers' true location and behavior, they used encrypted communication channels within Equifax's network to blend in with normal network activity, and afterwards they deleted files and wiped log files daily to hide the records of their activity.

Some aging military systems are more prone to deceptions in a cyber-attack [53]. For example, in a memo by the U.S. Navy, its aged computer networks offer limited capabilities, such as file sharing, cloud collaboration, chat communication, video communication and, more importantly, the ability to identify and thwart cyberattacks, allowing foreign countries the ability to steal information about the Navy's weapons systems. According to the memo, many sailors become vulnerable to these systems:

> Our adversaries gain an advantage in cyberspace through guerrilla tactics within our defensive perimeters ... Once inside, malign actors steal, destroy and/or modify critical data and information.

Deception can be deadly. Members of the Taliban recently infiltrated U.S. and Afghan forces by posing as soldiers to carry out an insider attack. A NATO analysis calculated that 10% of such "green-on-blue" attacks are directly tied to insurgents, with the large majority of these attacks caused by personal or cultural disagreements [54].

Moreover, the battlefield of the future is changing from a ground-war to cyberwar. From Kanno-Youngs and Perlroth [55],

> Iran's declaration on Wednesday that a missile attack on Iraq had "concluded proportionate measures" against the United States in response to the killing of its most important general may amplify the Trump administration's attention on computer systems as the next battlefield in its showdown with Tehran. Cybersecurity experts and government officials are already monitoring an uptick of malicious activity by pro-Iranian hackers and social media users that they believe are harbingers of more serious computer attacks from Tehran, including possible efforts aimed at destroying government databases.

Within the loosely regulated world of the Internet's infrastructure, the guise of deception is mutating as part of cyber threats. In the news recently [56], a small technology firm, Micfo, has been charged with the first federal case of fraud perpetrated against the American Registry for Internet Numbers (ARIN), illuminating the architecture of how fake internet addresses on the internet cloak the identities of bad actors (e.g., spammers and hackers). ARIN, located in Virginia, is a non-profit organization that assigns Internet protocol addresses, like a phone number, required for all online devices in North America and the Caribbean.

Funding for the ARIN registry comes from the fees companies pay for these services. But available IP addresses are currently scarce. About 4 billion exist of the current version, IPv4; it is being switched to a newer version that will make billions more available, but this undertaking remains years away to complete. ARIN said it asked the Federal Bureau of Investigation to investigate Micfo when it discovered a change in ownership of two identical blocks of IP addresses.

IP addresses allow devices to communicate with each other online. To get online with a cellphone or computer, users assigned an IP address gain access using an Internet service provider; some firms use thousands of IP addresses for their Internet platforms. In the Micfo case, it created shell companies to obtain false IP addresses that were then resold after lucrative markups to the Virtual Private Networks (VPNs) that gives users anonymity. By masking web traffic, some of these VPNs transmitted illicit content or perpetrated cybercrime.

For our last example of deception, Israel's military claimed that a Palestinian militant group, Hamas, duped dozens of its soldiers in an operation into downloading spyware under the ruse of exchanging photos of young women [57]. The scheme used fake profiles of supposedly young Israeli women, but the women were working as operatives for Hamas using Facebook, WhatsApp, Instagram and Telegram, highlighting the widening scope of these cyber-spying attempts. The Israeli military said that the scheme was discovered before its military secrets got out, however, and the servers used by Hamas were destroyed. Known as a honey trap, this phishing scheme shows how an enemy can exploit social media with deception to elicit information from enemy soldiers and how difficult it is to prevent these sophisticated attacks, the third by Hamas against Israel since 2017.

3   Reactive and Proactive Cyber-Defenses

We have predicted that boundaries are critical to teams, organizations and systems
that need to execute sensitive operations [4, 5]. Boundaries can serve to impede the
spread of diseases (e.g., [58]), political contagions and migration; boundaries reduce
external destructive interference. By extension, boundaries help to limit adverse
interference inside of a social unit, a deceptive agent's consistency providing
the means to hide the deception by cyber-criminals internal to an organization.
Boundaries that protect a team, organization or system can easily be defeated
with deception, making it an important tool for cybercriminals. There are at least
two means of protecting boundaries: reactive cyber-defenses and proactive cyber-
defenses.

Reactive cyber strategies must continue, however, whether or not proactive cyber
defense strategies are adopted. That is, Next Generation Fire Walls (NGFWs),
antivirus protections, junk and spam filters, multi-factor authentication techniques,
and breach strategy plans are needed today and in the future, as will keeping
lists of defeated cyber-threats, those cyber-threats currently in play, and rumors of
new cyber-threats. Reactive cyber-security strategies depend on a firm's ability to
strengthen its cyber defenses before cybercriminals can find, target and exploit a
new vulnerability [59]. Reactive cyber security includes the responses to alarms
that a network has been breached. In sum, reactive cyber-security defenses imply a
constant firefighting vigilance. But are reactive strategies sufficient today?

Reactive cyber-security remains important for organizations to block, or inter-
cept, the vectors that reflect expanding threats, emerging attack strategies, sophisticated cybercriminal communities, new malware, and zero day vulnerabilities (the
latter relying on surprise to exploit organizations on the day of release for an attack).
But reactive security alone can leave social units vulnerable. From Graves [59], the
time on average to identify a cyber-breach is less than 200 days, but once identified,
it takes another 70 more days to contain the breach. Almost 75% of organizations
report, however, that they are unprepared for future cyberattacks. This data indicates
a poor state of affairs for reaction-based security strategies.

One of the worst sources of breaches, however, about half of them, are initiated
either accidentally or purposely by insiders with malicious intentions [59]. The
breaches caused by insiders can be difficult to detect and expensive to fix. Almost
all organizations have policies that establish acceptable and unacceptable cyber
behaviors. Techniques like file fingerprinting and monitoring programs across an
organization's cyber-state can make insider breaches more difficult. But insiders,
however, are often the most trusted people in an organization; these malicious
insiders are users with extensive privileges, the very people who know where an
organization's cyber strengths and weaknesses are located, including the reactive
cyber defenses in existence, giving them the knowledge to leverage their use of
deception to avoid detection. Insiders know where an organization's most valuable
data, its intellectual property (IP) and its trade secrets are located. Together, this
makes the cyber threat by an insider too potent for the reactive model of defense.

Shifting cybersecurity from a reactive to a proactive posture requires an integrated approach that can operate across the full spectrum of prevention, detection, and hunting for breaches and responses; it requires robust threat intelligence to alert defenders to the emerging and evolving threats most likely to impact networks and systems; and for the organizations that can afford the expenses entailed, it requires advanced analytics and machine learning (ML) technologies to, for example, stitch seemingly unrelated events together occurring across an organization's architecture to produce high confidence and actionable alerts [60].

In addition to the reactive strategies already enumerated, several proactive defense strategies exist that should be adopted [59]: Stress-testing an organization's security infrastructure regularly; identifying and mitigating hazardous cyber conditions; tracking deviations from consistent behavior by regular and supervisory cyber personnel (however, consistency is part of the rational model; for a cyber-criminal using deception, their technique is to maintain consistent behavior, maybe even leading the charge to protect an organization until making a cyber-breach, such as moving key files to a new server; logging in to resources rarely used by this individual; or moving data in unexpected ways).

An example of a positive cyber-strategy was recently discussed at an RSA conference[3] by Michael Mylrea, Director of Cybersecurity R&D at GE Global Research. Mylrea recommended that utilities have a plan for their staff for communications and recovery in the event that a cyber incident has occurred. He also outlined how an open software search engine tool (i.e., Shodan) is available to crawl the Internet and identify cyber risks across a utility's energy infrastructure [61]. He further recommended that

> utilities not run ... a "flat network," where everything runs in the same network segment. Rather, he suggested that utilities should run segregated networks where operational and IT technologies are separated and secured from one another. ... Mylrea advised the audience that utilities should use Shodan, setting up automated queries to search for bad configuration, exposed services, and potential vulnerabilities.

Providing Defense of Department (DoD) policymakers with a proactive framework to measure the expected value of its cybersecurity investments, the National Security Agency (NSA) has established for DoD a cyber threat-based security strategy known as the NIPRNet SIPRNet Cyber Security Architecture Review, or NSCSAR (now referred to as DODCAR). But while DODCAR reviews have led adoptees to realize savings, improved user experiences and increased productivity with innovations like cloud technologies, they have also made it easier for adversaries to hide in a cloud's distributed network [60].

There is a danger, however, with the use of proactive cyber-defense strategies. Those firms with the most sophisticated cyber technologies know what is required to protect their organization's systems, including its customers, their networks, their IP and their trade secrets. But they are also more likely to have been well-trained and highly skilled cyber workers with the ability to track down hackers, to penetrate an

---

[3]RSA: public-key encryption technology.

attacker's cyber system, and to perpetrate revenge on them, like vigilantes from the Wild West (e.g., [62]). Shackleford [63] is satisfied with organizations that use some proactive defense measures, like identifying and gathering intelligence about potential attackers and intrusions. But when proactive defenses become too aggressive, he recommends that these maneuvers be discouraged or prevented because of the risk they pose to destabilize international interactions between corporations and also international governance.

Going well beyond the proactive position of Shackleford [63], in response to the rapid increase in cyber threats, several private firms and governments are hiring "red-hat" hackers, i.e., offensive cyber-security experts [43]. Compared to the better-known and friendly "white-hat" hackers who might help organizations react appropriately, red-hatters apply the methods of cybercriminals against the criminals themselves; rather than defending against attacks in cyber space, red-hatters counterattack cyber-criminals or use preemptive strikes against cyber-criminals. When red-hatters become aggressive, they act as cyber vigilantes. They work under the same rules as hackers, attackers, hacktivists, organized cyber-criminals, and state-sponsored attackers. The danger, however, is that the behavior of red-hatters can devolve into the unethical practices associated with cyber criminals.

Proactive cyber defenses have increased in sophistication. Constant vigilance for data systems, IP properties, and insider damage is good. When organizations take the law into their own hands with the rise of vigilantes, however, that means the worst practices from the Wild West may be overtaking cyber space.

Governments can and do take proactive cyber measures much further than private organizations. For example [64], more than a half century ago, during and following the Second World War, governments around the globe trusted Crypto AG, a Swiss company, to keep their communications with their spies, soldiers, diplomats and cables confidential. Crypto AG began with a contract to build a code-making machine for U.S. troops during the War. Wealthy as a result, the firm dominated the encryption device market for decades, adopting new technology from physical gears to computer chips and software. This Swiss firm sold equipment to more than 120 countries well into the twentyfirst century, including military juntas in Latin America, nuclear rivals India and Pakistan, Iran, and the Vatican. But none of its customers knew that Crypto AG supposedly was secretly owned by the CIA. According to Miller, Crypto rigged its coding devices so it could later access and break the codes whenever encrypted messages were sent, including to Iran's mullahs during the 1979 hostage crisis, Argentina's military for Britain during the Falklands War, and to Libyan officials congratulating themselves on the 1986 bombing of a disco in Berlin.

The aggressive cyber tactics used by governments become ethically dubious and possibly criminal when used by teams, firms and organizations. Instead, to govern proactive cyber defenses, we discuss a better way below with the checks and balances that reflect interdependence. But, supported by Grove, the conflict produced by checks and balances precludes the convergence to meaning as desired by rational choice theorists.

The elusiveness of meaning for rational choice theory applies to deception, too. Like quantum theory, however, interdependence accounts for the need for boundaries surrounding social units; the need to use deception by and to uncover deception against friendly forces; the use of consensus-seeking rules by gangs and dictatorships to maintain their rule; the intractability of deriving meaning from interactions; and more; e.g., the mergers discussed below and the operation of A-HMTs.

4   Interdependence Theory

For interdependence theory, we recognize that MI is unable to determine context [65], and, more fundamentally, it is unable to aggregate data from interdependent states (specifically, social psychologists actively try to remove its effects statistically; in [66], p. 235). We also address our findings that support interdependence theory, including redundancy, intelligence, tradeoffs, orthogonal relationships and social harmonic oscillators. We note similarities between interdependence and quantum theory. Finally, from the perspective of interdependence theory, we close by addressing Schrödinger's (1944) question, "*What is life?*"

Social effects arising spontaneously as individuals immediately begin to agree or disagree with each other in every social setting as they strive to determine the context. The social effects, reflecting the presence of interdependence, are ignored by rational choice theorists. Although conflict disables rational choice theory, conflict is of great value to humans freely able to exploit the effects of interdependence to self-organize and make decisions. We see the failure for context to be derived better illustrated, for example, when China's leaders are unable to suppress freedom in Hong Kong (e.g., [67]); with the inability of Nations in MENA countries, but not in Israel, to promote innovation [6]; and in 2019 after the extraordinary internal dissent in the alliance between Nissan and Renault caused Nissan to suffer its first loss in a decade [68]. Directly contradicting Axelrod [22], our case study below on the management of military nuclear wastes addresses how self-organized groups in a free society exploit the conflict between two bureaucracies not only to set the context in a way that highlights a problem, but also to solve the problem for the benefit of society.

Of importance to us, and relevant to this chapter, are the use of human-machine systems and other mechanisms for sharing, which invoke interdependence, a difficult concept to grasp in the laboratory ([35], p. 33) with exceptions (i.e., [69]), but even fewer exceptions theoretically [7].

By rejecting MI in favor of interdependence theory, we have hypothesized for teams, found and replicated that the optimum size of a team minimizes its member redundancy [4, 5]. With interdependence theory, we have also found that, proportional to the complexity of the barriers faced by a team to completing its mission, and while at the same time efficiently executing a mission, intelligence is critical to a team's maximum entropy production (MEP; [6]). We have also found that while physical training promotes physical skills and book knowledge promotes cognitive skills, these two skill sets are orthogonal to each other, resolving a long-standing experimental and theoretical conundrum. We have also found that the best determinations of social reality, decisions by a team, and decisions for the welfare of a society are based on the interdependence of orthogonal effects [7]. We have linked this finding to a social harmonic oscillation of information driven by orthogonal pro-con positions, alternatively presenting one argument before an audience of neutral judges countered by its opposing argument until a decision has been rendered.

From this foundation, unlike traditional models based on MI, interdependence theory scales to integrate wide swaths of field evidence; e.g., bacteria gene [70] and business mergers [71] seeking MEP, but, if failing, leading to collapse (weak entropy production, WEP). Instead of predictions which are likely to fail in interdependent situations, we propose that the way forward for autonomous systems is to limit autonomy with checks and balances, similar to how free humans limit autonomy [7].

Grove [72] has written about the rapid changes underfoot in American politics and law today as the result of political, judicial and cultural victories and defeats. Debates raging over economic protectionism and free trade now question the aims and principles of America's founding. By looking to an earlier age in the United Kingdom, Grove reviewed the UK's Parliamentary sovereignty over the American colonies, a time when Edmund Burke warned his opponents against forcing a comprehensive theory to fit reality. Parliamentarians considered the American crisis as one that the Americans had either to take or to leave the Commonwealth; i.e., accept the theory of Parliamentary sovereignty to allow it to tax the colonies whenever desired, or deny the sovereignty of the head of the empire over its parts. Britain's *Burke*, an Irish statesman and philosopher, argued that the politics of the British empire should not be forced to fit a single theory; in his *Observations on a Late State of the Nation*, Burke wrote that

> The old building stands well enough until an attempt is made to square it into uniformity. Then it may come crashing down upon our heads in much uniformity of ruin.

Grove makes the case that America is much like the "old building" Burke had described. Liberal, conservative, religious and other ideas, Constitutional rights, and institutions have combined to shape America in its development. Importantly, none of these ideas or institutions coheres theoretically with one another, nor should they. Grove has argued that the core essence of a nation need not be defined by a single ideology whether propagated by its state, its politicians or its intellectuals. Tocqueville agreed, observing "you must not judge the state of a people by a few adventurous minds that appear within it." There are pernicious ideologies at work today as in the past, all with an influence on American politics and its laws. But Constitutional habits, instincts, associations, and institutions remain intact.

From Grove, a rational consensus belief or ideology for the right way to govern the American States and peoples is unlikely. Instead, while resistant to comprehend theoretically, according to Madison [73], the best way to govern a people is not with the majority rule enshrined in the Constitution, nor with the people's right to choose its representatives also enshrined in the Constitution, but with the checks and balances afforded by the Constitution that limit the powers of politicians, judges, majorities against minorities, officials against the people, the police, the military, etc. We believe this is the key strategy to governing autonomous systems (A-HMTs), which we elaborate next. Before we begin, however, we underscore that checks and balances do not lend themselves to a rational consensus, such as subsequently described with the rational choice theory. This problem is not unique to governance; arguments about the meaning of quantum mechanics, likely the most successful theory ever, still rage a century after its discovery (e.g., [74]).

Our prior findings indicate that redundancy and emotion impede interdependence [4, 5]; that intelligence requires interdependence; that tradeoffs reflect uncertainty in a team's decisions [6]; and that the determination of social context operates like a harmonic oscillator [7].

Intelligence is needed by a team or society to self-organize sufficiently to overcome barriers, as with the superior patent productivity we found for well-educated researchers in Israel compared to their poorly educated research counterparts in neighboring MENA[4]countries [7]. By comparison, in a non-competitive society where individuals are dependent upon others, an education is less important than the street-smarts necessary to survive; e.g., in Samoa today, the average education typifies an uneducated country's "Backward March of Civilization" [75].

We consider that interdependence operates like a superposition to fully engage the members of a team in a state of communication. Mindful of this state, it was straight forward to theorize that redundancy contributes destructive interference interdependently to the operation of a team. We hypothesized and found that the cost to communicate in a team with redundant members acts like an impurity in a crystal, increasing entropy, whereas the perfect team acts like a pure crystal (e.g., the orthogonal members of a team performing a military mission, a research project, or the conflicting roles in a courtroom in the pursuit of truth).

Consider Von Neumann's [76] failure to construct a theory of self-replicating automata with thermodynamics from an individual automata's perspective. He concluded that it was not possible to choose the parts of a self-replicating automata in the right order. In contrast to this aggregation problem, we have argued that a team's perfect fit occurs when it minimizes its structural entropy sufficiently to allow the team to achieve maximum entropy production (MEP), demarcating the construction and in the right order of good from bad teams.

The search for the perfect team motivates mergers. For example, Lombardo and Cimilluca [77] reported on a merger between Intuit, the maker of TurboTax, and personal-finance portal Credit Karma. Intuit is a bookkeeping-software giant that is pushing itself further into consumer finance, while Credit Karma gives customers free access to credit scores, borrowing history, notices about possible data breaches, credit monitoring, tax preparation and tax filing. In turn, Karma's customers gain

---

[4]Middle Eastern North African countries.

offers for credit cards and loans to fit their credit history, giving money to Credit Karma when its customers use those products:

Adding … [Karma] to its stable would give Intuit a stronger foothold in the burgeoning realm of online personal finance. In addition to TurboTax, the online software that millions of people use to file their taxes, Intuit's offerings include QuickBooks bookkeeping software used by businesses and Mint, an online-budgeting platform that also pitches individuals financial products…. Best-known for its bookkeeping software [Intuit] … has said it wants to push further into the finances of the individuals and businesses it serves by adding more offerings to its platform.

Oppositely, when a team goes through a divorce, it requires energy to increase its *dof* by ripping apart its structure, increasing its joint entropy (i.e., $H_{A,B} \geq H_A$, H_B; e.g., divorce hurts all families; in [78]; preceding the ViacomCBS merger when the two firms openly shared hostilities, both companies lost money; in [79]; and to reiterate, Renault and Nissan were both harmed by their internal conflict; in [68]). But even if a firm does not go through a divorce, isolation from competition can lead it to make bad decisions; e.g.. Boeing over the last few years.

Dominant firms can become the only source for a vital product. After McDonnell Douglass merged into Boeing in 1997, the combined firm provided almost all domestic civilian aerospace business [80]. Boeing faced competition from Airbus, but its market power insulated it from the consequences of its mismanagement. Two deadly crashes over the past year of Boeing 737-Max passenger airlines, however, revealed the extent of the company's bad decisions. Moreover, with Boeing representing almost the entire U.S. aviation industry, its problems are rippling across suppliers and airlines; e.g., the scandal at Boeing has cost General Electric about $750 million in lost cash flow from the sales of its jet engines (e.g., [81]).

Based on the evidence for the structures that poor teams strive to destroy, we have assumed and found that the energy flowing into a team can be divided into two streams, one for its structure [82], and one that allows it to achieve MEP [7]. Minimizing the *dof* in a team's or organization's structure allows the maximum of its available energy to focus on achieving MEP.

Along the paths of entropy expenditures, as mentioned, we separate a team conceptually into its structure and its mission. Structurally, we have postulated that a perfect team operates at its lowest entropy, its ground state (like a biological enzyme, in [83]), allowing the perfect team to direct most of its available energy as it functions to achieve MEP. Thus, the best teams operate at ground states, the worst at excited states (e.g., marital divorce; the civil war in Syria; hostile mergers). In sports where it is more easily recognized, an excited negative state can produce adverse performance [84]:

Negative emotions can hurt performance both physically and mentally. They first cause you to lose your prime intensity. With frustration and anger, your intensity goes up and leads to muscle tension, breathing difficulties, and a loss of coordination. These emotions also sap your energy and cause you to tire quickly. When you experience despair and helplessness, your intensity drops sharply and you no longer have the physical capabilities to perform well.

Preferences and self-interest conflicts imply the existence of an uncertainty principle [6]. Tradeoffs underscore the need for intelligence to navigate barriers; e.g. the EU-UK negotiations for a new treaty imply "... difficult trade-offs because both sides say they want close economic ties but have conflicting agendas" [85].

As a case study [7], the Department of Energy (DOE) had been granted authority in 2005 to renew the closure of two high-level radioactive waste tanks (HLW). As part of the 2005 law that allowed DOE at its Savannah River Site (SRS), South Carolina (SC), to close these and its remaining 47 HLW tanks, the Nuclear Regulatory Commission (NRC) was given oversight of DOE's HLW tank closure. After the 2005 law was passed, the SRS Citizen Advisory Board (CAB) and State of SC restated their support of DOE's decision to renew the closure of its HLW tanks at DOE's SRS facility. Each month, however, DOE would propose a plan to close its next two HLW tanks, NRC would make an objection, which would force DOE to revise and resubmit its plan; precluding an objective interpretation for which tribe has the better grasp of social reality, this social oscillation continued until the fall of 2011 when SC complained in public before the citizens of the SRS-CAB in Aiken, SC, that DOE was going to miss its legally mandated milestone to close these two HLW tanks. At its very next public meeting, the SRS-CAB demanded immediate closure; both DOE and NRC agreed, and the two HLW tanks were quickly closed.

DOE's determination to close its tanks at SRS was insufficient to set the context. The conflict between DOE, NRC and SC was also insufficient. It took the citizens in a state of interdependence at SRS to demand that DOE and NRC close the tanks at SRS, an establishment of context that has continued to this day.

The SRS-CAB uses majority rules to make its decisions; in contrast, DOE's Hanford CAB uses consensus rules [86]. DOE's SRS and Hanford sites are the two largest military radioactive waste management sites in the DOE complex. Compared to DOE's Hanford site where no HLW tanks have yet been closed under the consensus rules used by its citizens, tanks at SRS have been closed regularly since its HLW tank closures restarted in 2012.

The European Union has experienced problems similar to those at DOE's Hanford site in that both Hanford and the EU used a forced-consensus consensus-seeking process for making its decisions ([87], p. 29):

> The requirement for consensus in the European Council often holds policy-making hostage to national interests in areas which Council could and should decide by a qualified majority.

There is nothing wrong with arriving at a consensus, only in forcibly seeking a consensus [88]. Authoritarians like forced consensus-seeking rules. If rules for seeking a consensus require a high degree of unanimity to reach a decision, it becomes relatively easy to block undesired changes. In particular, consensus-seeking rules have been described as minority rules [7].

Unlike quanta, few objective measures of interdependence are possible. Here is a summary of what can be measured for interdependence theory: N; the effects of aggregation and dof; comparative MEP and WEP between teams; structural entropy production [65]; imagination ([89]; e.g., perceived racism); orthogonal roles; beliefs and stories (the latter from [90]); rotations from oscillations [7]; the use of deception

and the techniques, primarily competition especially in the form of a challenge, to uncover deception; and the competition to determine social reality [65]. For the future, we are contemplating how to build an index of interdependence.

Based on what we consider to be objective measures, and ranged in order of the increasing entropy production reflected by a team's *dof* or structure (its structure is not its primary work output or mission, however, structural costs reduce MEP). We expect increasing entropy production for team structures, first, with minimum redundancy (viz., a team's structure functioning like a crystal with no impurities in it), we place least the entropy production by a perfect team's structure (i.e., dof_{PT}; [7, 82]). Second, from the National Academy of Sciences [15], next, we place the same individuals from a perfect team but now operating as individuals without a structure (dof_{IHT}; i.e., a "team" guided by the "invisible hand" of Adam [91]). Third, then we place interdisciplinary science teams based on Cummings [16] finding that they produce the poorest science (dof_{IDT}; we crudely co-locate here teams with redundancy). Fourth, and lastly, we place teams in distress or under duress (e.g., those structures under authoritarian rules) last in that they are consuming almost all of their available energy to depress innovation or to rip apart their team's structure, producing copious wasted entropy production (WEP; dof_{DT}):

$$\log\left(dof_{PT}\right) \leq \log\left(dof_{IHT}\right) \leq \log\left(dof_{IDT}\right) \leq \log\left(dof_{DT}\right)$$

Moreover, when the perfect team is constructed, simulating entanglement such as in a quantum system, information about how it functions as a whole team is gained in exchange for how information about how the team was constructed is lost (i.e., joint subadditivity: $S_{A, B} \leq S_A + S_B$); in agreement with what our model has predicted and found [7], Schrodinger [92] claimed that the perfect team loses internal information from its reduced degrees of freedom:

> ... those true lovers who, as they look into each other's eyes, become aware that their thought and their joy are numerically one, not merely similar or identical ...

Interdependence transmits constructive and destructive interference among the members of a social unit, whether as an individual (an actor or observer), team (including A-HMTs), organization, system or as a member of a tribe competing with another tribe. It functions like superposition in what appears to act like a sea of communication inside of, say, a team, allowing communication and changes to occur quickly, reflecting a team's intelligence [69]. Based on this theory, redundancy interferes with a team's operations. Boundary maintenance of a biological molecule, organism or team is needed to reduce destructive interference (e.g., prominent in a divorce; organizational split-up; etc.) and as a barrier to redundant team members [7].

Internal destructive interference occurs in teams, too; e.g., from Hackman [93], conflict in teams is common, but the best teams learn to adapt and to resolve internal conflict compared to the worst teams.

Information loss from joining two interdependent (social) objects together, that is, the sub-additivity (i.e., $S_{a, b} \leq S_a + S_b$), produces an effect that is similar to no-cloning (e.g., [94], p. 77), precluding the replication of perfect teams; redundancy, however, sheds light on the collapse of interdependence. In that two sides exist to every story accounts for the failure to find a unique meaning for quantum mechanics [74] and it accounts for the source of innovation and reflects checks and balances [7].

Tradeoffs that capture uncertainty in decision-making, and introduce intelligence for social decision-making, reflect a social harmonic oscillator, followed by the resistance to a judgement that determines social reality [7].

5 Conclusion

Deception allows cyberthreats to take root, countered by reactive cyber defenses. Proactive cyber-defenses can be successful if constrained to the organization itself and applied to active organizational defenses, to active vigilance against insider attacks, and to active vigilance on IP property and data bases. But if proactive cyber-defenses reflect a vigilante, the results can be counterproductive. Instead, that is when and where the State should become responsible. Checks and balances should also come into play; e.g., with cyber-police; cyber-courts; cyber national defenses.

Our best guess model of reality allows predictions based on what reduces interdependence (e.g., redundancy), exploits it (e.g., tradeoffs), or limits it (e.g., censorship; the inability to freely decide what workers and resources are needed). Regarding moment-to-moment decisions, a team or A-HMT will have a plan of action to accomplish its job or mission; the plan should be followed until a barrier is reached that cannot be overcome or until the plan fails; then, the team should debate a path forward, creating a social harmonic oscillator, working through tradeoffs until the team decides on a revised plan signified by a drop in entropy.

To Schrödinger's [92] question, *What is life?*, he answers what "an organism feeds upon is negative entropy ... [where] metabolism ... [gives] a measure of order ... the organism succeeds in freeing itself from all the entropy it cannot help producing while alive ... [allowing life to exist at a] fairly low entropy level ... "

To paraphrase Schrödinger's question whether "two souls become one," we postulate that the collectivism in a socialist country, like Cuba (e.g., [95]), blocks self-organization and interdependence in teams to force citizens to generate the WEP that benefits a country's masters or a gang's leaders, versus a country of free individuals able to self-organize into teams to compete and foster the team's intelligence that focuses entropy to produce the MEP that directly improves the team's performance and, indirectly, society's collective well-being.

Generalizing Arrow [21], in the absence of competition; or a scientist establishing a game theory's payoffs; or a military Commander Officer's intent; or, for example, the U.S. Federal Reserve changing the interest rate; etc. in these and other absences, it is impossible for an autonomous individual or team to determine social reality ([7]; also [65]); e.g., in the Carter Page matter, the FISA[5] court's chief judge, Rosemary Collyer, officially indicated that for every request to surveil by the Department of Justice, something is needed like a standing advocate who can challenge requests on behalf of the subjects the FBI wants to surveil to give FISA judges a counter-position to consider [96]; her indication underscores the value of a social harmonic oscillator process as part of every good decision made under uncertainty, i.e., a claim followed by a counter-claim and a decision by a neutral party, audience or jury.

Moreover, it is impossible to simply sum to aggregate the data from interdependent states, which leads to mistaken predictions; viz., explaining Tetlock & Gardner's [42] failed predictions that Brexit would never happen nor would Trump win the presidency in 2016 [7].

For several years, however, by focusing on the cognitive behavior of the individual, social scientific perspectives of teams and organizations have undervalued physical aspects of teams and organizations, notably the operational structures and resource boundaries that determine the context of and the information flows into cyber-defenses. The cognitive approach alone is likely why the self-reported observations that feed into group theories have been unsuccessful at unraveling the properties of teams, organizations and systems. Since then, we have theorized and found that while cognitive aspects remain important, such as a plan by a team or organization, physical and cognitive factors are orthogonal to each other, a solution to long-standing problems in social science. In contrast to the individual approach, based on the theory of interdependence for each social unit like teams (including A-HMTs), organizations and systems, interdependent units perform better than the same individuals independent of the team or organization. To further improve cyber-defenses and advance theory, we address cyber-defenses and A-HMTs from cognitive and physical perspectives.

Is it merely romantic, popular or religious to accept that the cooperation model of Axelrod [22] or the rational collective choice model [38] increases the value of meaning, but not survival or evolutionary outcomes? Is meaning even necessary, when the meaning of the successful quantum theory has eluded researchers after a century of fierce debate [74]? Natural selection, and the evidence we have assembled, appears not to care. More than likely, a single meaning of life does not exist, evidenced by our proposed function of opposing world views that generate tradeoffs and solutions to difficult problems as part of social harmonic oscillations (e.g., debates prior to voting in elections; prior to deciding by a jury; and prior to choosing the winner of a contest), adding value to Schrodinger's [92] question, *What is life?*

Acknowledgements This version of our manuscript was first published as: [97]. For this chapter, we have revisited the subject matter in the original chapter, revised it fully, and added new material.

---

[5]Foreign Intelligence Surveillance Court is a U.S. federal court established and authorized under the Foreign Intelligence Surveillance Act of 1978 (FISA).

References

1. Bacsh, M.: New counterintelligence strategy to boost sharing on cyber threats, defense one. https://www.defenseone.com/threats/2020/02/odni-plans-share-more-about-cyber-threats-under-new-counterintelligence-strategy/162896/?oref=d-river (2020). Accessed 2 June 2020
2. NCSC: Strategic plan–2018–2022, National Counterintelligence and Security Center. https://www.odni.gov/files/NCSC/documents/Regulations/2018-2022-NCSC-Strategic-Plan.pdf (2018). Accessed 29 Feb 2020
3. Tarraf, D.C., Shelton, W., Parker, E., Alkire, B., Carew, D.G., et al.: The Department of Defense Posture for Artificial Intelligence. Assessment and Recommendations, RAND Corporation. https://www.rand.org/pubs/research_reports/RR4229.html (2019). Accessed 2 Oct 2020
4. Lawless, W.F.: The entangled nature of interdependence. Bistability, irreproducibility and uncertainty. J. Math. Psychol. **78**, 51–64 (2017)
5. Lawless, W.F.: The physics of teams: Interdependence, measurable entropy and computational emotion. Front. Phys. **5**, 30 (2017). https://doi.org/10.3389/fphy.2017.00030
6. Lawless, W.F.: Interdependence for human-machine teams. Found. Sci. (2019). https://doi.org/10.1007/s10699-019-09632-5
7. Lawless, W.F.: The interdependence of autonomous human-machine teams: The entropy of teams, but not individuals, advances science. Entropy. **21**(12), 1195 (2019)
8. Wehrman, J.: "Draft of bipartisan driverless car bill offered by House panel. Bipartisan, bicameral bill authors try to avoid pitfalls that brought down previous attempts to get a federal handle on autonomous vehicle oversight," Roll Call. https://www.rollcall.com/2020/02/13/draft-of-bipartisan-driverless-car-bill-offered-by-house-panel/ (2020). Accessed 13 Feb 2020
9. Host, P.: "Top US Air Force officer sees MQ-9 Reaper UAV as prime candidate for armed overwatch," Jane's Defence Weekly. https://www.janes.com/article/94311/top-us-air-force-officer-sees-mq-9-reaper-uav-as-prime-candidate-for-armed-overwatch (2020). Accessed 15 Feb 2020
10. Mattis, J.: Summary of the National Defense Strategy of The United States of America. Sharpening the American Military's Competitive Edge. https://dod.defense.gov/Portals/1/Documents/pubs/2018-National-Defense-Strategy-Summary.pdf (2018). Accessed 29 Feb 2020
11. CRS: Defense Primer: U.S. Policy on Lethal Autonomous Weapon Systems, Congressional Research Service. https://fas.org/sgp/crs/natsec/IF11150.pdf (2019). Accessed 2 Dec 2020
12. Editors: "Ready for weapons with free will?" New York Times, https://www.nytimes.com/2019/06/26/opinion/weapons-artificial-intelligence.html (2019)
13. Host, P.: "AFRL delays first X-60A flight," Jane's Missiles & Rockets. https://www.janes.com/article/94285/afrl-delays-first-x-60a-flight (2020). Accessed 15 Feb 2020
14. Mizokami, K. "The Navy's Surprise Unmanned Fighter Is a Glimpse of War's Near Future. The Navy converted manned combat jets into unmanned ones. Nobody had any idea they were doing it," Popular Mechanics. https://www.popularmechanics.com/military/aviation/a30771030/growler-unmanned-navy/ (2020). Accessed 2 June 2020
15. Cooke, N.J., Hilton, M.L. (eds.): Enhancing the effectiveness of team science. Authors: Committee on the Science of Team Science; Board on Behavioral, Cognitive, and Sensory Sciences; Division of Behavioral and Social Sciences and Education; National Research CouncilNational Academies Press, Washington, DC (2015)
16. Cummings, J.: Team science successes and challenges. National Science Foundation Sponsored Workshop on Fundamentals of Team Science and the Science of Team Science (June 2), Bethesda, MD. https://www.ohsu.edu/xd/education/schools/school-of-medicine/departments/clinical-departments/radiation-medicine/upload/12-_cummings_talk.pdf (2015)
17. Amadae, S.M.: Rational choice theory. Political science and economics, encyclopaedia britannica. https://www.britannica.com/topic/rational-choice-theory (2016)
18. Israel, J.I.: The Enlightenment that failed. Ideas, revolution, and democratic defeat, 1748-1830Oxford University Press, Oxford, UK (2020)

19. Nell, E.J., Errouaki, K.: Rational economic manEdward Elgar Publisher, Cheltenham, UK (2011)
20. Kelley, H.H.: Personal relationships: Their structure and processesLawrence Earlbaum, Hillsdale, NJ (1979)
21. Arrow, K.J.: Methodological individualism and social knowledge. Am. Econ. Rev. **84**(2), 1–9 (1994)
22. Axelrod, R.: The evolution of cooperationBasic, New York (1984)
23. Rand, D.G., Nowak, M.A.: Human cooperation. Cogn. Sci. **17**(8), 413–425 (2013)
24. Folds, D., Lawless, W.: Naval Research & Development Enterprise (NRDE). Applied Artificial Intelligence (A2I) Summit. An Anthology of the Dialog of the Summit, San Diego, CA. 15–19 October, 2018 (2018)
25. Friedman, G.: "The Pressure on China," Geoploitical Futures. https://geopoliticalfutures.com/the-pressure-on-china/ (2019). Accessed 12 July 2019
26. Lai, J.: "China's facade of stability. Recent stresses have exposed the lack of trust at the core of Beijing's repressive model," Wall Street Journal. https://www.wsj.com/articles/chinas-facade-of-stability-11582156842 (2020). Accessed 20 Feb 2020
27. EB: The Editorial Board: *"Arrested in Hong Kong.* Publisher Jimmy Lai is charged for taking part in an August protest," Wall Street Journal. https://www.wsj.com/articles/arrested-in-hong-kong-11582934933 (2020). Accessed 2/29/2020
28. Trofimov, Y.: "From Chernobyl to the Coronavirus. In the U.S.S.R. in 1986, as in China today, a public health disaster exposed the limits of dictatorial rule," Wall Street Journal. https://www.wsj.com/articles/from-chernobyl-to-the-coronavirus-11581610088 (2020). Accessed 15 Feb 2020
29. Su, A.: "He filmed corpses of coronavirus victims in China. Then the police broke into his home," Los Angeles Times. https://www.latimes.com/world-nation/story/2020-02-03/china-wuhan-coronavirus-censorship (2020). Accessed 28 Feb 2020
30. Yu, V.: "Senior Wuhan doctor dies from coronavirus as authorities start to 'round up' patients. In city of 11m, officials threaten with punishment those who delay reporting symptoms," The Guardian. https://www.theguardian.com/global-development/2020/feb/18/senior-wuhan-doctor-dies-from-coronavirus-as-authorities-start-to-round-up-patients (2020). Accessed 28 Feb 2020
31. Davidson, C., Gedmin, J.: China, world leader in graft. The country is stealing from its people. America can stop it, Politico. http://www.politico.com/magazine/story/2015/09/china-us-visit-213169#ixzz3mTDbmziE (2015)
32. Foxall, A.: Russian Kleptocracy and the rule of law: How the Kremlin Undermines European Judicial SystemsThe Henry Jackson Society, London (2020)
33. Rovelli's, C.: "Seven Brief Lessons on Physics"; reviewed by Garner, D. (2016, 3/22), "Book Review: 'Seven Brief Lessons on Physics' Is Long on Knowledge", New York Times, (2016)
34. Zell, E., Krizan, Z.: Do people have insight into their abilities? A metasynthesis. Perspect. Psychol. Sci. **9**(2), 111–125 (2014)
35. Jones, E.E.: Major developments in five decades of social psychology. In: Gilbert, D.T., Fiske, S.T., Lindzey, G. (eds.) The handbook of social psychology, vol. I, pp. 3–57. McGraw-Hill, Boston, MA (1998)
36. Kahneman, D.: Thinking, fast and slowMacMillan (Farrar, Straus & Giroux), New York (2011)
37. Robb, R.: Willful. How we choose what we doYale University Press, New Haven, CT (2019)
38. Mann, R.P.: Collective decision making by rational individuals. PNAS. **115**(44), E10387–E10396 (2018)
39. Lawless, W.F., Mittu, R., Sofge, D.A., Shortell, T., McDermott, T.: AI welcomes systems engineering: Towards the science of interdependence for autonomous human-machine teams. AAAI-Spring 2020 Symposium, University of Stanford, CA (2020).
40. Blanton, H., Klick, J., Mitchell, G., Jaccard, J., Mellers, B., Tetlock, P.E.: Strong claims and weak evidence: Reassessing the predictive validity of the IAT. J. Appl. Psychol. **94**(3), 567–582 (2009)
41. Baumeister, R.F., Campbell, J.D., Krueger, J.I., Vohs, K.D.: Exploding the self-esteem myth. Sci. Am. **292**(1), 84–91 (2005)

42. Tetlock, P.E., Gardner, D.: Superforecasting: The art and science of predictionCrown Publishers, New York (2015)
43. Withers, K.L., Parrish, J.L., Smith, J.N. & Ellis, T.J.: Vice or Virtue? Exploring the Dichotomy of an Offensive Security Engineer and Government "Hack Back" Policies, Proceedings of the 53rd Hawaii International Conference on System Sciences: 2020. https://scholarspace.manoa.hawaii.edu/bitstream/10125/63963/0180.pdf (2020). Accessed 2 July 2020
44. Kaste, M.: "Cybercrime booms as scammers hack human nature to steal billions," NPR. https://www.npr.org/2019/11/18/778894491/cybercrime-booms-as-scammers-hack-human-nature-to-steal-billions (2019). Accessed 24 Feb 2020
45. Vigna, P., Jeong, E.Y.: "Cryptocurrency Scams Took in More Than $4 Billion in 2019. Ponzi schemes are the latest form of bitcoin fraud big platforms like one called PlusToken drawing the most most money," Wall Street Journal. https://www.wsj.com/articles/cryptocurrency-scams-took-in-more-than-4-billion-in-2019-11581184800?mod=hp_lead_pos4 (2020). Accessed 2 Aug 2020
46. Diamond, J.: 'Dark Arts' and 'Codebreaker': The Origins of the Houston Astros Cheating Scheme. MLB Commissioner Rob Manfred's previously undisclosed letter to Astros GM Jeff Luhnow details the team's spreadsheet and algorithm to steal signs in one of the biggest scandals in baseball history, Wall Street Journal. https://www.wsj.com/articles/houston-astros-cheating-scheme-dark-arts-codebreaker-11581112994?mod=trending_now_pos1 (2020). Accessed 2 Aug 2020
47. Patrick, M.: "Bank Boss Resigns Amid Spying Scandal. Credit Suisse's Tidjane Thiam oversaw huge restructuring at the lender," Wall Street Journal. https://www.wsj.com/articles/credit-suisse-ceo-resigns-amid-spying-scandal-11581057307 (2020). Accessed 2 Aug 2020
48. Michaels, D.: "Justice Department Presses Ahead With 'Spoofing' Prosecutions Despite Mixed Record. Crackdown in futures markets is yielding new wins for prosecutors, but several coming trials will show if tactic is ultimately successful," Wall Street Journal. https://www.wsj.com/articles/justice-department-presses-ahead-with-spoofing-prosecutions-despite-mixed-record-11581095386 (2020). Accessed 2 Aug 2020
49. Krouse, S., Hagerty, J.R.: "Fall of WorldCom's Bernard Ebbers Sent Chilling Message to CEOs. Ebbers's conviction and imprisonment demonstrated the risk of pleading ignorance of wrongdoing," Wall Street Journal. https://www.wsj.com/articles/fall-of-worldcoms-bernard-ebbers-sent-chilling-message-to-ceos-11581019119 (2020). Accessed 2 Aug 2020
50. DOJ: Chinese Military Personnel Charged with Computer Fraud, Economic Espionage and Wire Fraud for Hacking into Credit Reporting Agency Equifax. Indictment Alleges Four Members of China's People's Liberation Army Engaged in a Three-Month Long Campaign to Steal Sensitive Personal Information of Nearly 150 Million Americans, Department of Justice. https://www.justice.gov/opa/pr/chinese-military-personnel-charged-computer-fraud-economic-espionage-and-wire-fraud-hacking (2020) Accessed 2 Nov 2020
51. Lucas, R.: "Justice Department Charges Chinese hackers in bid to curtail cyber-theft," NPR. https://www.npr.org/2018/12/20/678587956/justice-department-charges-chinese-hackers-in-bid-to-curtail-cyber-theft (2018). Accessed 2 Aug 2020
52. Sherman, E.: "One in Five U.S. Companies Say China Has Stolen Their Intellectual Property," Fortune. from https://fortune.com/2019/03/01/china-ip-theft/ (2019). Accessed 2 Aug 2020
53. Volz, D. & Lubold, G.: "Navy, Beset by Aging Tech, Pushes for Rapid Modernization. Shortcomings hamper ability to fend off hackers, top official says; Navy, contractors 'leak like a sieve'," Wall Street Journal. https://www.wsj.com/articles/navy-beset-by-aging-tech-pushes-for-rapid-modernization-11582138002 (2020). Accessed 20 Feb 2020
54. Pearce, T.: "Pentagon identifies two special operations forces soldiers killed in Afghanistan ambush," Washington Examiner, https://www.washingtonexaminer.com/news/pentagon-identifies-two-special-operations-forces-soldiers-killed-in-afghanistan-ambush (2020). Accessed 2 Sept 2020
55. Kanno-Youngs, Z., Perlroth, N.: Iran's military response may be 'Concluded,' but cyberwarfare threat grows cybersecurity experts are seeing malicious activity from pro-Iranian forces, and

warning that Iran has the capacity to do real damage to American c[...]
York Times. https://www.nytimes.com/2020/[...]/06/us/politics/iran-atta[...]
Accessed 2 Dec 2020

56. Tan, H., Volz, D.:"Fraud Case in Charleston, S.C., Shines Light on Web's [...]
and its founder, [...] not guilty in case revolving around IP addresses and th[...]
istry [...] Numbers," Wall Street Journal. https://www.wsj.com/articl[...]
[...]on-s-c-shines-light-on-webs-dark-corners-11581944400?mod=hp_lead[...]
Accessed 17 Feb 2020

57. Fisher, D.: "Israel Says Hamas Targeted Its Soldiers in 'Honey Trap' Cy[...]
atives duped soldiers with false promise of exchanging illicit photos with [...]
military says," Wall Street Journal. https://www.wsj.com/articles/israel-says-ha[...]
its-soldiers-in-honey-trap-cyberattack-11581874401?mod=hp_lista_pos4 (2020). A[...]
2 Feb 2020

58. Yang, S., Li, S. & Arauly, J.T.: Unarmed. Reporting on an Epidemic Under
Watchful Eye. Three Wall Street Journal reporters experienced the scope of the
government's response to a deadly viral epidemic," Wall Street Journal. https://www.w[...]
articles/quarantined-reporting-on-an-epidemic-under-chinas-watchful-eye-11590301786
(2020). Accessed 23 Feb 2020

59. Graves, J., Reactive vs. proactive cybersecurity. 5 reasons why traditional se[...]
no longer works, Fortinet. https://www.fortinet.com/blog/industry-trends/reactive[...]
[...]D%2D-proactive-cybersecurity%2D%2D-reasons-why-traditional.html (20[...]
Accessed 2 July 2020

60. Barber, C.: Get Proactive to Better Arm Yourself Against Cyberattacks. Agencies must
move to an integrated data-driven approach aimed at predicting and preventing cyber
threats. Nextgov. https://www.nextgov.com/ideas/2019/09/get-proactive-better-arm-yourself-
against-cyberattacks-160691/ (2019). Accessed 2 July 2020

61. Kuhrer, J.M. (2020), "How Should Has Been Improved to Help Protect Energy Utilities,"
InfoSecurity Magazine. https://www.infosecurity-magazine.com/news/isac-how-should-has-
been-improved/ Accessed 21 Feb 2020

62. McKenna, [...]: Vigilance. In D.J. Wisehart (Editor), The Encyclopedia of the Great
Plains. http://plainshumanities.unl.edu/encyclopedia/doc/egp.law.051 (2011), Accessed 2
Sept 2020

63. Shaikh, Mu., S.: How far should organizations be able to go to defend against cyberattacks? When it Comes to Cyber Security Passive Defense is Best. Employing aggressive defensive tactics to respond that would have dire global consequences," The Con-
servation. https://theconversation.com/how-far-should-organizations-be-able-to-go-to-defend-
against-cyberattacks-110143 (2019), Accessed 2 July 2020

64. Miller, [...]: 'The intelligence coup of the century.' For decades, the CIA read
the encrypted communications of allies and adversaries," Washington Post. https://
www.washingtonpost.com/graphics/2020/world/national-security/cia-crypto-encryption-
machines-espionage/ (2020). Accessed 2 Nov 2020

65. Lawless W.F., Mittu, R., Sofge, D.A., Hiatt, L.: Introduction to the special issue, "Artificial
intelligence (AI), autonomy and human-machine teams: Interdependence, context and explainable AI". AI Mag. **40**(3), 5–13 (2019)

66. Kenny, D.A., Kashy, D.A., Bolger, N.: Data analyses in social psychology. In: Gilbert, D.T.,
Fiske, S.T., Lindzey, G. (eds.) Handbook of social psychology, vol. 1, 4th edn, pp. 233–265.
McGraw-Hill, Boston, MA (1998)

67. Mangan, L.: "Give me death or freedom – The battle for Hong Kong review," The Guardian.
https://www.theguardian.com/profile/lucymangan (2020). Accessed 23 Feb 2020

68. Roca, C.: "Renault Swings to Loss, Hit by Nissan Woes, Falling China Sales. Net
loss in 2019—its first in a decade—caps a tumultuous year for the French car maker,"
Wall Street Journal. https://www.wsj.com/articles/renault-swings-to-loss-hit-by-nissan-woes-
falling-china-sales-11581684013 (2020). Accessed 15 Feb 2020

69. Cooke, N.: Effective human-artificial intelligence teaming, AAAI-2020 Spring Symposium,
Stanford, CA. https://aaai.org/Symposia/Spring/sss20symposia.php#ss03 (2020)